THE WILD ANIMAL TRAINER IN AMERICA

THE
WILD ANIMAL TRAINER IN AMERICA

JOANNE CAROL JOYS

Foreword by Tom Parkinson

PRUETT PUBLISHING COMPANY
Boulder, Colorado

First Edition
1 2 3 4 5 6 7 8 9

Printed in the United States of America

Library of Congress Cataloging in Publication Data

Joys, Joanne Carol, 1940–
    The wild animal trainer in America.

    Bibliography: p.
    Includes index.
    1. Animal trainers—United States—Biography.
2. Animals, Training of—United States—History.
I. Title.
GV1811.A1J69   791.3′2′09   82-436
ISBN 0-87108-621-2   AACR2

All photos courtesy of the author unless otherwise credited.

CONTENTS

FOREWORD

It was a famous animal act that I had seen twenty times in as many seasons—regal tigers and proud lions. Audiences thrilled to the doings of the trained and the trainer. But this time there was a difference.

A cat had balked at its cue. The trainer bonked it on the nose to get attention and poked its flank to prompt it—a mild reprimand such as one might give a dog that chewed the newspaper. The fine cat was unhurt, even unimpressed. It barely noticed the rap, but the audience noticed; people groaned in disapproval. Not long before, any audience would have cheered the brave trainer. Now the lesson was that a trainer can't scold an animal, no matter how deserved that might be.

Fashion has changed. The world of animals is in a turmoil. It almost always is. Today there are over-riding questions of ecology and endangered species. An animal protective association declares that it wants circus acts and zoos disbanded, the animals sent back to their ancestral habitats. The government is pressed to formulate animal regulations; socialites and celebrities lobby to prevail over professional handlers.

These quandaries point up the contradictions that one faces when venturing into such a study. Is the association justified? Can the government discover correct standards? Are zoos educational? Are trainers abusive? Or, if a dog can be a shepherd or a guard, can it not be an entertainer? What then of elephants? Or the big cats? Is it better for a tiger to risk disease and poachers and shrinking habitat in the wild or to take its vitamins and have its tooth filled and gain alertness, breed well, and eat regularly with the circus?

To consider such questions, Joanne Joys has completed this study, seeking out the evidence that only good research develops. That quickly turns up another echelon of queries.

Once, Americans preferred the "fighting" style of animal acts; Europeans liked the quiet, sophisticated style. It was a difference between tamer and trainer, subjugator and educator. Or was it largely the contrast between what different audiences wanted to see in their turns? Which is better? Is the ferocity just playacting? Is the loving treatment foolhardy? Fundamental questions have to do with whether training methods vary and whether abuse is involved.

Everyone endorses kind treatment and abhors cruelty. Certainly circus trainers do so. They evince love and respect for their animals and regard for their well-being. But opponents claim training never can be humane. Trainers are put into the impossible position of seeking to prove a negative, of denying unsubstantiated charges.

In an era when the public wanted to hear about a man so brave he would enter the cage of lions and fight them to a standstill, press agents filled that desire with inside information about fearless trainers. In another period, when the public wants assurance that the animals are well treated, there are background articles about training through kindness and reward.

Novelists and their movie counterparts know that an easy way to paint a character as a villain is to have him abuse an animal, whether it be Lassie or Jumbo. A circus novelist may hide his evil characters behind clown white or have them jimmy the aerialist's rigging. More often, the novelist writes about a Teutonic trainer and moronic cage boy. The reader must ask when is the Teuton just representing an easy villain and when is the author claiming to reveal some truth about training.

Into this jungle Joanne Joys moves with skill and objectivity. As she notes, it would have been easier to write a book that buttresses one side or the other, but she opted to sort out the protective, the prejudiced, the promotional, and the emotional, all to seek balanced conclusions. It is not the easy exposé, not the tempting whitewash. By noting shortcomings and excesses, she has strengthened her commentary and conclusions.

Nor is this merely a consideration of arguments about treatment of animals; equally, it is a study of the trainers, their biographies and their circuses. A specialized section of circus history, the book probably could not have been written much earlier. Historiography of the circus has developed rapidly in recent years, providing the basics from which an author can draw historic sequence and depth of understanding. For this book the author has used the body of knowledge to the fullest, revealing a good appreciation of circus history and operation. Adding her own specialized research, interviews, and observations, she presents qualifications perhaps unmatched among those who have commented about wild animal trainers and their unique circle in the circus world.

TOM PARKINSON

PREFACE

I have always found the circus an extremely entertaining area of study. But as my research grew more and more serious, I could increasingly see it in the context of American historical development. The circus, in fact, is unique in that its history virtually spans our nation's history. It has thus both reflected changing American life-styles and has led, for example, in the introduction and usage of the modern techniques of mass advertising and railroad transportation. Circuses also brought many Americans their first look at inventions such as the automobile and the electric light bulb. The great impact of circus day on small town and rural Americans can be seen through the reminiscences of authors like Hamlin Garland, John Steinbeck, Joyce Kilmer, and Thomas Wolfe. Its momentary glimpse into a bigger, more wondrous world stirred the imaginations of countless youth.

My favorite aspect of the circus has always been the wild animal act. Through its study can be seen the changing attitudes of Americans toward wilderness, conservation, and animal rights legislation. The animal trainer, from his first appearance, has been a character of mythic aura. His willingness and ability to face beasts that terrify the general public has given him slightly superhuman status. Like "cowboy" the term "lion tamer" immediately creates a plethora of positive and negative images in the reader's mind. The purpose of this work is not to discuss every wild animal trainer who ever practiced his trade in America (many excellent ones are not covered), but instead those that made the greatest impact on the public through their sense of showmanship or their importance to the history of the wild animal act or the circus.

From its earliest inception the wild animal act proved controversial. Today stringent legislation involving the importation, trading, and transportation of endangered species could perhaps end this colorful, exciting form of entertainment. The blame for these laws could easily be placed entirely on ignorant legislators, unrealistic conservationists, and celebrities who vociferously take up the humanitarian movement. Actually the onus also rests on the circuses and trainers themselves.

The wild animal trainer reached the heights of professionalism in the first half of this century. But with the end of the giant circus operations of the past and the decline or closing of training centers, the general quality of wild animal acts has deteriorated. Of course some excellent practitioners, throwbacks to the old American or European schools still exist, but their number is diminishing. Jack London's characterization of preconceived brutality is not as true today as cruelties arising from ignorance, negligence, amateurism, inadequate help, and cheap, inexcusable cage conditions. This is particularly true in the small "mud shows" that believe they need a wild animal act to prove their worth as a circus, since the success of a show that can offer no more than acrobatic demonstrations would be very doubtful.

Trainers, even in the heyday of the circus, according to some of their contemporaries, often did not live up to their press agents' notices. Rather than "all-American boys" or "gallant" Europeans, they have been described as hard-drinking, fast living spendthrifts. Little cooperation exists even today among circuses and trainers to improve their collective images or constructively fight governmental legislation. These assessments plus the frequently abominable conditions existing now, cause even the staunchest advocates of wild animal acts to question their future.

As much as I enjoy a well-staged wild animal presentation, I also consider myself very much in favor of the majority of conservation and humane legislation. Hopefully legislation will prove to be constructive rather than destructive and the wild animal act, free from abuses, will entertain future circus crowds. For it is difficult to imagine the American circus surviving without elephants or big cats. Those of us who love this longest-lived national entertainment, find its possible demise a gloomy proposition. The confrontation of caged beasts and man has provided thrills and excitement for over one hundred fifty years. It still takes constant work and dedication, the ability to withstand pain, a sense of showmanship, and a thorough understanding of animals to make a success-

ful trainer. A few still possess these extraordinary capabilities and their presentations give audiences the opportunity to see the grace and power of these great animals in dramatic action rather than repose. Indeed, the public's positive response to the strength and beauty of these creatures may contribute to their willingness to support legislation to preserve these species.

I tend to agree with New York *Daily News* critic Patricia O'Hare who wrote in 1979 that the circus is "more glitter and glitz than anything else. . . . But the circus is the circus, and people love it. I loved it too, while I was sitting watching it. It really is the Greatest Show on Earth.

"However, it had better thank God it has the animal acts."

ACKNOWLEDGMENTS

I would like to offer my heartfelt thanks to the following people who helped make this project possible. At The University of Toledo: Dr. W. Eugene Hollon, who encouraged me to begin this unusual study and my advisor, Dr. William H. Longton, who patiently clarified and gave continuity to my manuscript, and Dr. Richard Boyer, who obtained some very useful material for me from the British Museum. Research of this type is impossible without the aid of a good library, and I would especially like to thank Alice Weaver, Joanne Hartough, Della Ward, Lucille Emch, and Nancy Kemper of the University Library. James L. Murphy, reference librarian of the Ohio Historical Society and Celeste L. Koerner, librarian of the Martha Kinney Cooper, Ohioana Library also helped. Exceptionally helpful were Jeff Gunderson, assistant reference librarian, Indiana Historical Society Library (William Henry Smith Memorial) and Charles A. Wagner, director of the Peru (Indiana) Public Library. Pamela J. Bennet, director of the Indiana Historical Bureau and Martha E. Wright, reference librarian, Indiana Division of the Indiana State Library both contributed. Special thanks are due the *Chillicothe* (Ohio) *Gazette*. Alice Herrington, president of Friends of Animals, Inc. made a very valuable contribution.

Any book about the circus would be impossible without the help of fellow circus historians, and circus people themselves. One invaluable resource is the Circus World Museum at Baraboo, Wisconsin. The chief librarian and historian, Robert L. Parkinson, was not only a contributor but also was kind enough to read my manuscript for accuracy. Fred D. Pfening, Jr., editor of *Bandwagon*, journal of the Circus Historical Society, very generously provided me with many of the photographs that appear in this volume along with reference material, as did his son, Fred D. Pfening, III, an excellent historian in his own right. Circus historian John Polacsek contributed some valuable material. Ken Hasselkus and Joyce Ferguson of the Circus City Festival Museum, Inc. in Peru were very thoughtful in providing photographs. Dave Price graciously shared his expertise on Clyde Beatty. Stuart Thayer was extremely kind in letting me utilize materials he has researched and gathered on the early American circus and menagerie. Al Conover of the Circus Model Builders provided excellent help on photographs. Tom Henricks, president of the Albert and Jeannette Rix Tent of the Circus Fans of America, provided some helpful articles, as did the Rixes—thanks to all of them. The very knowledgeable animal man, Roger Smith, brought the book alive with his wonderful reminiscences. Dave Hoover, wild animal trainer of Clyde Beatty-Cole Bros. contributed the prologue, an excellent insight into animal training, and gave me some valuable interviews that were extremely helpful. Thanks also to the staff of the Clyde Beatty-Cole Bros. Circus for reading my manuscript for accuracy and allowing me to utilize ads with titles they own. The author thanks Ringling Bros. and Barnum & Bailey Combined Shows, Inc., for permission to reproduce material involving circus names it owns, among them Ringling Bros.–Barnum & Bailey Circus, Barnum & Bailey Greatest Show on Earth, Ringling Bros. World's Greatest Shows, Sells-Floto Circus, Hagenbeck-Wallace Circus, Sparks Circus, John Robinson Circus, Al G. Barnes Circus, Buffalo Bill's Wild West and Forepaugh-Sells Bros. Circus.

(Finally I must give a big thank you to my patient colleagues in the Publications Office at The University of Toledo, who bore up well during my project, and my mother who suffered through three years of this endeavor.)

PROLOGUE

by Dave Hoover

A wild animal trainer must be an animal lover. A wild animal trainer has to spend his life with his animals—365 days a year. There is never a day off—never a two-week vacation. And, contrary to popular belief, it is not a big-profit business. In fact a full eighty percent of my income goes to feed and care for my animals. Even the glory that many people believe to be one of the main incentives of the wild animal business wears thin after a few years. So, if you want glory or riches instead of work or satisfaction, don't waste your time becoming a wild animal trainer. I'm well-educated and could have done much better financially in another trade. But I'm doing what makes me happy.

Concerning the cat acts today, I think I find the public more appreciative. People really enjoy the wild animal acts and expect to see them in circuses. But some have funny ideas about wild animal acts. Some people think the animals have been kidnapped from their native environment and are being beaten or forced to perform. It's not the truth. Some think it awful that animals must work. Some think that even people shouldn't work—that the world owes all of us a living. But an animal, like a person, must justify his existence. A performing animal works and receives his care as his just pay. In his native environment, a wild animal works for his feed and helps balance nature.

But more and more areas of Africa and India are going into agriculture to feed the starving. World population is getting out of hand. This means that much more land has to be converted, and that grazing animals must go because they damage the crops and aren't needed to keep the natural vegetation in balance. So too, the carnivorous animals that feed on grazing animals also start disappearing. Unlike human beings, big cats stop reproducing when there are not enough grazing animals to feed them, so, without grazing animals to be kept in balance there are fewer carnivorous animals. This is why tigers are endangered in the wild state, and not because they are being captured for circuses and zoos. In all my years as a wild animal trainer, I've never seen an imported tiger, or a lion, for that matter.

Each year, more tigers are raised in the United States than the entire known number in India. Yet in 1973 Congress passed the Endangered Species Act that, in effect, stopped major breeding of tigers and leopards in this country and made it illegal to sell them. I raised nearly three hundred cubs prior to that law's passage: ten percent were used in my act, and the balance was sold to zoos, other circuses, and dealers all over the world. Since then I have raised only six—just what I need for my own use. Prior to this law, zoos raised cubs each spring and had a nice family group for summer exhibition. Come fall, the cubs were sold, in order to reduce feeding costs during the winter and to breed the parents again for another family group the following summer. Of course this cycle stopped since zoos need only one pair for each exhibition, and few could raise tiger cubs and then keep them. The cost alone is tremendous—I spend approximately $1,800 to $2,000 a year to feed each animal. Zoos just don't have that kind of money. Tigers breed like housecats, and a pair can reproduce themselves by thirty-two in a lifetime, so zoos either had to stop breeding, or breed the animals only to destroy the cubs later on. Unfortunately, many chose to illegally destroy these animals. Since this law has gone into effect, I estimate zoos have destroyed enough animals to put fur trim on the coats of every woman in America today. The law removed a very important source of zoo revenue because the cubs not only made a nice exhibition during the summer months, but the money derived from selling the animals helped support the parents of these animals. I feel it's a bad law.

I think it's time animal lovers, environmentalists, and conservationists stopped looking at wild animal trainers as foes and joined them as allies to preserve these creatures of God. Soon the animals' natural environment will be gone, and they will disappear if man doesn't care for them in zoos, parks, and circuses. Circuses help preserve the tiger; they generate the necessary finances to feed the animals and to make them self-sufficient; in fact, more tigers work in acts throughout the world than live in zoos.

Even our interior department (try as they may) cannot protect our national wildlife. The bald eagle, the golden eagle, and the California condor are good examples. Ranchers and farmers regard these birds as a menace and shoot them, law or no law. The cheetah is another good example. They are hunted as pests in South Africa, yet we are not allowed to import these animals into the United States because they are an endangered species. America cannot police the world, and it is silly for us to pass a law concerning wildlife outside our borders. The country of origin should have that responsibility, and they must be encouraged to protect their wildlife locally.

But the American wild animal trainer may be the endangered species himself. I'm the last American-style wild animal trainer left, the so-called fighting act, for which Mr. Beatty was well-known. All the rest of the acts in the United States today are either from Europe or have trainers using the European style. The public, not understanding wild animal training, probably thinks that a fighting act is trained with a lot of force, and a quiet act is trained with love and kindness. Not entirely true! If you have ever owned a housecat, you know they are very independent animals. They attach

themselves to one person, and usually, even with that one person, it's a very, very strained relationship. So common sense should tell you that if a lion or tiger is told to do something on command, and he does it at once on cue without any argument, he has to have been trained with a great amount of force. On the other hand, a balking, noisy animal that fights and protests still has his spirit. My animals learn by taking a piece of meat off a stick. This is one way to break an animal act. Each time he does the routine in training, he gets a piece of meat along with a word command, so he learns by repetition, not by force. He's also not becoming a pet. He hears the same verbal command and soon he associates the command with what he is doing; later, when the meat is removed, he performs it on command. But, being lazy and independent, the cat soon balks and that is when the noise and the fighting come in — not because of force or clubs, as some people think.

Everything I use in my act is a psychological weapon. Animal training is actually based on animal psychology. For instance, the chair has four legs and an animal has a one-track mind. When the chair is held up, the big cat must face four legs —four points of interest. He becomes confused, forgets the trainer, and takes his wrath out on the chair. His chain of thought has been interrupted. The blank gun serves the same purpose: when the gun fires off, the report breaks the animal's chain of thought. Usually the trainer will immediately use a familiar command, and the cat automatically executes that command because he has forgotten his original thought. The whip is used only for cueing: a flip brings the animal forward or backward. And the stick, of course, replaces the meat stick he followed in his original training.

I never train an animal to do a trick that I feel might be unnatural for him. The barrel roll is a good example. I turn my animals out in the big cage for exercise every day, and all the props that we use in the act are left in the cage; invariably, several cats will mount and roll the barrel just in play. While playing they will try almost everything in the act, and sometimes they do things I didn't think they could do. This is a good time to observe the animals and work into the routine something they might tend to do themselves.

The European act is very precise and the animals are usually very quiet and docile. Many of these animals have been declawed, and some are

Chapter I

THE WILD ANIMAL TRAINER IN AMERICA
THE EARLY YEARS

He stood alone, like another Daniel, in the midst of the fierce, mismated family, with absolutely no weapon but the small whip in his hand. It was an impressive sight—this human being, unarmed and unarmored, in the cage of great cats. In these animals ages of conflict have brought the organs of destruction to the highest perfection. The great muscles of limb and jaw, the long curving teeth, the cruel talons, all spell Death—sudden, cataclysmic death; and behind them lies a sleepless, untamable ferocity. Yet [he], in the tricks which followed, bent each brute to his will, rendered nugatory, the first laws of being; yes held in abeyance, its very God-given instincts of self preservation, and forced it to acts—such as leaping through a hoop of fire—from which its every fiber recoiled in repugnance and terror . . . never losing patience but bound to conquer—as he must or abdicate his power forever.

Elmore Elliott Peake
"The Wrath of Afric"

This 1902 passage describes the mystique that the wild animal trainer has had for American audiences for nearly one hundred fifty years. He is an artist who makes "living animals exhibit endless graces of subtle line and lovely color." When he thrusts his head in the lion's mouth it is a vulgar concession to the "groundlings," but when he faces a lion and "compels the great tawny thing to repeat the grace of a natural movement . . . and leap in a long gracious curve across the arena to an unstable landing on a rolling sphere, he feels he is doing something worthy of himself and his animals."[1] Yet each time he enters the cage he gambles with the chance of a bad mauling or death. As the riskiest of all circus acts it is small wonder that its performers marvel not that some of them are occasionally killed but that so many have survived.[2]

A circus man's relationships with animals involve a curious combination of danger, affection, and cruelty, and he himself often appears as a hero, fool, or villain. He is a hero in the primitive sense of being an invincible conqueror with magical powers, or as a self-made man, epitomizing the popular underdog.[3] The shining impression of doing something remarkable before an audience, of being the "splendid performer," "clicking" or "wowing" the crowd, attaches heroism to him.[4] But he is just as often a daredevil, less heroic than reckless, an exhibitor of foolish courage for the sake only of notoriety and money.[5] Finally, he is an oppressor who misuses power over weaker rivals—a proud, powerful, cruel, unfair, relentless bully.[6]

Courageous hero or oppressive villain? The question is confused by the aura of romance that sur-

1

rounds circus life. The circus is a world of story-books and fairy tales, a delightful world of monkeys and clowns, balloons and spangles, and elephants and lion tamers named Dumbo and Bosco. It is a dramatic show of drum rolls, the high wire, and the Bengal tiger, of pomp, pageantry, and excitement, and of a beauty and grace that relieve the drabness and clumsiness of ordinary life.

But analysis is also complicated by the mixture of legend and fact that make up so much of circus history. Because of its rootless geographical mobility, the circus, with its braggadocio and bravado exists in an unusually insulated world. What this has meant is that most of its cultural elements have been transmitted orally within it. Techniques of circus production and the various skills involved in circus acts have traditionally been acquired almost exclusively from training by older practitioners. Even this training is not formal but instead involves repeated observation of the basics of the acts. Commonly related myths are used to describe the origins of standard circus items, while other legends ascribe impossible capabilities to performing animals and exceptional character and skill to circus "greats."[7]

Many of these circus techniques and legends date back to the English fairs of the seventeenth, eighteenth, and nineteenth centuries. The modern American circus originated in those festivals of dancing, fiddling, drinking, wrestling, and bull-baiting for they also included menageries and circuses. The original circus was a stationary exhibition of riding skills while menageries developed as animal shows only. Gradually these two features became main attractions and then specialized to become independent of fairs and of each other.[8]

The menagerie was the first phase of the modern circus exploited in America. In pioneer days an occasional hunter brought down from the hills a tame bear which he exhibited at frontier taverns or the village commons. Then he passed the hat to sustain himself until he reached the next village. Sometimes a sailor delighted the patrons of a tavern with his pet monkey. But it took the shrewd speculative Yankee ship captains to introduce foreign wild animals to this country. They sold their animals at good profits to local exhibitors when they showed them in hotel stables or canvas-sided enclosures. In 1716, the first lion arrived in Boston. Five years later an announcement in a Boston newspaper called the lion not only "the largest and most noble, but the tamest and most beautiful creature of his kind, . . . [it] grows daily and is the wonder of all that see him."

Typical early nineteenth-century English menagerie.

Preceding by nearly one hundred years the regular exhibition of polar bears in menageries, *Ursa major*, or the great white bear, arrived in New York in 1733. Tigers came later, the first being introduced in New York in 1789.[9]

The popularity of these exhibits led to the development of traveling menageries, offering a wide variety of animals. By the 1820s as many as a dozen menageries toured the eastern United States from Maine to Alabama and west to the Appalachians.[10] The same spirit which sent settlers across the mountains and down the Ohio River into the Northwest spurred these exhibitors to fight almost impassable roads, flooded streams, disease, horrible weather, and murderous outlaws for the sake of possible profits.

Divorcing themselves entirely from circuses in their advertising by emphasizing educational values, traveling menageries brought directly to a great portion of America a certain knowledge of wonderful natural history. Their value was limited, however, because showmen often mislabeled their exhibits. Records indicate a gemsbok being called a James Bock; a mandrill, a "blue faced mongrel"; an aardvark, a valk valk; and a gnu, a horned horse. An Egyptian valpus was exhibited as part horse-part cow, along with a rompo, a cammouse, and an African Potchan, "the only one in America." Undoubtedly it was the only one that had ever been, or ever would be in this country.[11]

While menageries were deemed respectable, ministers in Puritan New England denounced the circus as an invention of the devil. As late as 1832, the *Massachusetts Spy* referred to "circus riders exhibiting their fooleries" in Worcester and declared that those who attended the show encouraged vice, idleness, cruelty, and dissipation. It hoped "that this is the last time we shall be troubled with such unwelcome visitors."[12] The Chillicothe *Weekly Recorder* in an 1815 editorial defined antishow bias when it pronounced the circus an "unlawful calling that cannot be defended on scriptural ground." Performances, it warned, were calculated to amuse the "giddy and thoughtless and excite the laughter of fools," and it solemnly concluded that there was nothing useful or rational about it. Thayer called it "double-damned" since critics argued that it excited "fools without instructing them and fails to entertain people of intelligence."[13]

Menagerie men resisted hostility to their form of amusement by turning to scripture in their advertisements, transforming the lowly hippo into "the blood-sweating behemoth of holy writ, spoken of in the book of Job"; the zebu into the "sacred cow"; the warthog into the "prodigal's swine"; the water buffalo, "the ox that treads out the corn"; the camel, "the ship of the desert"; and the lion's cage into a biblical symbol made obvious by painting on it a scene of the story of Daniel.[14] Heralding their show as a "dignified and refined Sabbath day diversion," menagerie directors protested that they attracted only "pious" minded crowds.[15]

The first of the modern traveling shows was born within a twenty-mile radius of Brewster, Putnam County, New York. Enjoying few amusements, the largely agricultural population there was ripe for entertaining diversion. In 1815, an American sea captain bought an elephant for twenty dollars at a London auction and brought it to New York, where he invited his brother Hackaliah Bailey, of Westchester County, to see it. Having heard about a previous elephant that had been purchased for ten thousand dollars and exhibited in New York and other commercial centers, Hackaliah Bailey bought the London elephant, Old Bet, for one thousand dollars, and began touring his Somers, New York, neighborhood with it. The profits he reaped soon pushed his farm into the background and he contracted for some monkeys and bears. With this small menagerie, with which he traveled at night to discourage free peeks at the animals, Bailey became the precursor of all later traveling menageries and wagon shows.

Bailey's elephant and the success of his new venture stirred the imaginations of local prosperous farmers. The elephant fascinated young America and that great beast's response to its comparatively puny masters came to symbolize all the mysterious workings of the circus. Sometime prior to 1820 John J. June, Lewis B. Titus, and Caleb S. Angevine gathered at Yerke's Tavern, the nerve center of North Salem, New York, to discuss Bailey's elephant and the business possibilities it suggested. The urge to troupe overpowered these highly respected citizens and they began a show entitled the June, Titus & Angevine Menagerie. The little town of Brewster soon became the hub of America's fledgling circus world. Other prominent landowners in the neighborhood—the Howes, the Turners, and Hackaliah's nephew, George F. Bailey—entered the menagerie business.[16]

These shows prospered and during the winter of 1834–35 grouped themselves into an association or

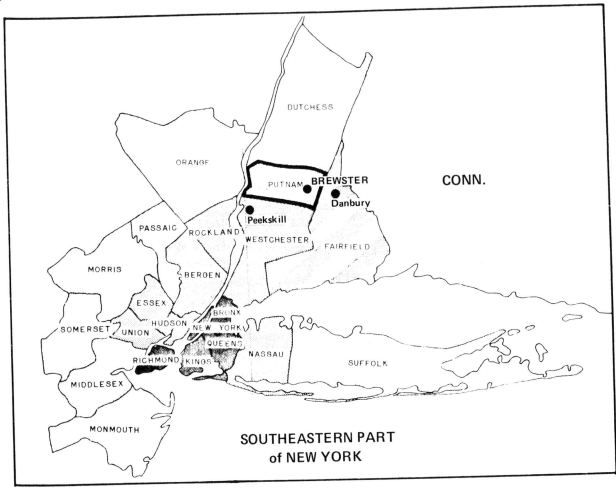

SOUTHEASTERN PART
of NEW YORK

corporation called the Zoological Institute with headquarters in their own building at 37 Bowery, the great amusement street of early New York.[17] The Articles of Association of the institute—by then an organization of nine shows valued at $329,325 and owned by one hundred and twenty-eight shareholders—called for the erection of these permanent indoor zoos with "the proper saloons, decorations, and accommodations" to attract the public. By careful routing of their season tours, the shows could finish the season in a city where the institute had an exhibition building. The five directors attempted to end cutthroat competition in the menagerie business by judicious allocation of animals, and the assignment of nonconflicting routes to member shows. The institute was now wealthy enough to send its own expeditions to Asia and Africa to supply the growing demand for wild animals. The powerful menagerie owners reputedly acquired the title "the Flatfoot Party" when they tried to monopolize the state of New

York. "We put our foot down flat and shall play New York State, so watch out" was the warning issued to rivals.[18]

The stiff competition called for a dramatic new attraction. It materialized in the person of Isaac A. Van Amburgh, a native of Fishkill, New York. Like many residents of this region, Van Amburgh was excited by the traveling shows and at the age of thirteen he joined the Zoological Institute as a cageboy. He served in this capacity for a Mr. Roberts, who was supposedly a former keeper of animals in the Tower of London. Roberts's performance consisted of entering the cage of a Bengal tiger, but in November of 1833 he was severely mauled.[19] This tragic incident gave Van Amburgh his chance. According to circus folklore, he was impressed by the story of Daniel in the lions' den and he convinced himself that he too could walk into wild animals' cages, confront the big cats, and bring them under his control. In 1833, at the age of twenty-two, he gave notice that he intended to

Engraving from Landseer's painting of Van Amburgh, which was painted at Queen Victoria's command.

enter "the following cages at 3½ o'clock, the lion, lioness, leopard and leopardess, all in one cage, to the black-maned caped lion, leopard and panther in the same cage." It was at the Richmond Hill Theater in the Bowery that Van Amburgh first entered the den of lions it had been his responsibility to clean, and so became the first modern wild animal trainer and the first legendary performer in circus history.[20] His performance has been graphically described by O. J. Ferguson:

He was attired in a dress designed to convey an impression to the beasts of the field that man, in accordance with the decree of God, was and should be the Monarch of the Universe. The daring pioneer approached the door of the den with a firm step and unaverted eye. A murmur of alarm and horror involuntarily escaped the audience. If Van Amburgh had possessed a nerve like ten thousand, nay, ten million men, he would have quailed and fallen victim to the fury of the animals. But the effect of his power was instantaneous. The Lion halted and stood transfixed.

An 1848 illustration of Van Amburgh and his big cats.

Article in the Aug. 8, 1838, London *Times*
announcing the planned arrival of Van Amburgh. ➤

The passage in Scripture "The lion and the lamb shall lie down together, and a little child shall lead them," has lately been literally realized by a most extraordinary exhibition of Mr. Van Amburgh, at the New York Zoological Institute. The gentleman enters a cage containing lions, tigers, and other beasts of prey, accompanied by a child nine years old and a pet lamb, and after the whole have gone through various groupings, he fearlessly places his bare arm, moist with blood, in the lion's mouth, and thrusts his head into the distended jaws of a tiger. The animals, we believe, are now on their way to the metropolis, and Mr. Van Amburgh, who has lately arrived in Liverpool, is about to follow them. —
Sheffield Mercury

London *Times* story describing Van Amburgh and his act. ➤

SEPTEMBER 19, 1838.

Van Amburgh, the Lion Tamer.

(From a Correspondent)

This remarkable man is a native of the state of New York, in the United States. He was born in Fishkill, a beautiful town on the North or Indian River, about 30 miles from New York. He is descended from one of the original Dutch settlers of that state, better known under the title of "Knockatokkers," a name which was given them since the early works of Washington Irving were published.

When about 15 years of age, with a fine constitution and a good temper, Van Amburgh left the little village of Fishkill, and visited New York. He became there for several years a clerk in the warehouse of a relative. But this kind of life not suiting his enterprising spirit, he packed up, and set out on his travels, as every adventurous Yankee or Yankee Dutchman does. In the ups and downs of life he became connected with a caravan of living animals that belonged to a company in the United States. By this time young Van Amburgh had reached his twentieth year. His fine figure, iron frame, and Herculean strength, fitted him admirably for his new vocation. At this present writing Van Amburgh is probably about 26 years of age, but one of the most athletic men of his size in the world. He is singularly made. His body is perfectly round, but rather thicker than broad. His bones large and firmly set, and his flesh almost muscle. Yet, from the peculiar conformation of his body, he seems to have all the grace and lightness of a Mercury.

His first intercourse with lions, &c., was accidental. At a little town in New Jersey, near New York, a caravan of living animals was exhibited. The lion was uncommonly good tempered, and one of the keepers was in the habit of going into his cage as a part of the exhibition. On a certain occasion this person was absent, the audience impatient, no one to enter the lion's cage, and a terrible row in prospect. In the extremity of distress, Van Amburgh had charity. "I'll go into the cage," said he to the managers. He took a cane, entered the cage, walked up to the lion, talked to him, and in a few seconds they became quite intimate. "In approaching wild animals," says Van Amburgh, "courage is every thing."

After this success, he went further. The lion soon died, and the company broke up. He then joined a caravan, called

the Zoological Institute, in New York, which contained some of the choicest animals ever exhibited. He there prosecuted his favourite pursuit—studied the temper of the animals, and proceeded step by step till he brought them all into a singular state of civilization.

His first association, in the same cage, of a lion and a tiger, presented remarkable scenes. These two animals would fight whole months, and sometimes he would give over one of them for dead. On such occasions Van Amburgh, after they had exhausted each other, would enter the cage, and begin his course of discipline to control both. Gradually he added animal to animal till he got as far as ten animals in one cage. On many occasions he had severe conflicts, with the tiger particularly, but nothing dangerous. When he talks of those animals he is highly interesting. "The tiger," says Van Amburgh, "is like a reckless, good-for-nothing, drunken rascal, who spends his time carelessly at taverns, and fights in a moment. Tigers have all bad spiteful tempers. The lion is not so irascible; he is slower and cooler, but there is not the generous feelings about him which he has been cracked up for. The leopards are like cats — playful, but easily provoked."

There is nothing more interesting than to hear Van Amburgh give a history of his intercourse with these animals..

Van Amburgh has a novel and practical theory to account for his power over them. From the first moment of his intercourse with them, he talked to them as he would to a human being. "They believe," says he, "that I have power to tear every one of them in pieces if they do not act as I say. I tell them so, and have frequently enforced it with a heavy crowbar." The personal strength, the peculiar cast of his eye, the rapidity of his movements, the tone of his voice, all tend to present to these animals an idea of superior power, which in sudden bursts of passion makes them crouch in the corner of the cage. Van Amburgh's eyes are peculiar; one of them has a remarkable cast, which rather heightens the effect of his expressive face, as is said of the "terrible eye of Caliph Vatheck." On one occasion in New York the tiger became ferocious. Van Amburgh very cooly took his crowbar and gave him a tremendous blow over the head. He then said to him, in good English, as if he was a human creature. "You big scoundrel, if you show me any more of your pranks, I'll knock your brains out," accompanying it with loud menaces and strong gesticulation. After this the tiger behaved like a gentleman for a couple of months.

In coming over to this country Van Amburgh was separated from these animals for several weeks. They arrived in London, he in Liverpool. As soon as he reached London, he went to see them. On his appearance outside the cage, one of the strangest scenes was presented that was ever beheld. The lions, tigers, and all recognized him at once. When he entered among the group, they crouched, they crawled, they lashed their tails with every demonstration of delight at beholding him again. He scratched the neck of the big lion, and his majesty growled forth his pleasure in tones like the sound of distant thunder.

In ancient and modern history we have heard of attempts made to tame single animals; but until the present era we have never seen such a mighty exhibition of human over animal power as Mr. Van Amburgh presents. The lion and the lamb literally lie down together. Yet the feats of familiarity performed nightly at Astley's are nothing, it is said, to those which he performed at New York.

The Tiger crouched. The Panther with a suppressed growl of rage sprang back, while the Leopard receded gradually from its master. The spectators were overwhelmed with wonder. Then came the most effective tableau of all. Van Amburgh with his strong will bade them come to him while he reclined in the back of the cage—the proud King of animal creation.

Consorting with ferocious beasts with calm and daring so thrilled spectators that they made few demands on him by way of performance. His bravery brought him an instant fame which "spread through civilization," his awed biographer observed, "and is now extensive with the Universe itself."[21]

Van Amburgh was not the first man to enter a cage with the big cats. The Frenchman Henri

Martin had presumably done so with a tiger as early as 1819 in Germany. In America keepers were advertised who combed their lion's mane through the bars or allowed the beast to lick their hands. The earliest Americans to actually enter a cage seem to be William Sherman, who in 1829 broke a lion and lioness presented to Andrew Jackson and later sold to menagerie man Rufus Welch, and Charles Wright, another Putnam County, New York, showman who may have entered the cage of a lion and lioness in 1827. In all perhaps seven keepers preceded Van Amburgh. Their performances were greatly limited by the small size of the dens in which the animals were kept. But they managed to enthrall their audiences by playing with their big cats, opening their jaws, and even thrusting their hands in the beasts' mouths.[22]

But Van Amburgh's notoriety quickly generated legends about him, the most peculiar of which concerned his early life. His real grandfather was an American, Worboys Van Amburgh, but contemporary biographers endowed him with a Tuscarora father who met his mother when he saved her from the claws of a rampaging bear. The Indian married her, took her name, and became a successful planter in Kentucky. Ephraim Watts, a New York gundealer, wrote a fanciful account of Van Amburgh's exploits. According to him, the youngster's father had an uncommon terror of wild animals and died in the prime of life when he unsuspectingly came upon the picture of a wild boar he saw on a new-painted sign. But Isaac was reared as a dedicated woodsman, fond of the wilds, affectionate of animals. Even as an infant he displayed his budding powers by subjecting insects to his will. In a few years he demonstrated his command over rats, mice, efts, and toads. By five, he was the most capable horse breaker in Kentucky. When two hunters killed a bear that he had raised from a cub, Isaac attacked them murderously, and leaving them for dead, he fled the state. In the North, he took a job as a cageboy with a traveling menagerie. Five years later he learned that the hunters had not been killed, but he had already developed his sensational cat act and had no desire to return home.[23]

Van Amburgh's training methods also became legendary. His eyes seemed to have a special power. Watts's 1838 biography of Van Amburgh has it that wild beasts are cowards at heart and that only their immense strength and ferocity give them an undeserved reputation of courage. When they are faced boldly and shown what the trainer can do "it's all over with their terribleness."[24] Van Amburgh's eyes were most extraordinary since the balls "project exceedingly, and it seems as if he could look all around him without turning his head the least." They also had a "cold whitish appearance and would resemble a dead ghost's only that they move in a quick circle and seem to visit all places at once."[25] Perhaps more effective was his allegedly disciplining the savage creatures with a crowbar, which he called the "silent system." In a tiger's den "he introduced himself with his crowbar and continued presenting his calling card until the tiger crouched down in one corner and expressed

himself happy to make his acquaintance."[26] The trainer once received a silver crowbar from the staff of the Theatre Royal, Drury Lane, where he had performed for an unprecedented one hundred and fifteen nights to overflow crowds. The crowbar had been "potently magnetised by three German Barons," who had promised to look at the weapon during a whole day before the presentation to "impregnate it with the magnetic power."[27]

How much of Van Amburgh's vaunted cruelty was real and how much showmanship is difficult to determine. Prior to Van Amburgh, the keepers demonstrated a benevolent and friendly approach to their beasts and they did not enter their dens before a long, patient introduction of themselves to the wild animals.[28] In contrast, Hyatt Frost, another biographer, charged that Van Amburgh once starved his lions for thirty-six hours prior to an important appearance and that he lashed them into "abject and crouching submission."[29] It seems questionable that any trainer would starve valuable animals, but it is certain that he deliberately created an atmosphere of noise, excitement, and cruelty designed to make the big cats act as ferocious and savage as possible.

Like other menagerie men, Van Amburgh combined deference to piety with blatant showmanship. He frequently argued that since God had created man and made him superior to the beasts of the field, it was a religious act for trained animals to kneel at his feet. Part of his act consisted of making a lion and lamb lie down together. Later he brought a child into the den, "thus completing the picture of the triumph of faith and innocence over the savage beast."[30] He also gave prominence to ostentatious display when he introduced the "head in the lion's mouth" trick and wore a Roman toga, linking himself with the ancient combination of lions and gladiators. At one time he employed a huge showboat, the *Floating Palace*, actually a barge towed by a steamboat, the *James Raymond*, as his arena for the animal trainer acts.[31] His bandwagon, displayed first in 1846, was enormous, measuring over twenty feet long and seventeen feet high, leading a Grand Procession of "carriages, cages and performing caravans, thirty in number and all entirely new."[32]

Van Amburgh began traveling with a menagerie that bore his name when he was twenty-three. He was still "Flatfoot" property then, but he was such a versatile performer that between regular circus

VAN AMBURGH & COS GREAT GOLDEN MENAGERIE.

Van Amburgh's name was active for years in circus titles. —Fred D. Pfening, Jr.

seasons he took theatrical roles, thus beginning the trek of circus performers from the sawdust ring to the vaudeville stage that has lasted down to the present.[33] He played the part of Constantius the Greek in the *Lion Lord* at the American Theater in the Bowery, and he was again on stage with his animals in *Bluebeard* at Wallack's National Theater. As the Arab who rescues a princess thrown to his cats in *The Daughter of the Emir*, Van Amburgh forced the animals to approach him and lick his boots as a sign of submissive obedience.[34]

In 1838, "Flatfoot" Lewis B. Titus sent Van Amburgh to England, allegedly to get him out of the way, since Titus's daughter had fallen in love with the animal trainer. The menagerie owner objected although he respected his employees. He could not tolerate that "so accomplished and proper a young lady as the elder Miss Titus could fall in love with anyone who valued her devotionate charms at a lower rate than the roaring society of the wilder animals of creation."[35] Making his debut at Astley's on August 27, 1838, he went on to appear at the Drury Lane Theater where Queen Victoria went to see his performances no less than six times in six weeks.[36] When the Queen expressed the wish of seeing the animals in their "more excited and savage state, during the operation of feeding them," the American kept them without food for thirty-six hours. During the performance, it took extremely strong handling to control the beasts. When the cats were finally fed, "the dash against the sides of the den sounded like the felling of huge

trees, and was enough by its force and fury to shake the strongest of nerves." Although most of the onlookers hastily retreated, the youthful Queen "never moved either face or foot, but with look undiverted and still more deeply rivited, continued to gaze on the novel and moving spectacle."[37] After one performance, the Duke of Wellington asked him: "Do you ever know fear while surrounded by your pupils?" "No, your Grace," was the reply; "The first time I am afraid or that I fancy my pupils are no longer afraid of me, I shall retire from the wild beast line."[38] In fact Watts bragged that Van Amburgh turned topsy-turvy all the ideas "previously set up by mankind on this important subject and instead of regarding lions and tigers and leopards and hyenas as objects to be feared, he looks upon himself as an object for them to fear."[39] The trainer was himself lionized. Victoria supposedly offered him a private order of knighthood, which he respectfully declined. He did, however, agree to the Queen's request that Edwin Landseer paint his portrait, which was later exhibited at the Royal Academy.[40]

There is a story that Van Amburgh declined a challenge to match skill and daring with "Manchester Jack," the lion king of Wombwell's in Southampton, but why he may have refused is unknown.[41] In any event, when he returned to America after seven years abroad, he was the titular king of trainers both in Europe and the United States. C. T. Miller wrote a song about him that remained popular for decades:

ASTLEY'S

ROYAL AMPHITHEATRE,
WESTMINSTER BRIDGE ROAD.

Proprietor and Manager, Mr. WILLIAM BATTY, Amphitheatre House, Bridge Road, Lambeth, Surrey. Licensed by the Lord High Chamberlain.

Under the Patronage of Her Most Gracious Majesty the QUEEN, H. R. H. PRINCE ALBERT, &c.

The New and Costly Decorations
Of the interior of the Theatre have been designed and executed by Mr. C. NORWOOD, of Hoxton.

Immense Hit of the Easter Spectacle!
OVERFLOWING HOUSES!
Hundreds have been nightly unable to gain admission to witness Mr.

VAN AMBURGH
IN HIS
WONDROUS PERFORMANCES!
Who has on each representation been hailed, with an **enthusiasm unparalleled**, by the most brilliant and **Crowded Audiences** ever assembled within the walls of this Theatre.

EVERY EVENING,
Until further notice, the curtain will rise at
Seven o'clock precisely,
To the **entirely New, Grand and Romantic Spectacle**, written expressly for the occasion by BAYLE BERNARD, Esq., the incidents of which have been suggested by a passage in EUGENE SUE's celebrated Novel of

THE WANDERING JEW,
And will be presented under the title of

MOROK

THE BEAST TAMER!
IN WHICH
MR. VAN AMBURGH
Will appear with his
UNEQUALLED COLLECTION OF
Trained Animals
Among which will be found one of the greatest novelties ever seen,
A BLACK TIGER!
The first ever known to mingle in a group with other animals, and has hitherto been considered **Untameable**, but which Mr. **Van Amburgh** after the most untiring exertion has succeeded in training.

The **Spectacle** has been produced with entirely **New Scenery, Machinery, Costumes, Music,** and **Decorations**, on a scale of **Unprecedented Grandeur!** under the exclusive direction of **Mr. W. West.**

The part of Armand Dugard, afterwards Morok the Beast Tamer, by Mr. VAN AMBURGH.

For particulars of this highly interesting Spectacle, see Full Bills.

The Spectacle will be succeeded by an incomparable routine of BATTY's
SCENES OF THE ARENA,
IN WHICH THE
BRITISH & FOREIGN ARTISTES
Will appear in their extraordinary and elegant
Equestrian Performances!

The Scenes of the Circle enlivened by the Drolleries of the unrivalled Jesters, M. ROCHEZ, Grotesque, and Mr. ADRIAN, the celebrated Provincial Clown. Riding Masters, Signor CHIARRINI and Mr. WIDDICOMB.

The Entertainments will conclude with a
LAUGHABLE FARCE.

Stage Manager - - Mr. W. WEST,
Late of this Theatre, and from the Theatre Royal, Drury Lane.

Box Office open daily from 11 till 5.   No remuneration to Place-keepers.
Box Book-keeper....Mr. JOHN.
ADMISSION:—STALLS, 5s. DRESS BOXES, 4s. UPPER BOXES, 3s. PIT, 2s. GALLERY, 1s. UPPER GALLERY, 6d. Children under Ten Years of age, Half-price to all parts of the House (the Upper Gallery excepted). Second price at half-past Eight, as usual. Doors open at HALF-PAST SIX; Performance to commence at SEVEN o'clock.

MATSON'S Omnibusses to Greenwich, and the "Atlas Association" ditto to Paddington, at the termination of the Performance, every Evening.

J. W. LAST, Steam Press, 59, West-street, West Smithfield.

English announcement for Van Amburgh's appearance at Astley's.

Van Amburgh is the Man
*   Who goes with all the shows,*
He gets into the lion's cage
*   And tells you all he knows,*
He puts his head in the lion's mouth
*   And keeps it there a while,*
And when he takes it out again
*   He greets you with a smile.*

A great performer, a shrewd promoter, one of the first circus men to court personal publicity, and the most accomplished press agent of his day, Van Amburgh pioneered the path Phineas T. Barnum followed so spectacularly.[42]

Over the years newspapers reported that Van Amburgh broke his back twice and died six times, once when a tiger bit off his head.[43] One mistaken report of his death claimed that a tiger attacked him and dragged him to the floor. Although he managed to stab the cat, he died two days later.[44] Early lion kings usually did meet with violent ends, but the truth is that Van Amburgh, a wealthy man, suffered a fatal heart attack in a Philadelphia hotel room in 1865. The legendary "Monarch of the Forest" initiated a long, colorful line of wild animal trainers on two continents. His name remained part of circus titles for ninety years.

A contemporary of Van Amburgh was the indomitable and colorful mountain man John Capen Adams. Because of his uncanny ability to capture and train wild animals, especially bears, Adams earned the nickname "Grizzly." A native of Medway, Massachusetts, and a bootmaker by trade, he joined a traveling menagerie when he was twenty-one in 1833, capturing wildcats, panthers, wolves, and foxes to exhibit in it. His career in the menagerie ended when an unruly tiger he had once quieted nearly mauled him to death. After recovering from his severe wounds, he went back to bootmaking and settled down to married life. Within a few years, however, Adams's adventurous spirit caused him to leave his family in Massachusetts and strike out for the California goldfields in 1849. Having little success as a miner, he went into the mountains to hunt and trap. Killing a female bear one day, he took her two cubs into his custody and raised them with great perseverance and patience, training them to carry loads, to wrestle with him, and to trust him as a friend. Grizzly once again went into the animal trade, capturing, exhibiting, and selling wild beasts.

In the winter of 1855, he came out of the mountains for good. First setting up his menagerie in San Jose, California, he soon moved to San Francisco. There, Theodore H. Hittell of the San Francisco *Evening Bulletin*, noticing a sign on a basement door announcing the exhibition of "The Mountaineer Museum," saw him and left this description of his experience. Hittell entered a large and dingy basement where he discerned chained to the floor two grizzlies, whom he subsequently learned were named "Benjamin Franklin" and "Lady Washington," pacing restlessly in circles. On one side of the cellar were seven more bears, all fastened with ropes, and on the other side two large elk stood haltered. Farther back was a row of cages containing cougars, eagles, and other local wild animals. At the rear in an iron cage was "Samson," the largest grizzly bear ever caught, weighing over 1,500 pounds. In the middle sat Adams, whom Hittell found as strange as any of the animals. Muscular and wiry, of about average height, he had grey hair and a white beard, sharp features, and penetrating eyes.[45] Dressed in fringed buckskins and a deerskin cap with a foxtail, he called himself "the hardest animal in the collection."[46] Under his command the bears did several tricks, walking on their hind legs, "talking" on cue, bowing, and wrestling. Hittell was fascinated. He

Grizzly Adams and his Family from *Struggles and Triumphs or, Forty Years' Recollections of P. T. Barnum written by Himself* (1871).

wrote several articles about the "Californian Van Amburgh," "one of the most complete examples of the power of man over the savage denizens of the forest," causing Adams's business to pick up so much that he was able to move his "Pacific Museum" to the spacious first floor of the California Exchange.[47]

Adams's favorite bear, "Benjamin Franklin," allegedly served as the model for the California state flag based on drawings Charles Nahl made of him.[48] When "Benjamin Franklin" died in 1858, the *Bulletin* ran an article on him entitled "Death of a Distinguished Native Californian."[49] Adams was deeply affected by the loss. He had been able to ride "Ben" and at the command (Ste' boy!) the huge bear would fight shoulder to shoulder with his master against another bear. In one such encounter, a hostile grizzly had scarred "Ben's" muzzle and punched a hole in Adams's head which was visible for years as a deep depression.[50]

In 1860, Adams and his menagerie left for New York on board the *Golden Fleece*. He was always careless with his animals, and during the voyage a bear reopened the depression in his forehead and a monkey bit him. He grew extremely sick and when New York doctors examined his exposed brain, they gave him no chance for recovery. Despite his grave injury, Adams opened his California Menagerie on schedule at Thirteenth Street and Fourth Avenue. On opening day he paraded down Broadway with his animals in procession and a band playing. Riding with him in a wagon were two bears while he sat astride a third. Meanwhile hawkers sold a biography that P. T. Barnum had commissioned for the occasion.[51]

Barnum had been immediately attracted to Adams. He grasped at once the possibilities this strange man presented, noting that together with his bravery "there was enough of the romantic in his nature to make him a real hero," and that his "recklessness which added to his natural, invariable courage, rendered him one of the most striking men of his age—quite as much a show as his beasts." Barnum promoted Adams's menagerie in New York, where Grizzly handled his animals magnificently. But spectators never suspected that the rough looking mountain man was running a high fever and suffering intense pain from his broken skull.[52] Fearing death, he begged Barnum to allow him to take his show on the road so he could leave some money to the wife he had left

years before. The menagerie was to tour Connecticut and Massachusetts for ten weeks during which Adams was to receive sixty dollars per week plus expenses and a five-hundred-dollar bonus if he completed the tour. Grizzly finished the route and collected the bonus, but Barnum had already chosen his successor.[53]

The man he selected was Herr Driesbach, who had always traveled in Van Amburgh's shadow. Called the "fearless Driesbach who plays with lions and leopards," the show claimed the largest circus and menagerie in America and boasted possession of the "only living giraffe in captivity."[54] When Barnum had a one-hundred-fifty dollar beaverskin shirt made for Driesbach, Adams asked if he could wear it. Knowing Grizzly only had a short time to live, Barnum agreed. Adams left for his home in Massachusetts in the fall of 1860, where his last words to his wife and daughter reportedly were, "Won't Barnum open his eyes when he finds I have humbugged him by being buried in his new hunting dress!"[55]

Concerning his death, *Harpers* said "his tastes led him to cultivate the society of bears . . . which he did at great personal risk but with remarkable success. He could conquer the passing obstinacy or ugliness of his animals but the strife left its marks and repeated attacks of bears were at last, too much for him."[56] Barnum allegedly visited Adams's unmarked grave some time later and had a stone picturing a hunter and a grizzly bear carved and placed on the site, a mark of the deep respect he had acquired for the trainer of the fiercest of all wild animals.[57]

Gradually the menagerie and circus merged. In 1828, the New Caravan of Living Animals became the first recorded menagerie to travel with a circus.[58] Circuses acquired animals usually one at a time. For example, by 1850 Hemmings, Cooper, and Whitby had five lions, an elephant, a camel, a llama, and a zebra, advertising as an "unprecedented attraction, a daily exhibition of nerve, daring and courage in which the keeper of the lions would enter the den of these bloodthirsty beasts and feed them raw meat."[59] At this time the "lion tamer" entered the cage in which lions, tigers, and leopards were transported, and had the animals perform simple tricks. The primary emphasis was on the man's fearlessness, not the animals' cleverness. Early advertisements stressed the amazingly friendly relations developed between man and beast. The Baltimore *Gazette* reported in 1835 that Solomon Bailey played and frolicked with his big cats, "all enjoying their wild pranks with as much seeming delight and innocence as children do their holiday gambols." Another advertisement in the Macon, Georgia, *Messenger* that same year claimed "The animals appear pleased with the visits of their keeper, and in no instance have they ever attempted to injure him. It is powerful proof of the injunction, 'the brute shall be subject to the will of man.'" Eight years later the Cincinnati *Daily Gazette* wrote that [John] "Schaffer's feats are wonderful—the lion, the tiger, the panther are put into one cage—he enters it, he plays with them, goes through a mock fight with all; harnesses the lion by whom he is drawn in a car; and not only keeps them at peace with each other, but makes them obedient to all his commands."[60] Another favorite circus attraction was a "living lion . . . loose in the streets!" The original animal to do this trick was "Old Parker" in 1864, who rode peacefully atop the big tableau wagon with the Howe's show.[61]

Van Amburgh's seven year European tour stimulated the introduction of many "lion kings" to English menageries and circuses. In England the menagerie movement had begun with the purchase by a speculator named Cross of the Royal Menagerie of the Tower of London in the early eighteenth century who then exhibited the animals publicly at Exeter. About 1805 Wombwell's and Atkin's menageries became chief attractions of British fairs. A great crowd pleaser of the day were the lion-baitings that Wombwell staged.[62]

"Manchester Jack" was Wombwell's first lion trainer before he retired to enter the hotel business.[63] Batty, Carter, and White were also early "lion kings." In 1857 when the American circus of Howes and Cushing visited Britain, it proved to be a formidable rival to English shows and led George Sanger's circus to introduce a lion act. An

Crockett, the English ex-musician, performed with three lions and a lioness and was called the equal of Carter and Van Amburgh. He began his career in 1858 and later was brought to America.

The American trainer Carter as "Karfa, The Lion Tamer of the Niger" in the spectacle *Mungo Park* at Astley's (London, 1844).

inexperienced but handsome band musician named Crockett, who suffered from a pulmonary disease so badly that he found it difficult to play a wind instrument, agreed to handle the cats for Sanger's.[64] He became very popular, demonstrating a great deal of courage and coolness. Sanger's later sold the act to Howes and Cushing, who took Crockett and his lions to America. Like many early "tamers" Crockett was a heavy drinker, "tossing it off by the tumblerful." On the day of his arrival in Chicago with the Howes and Cushing circus he supposedly fortified himself for the parade with copious amounts of whiskey. The morning was hot and the combination of sun and whiskey was devastating. Back at the circus grounds, Crockett fell over dead on his way to the ring.[65]

In England, "lion queens" became the next great attraction. Circus owner Joe Hilton introduced his daughter as a lion queen in 1846 to counter the popularity of Crockett. Mrs. George Sanger was another who entered a cage with a group of lions, tigers, and leopards, and a third "queen" was Helen Bright, daughter of a circus band musician. She came to an unhappy end. Peevishly striking a reluctant tiger with her riding whip one day, she infuriated the beast, who seized her by the throat and killed her.

"Lion kings" were recruited from unusual occupations, among them being a gingerbread salesman and a Negro sailor. The black seaman, Macomo, was extremely popular into the 1860s because of his courage and showmanship. Audiences believed lions were mad after the flavor of Negro flesh, but Macomo, although mangled many times, did not feed himself to the lions. He died of consumption in 1870. An Irishman named Macarthy succeeded him at Sanger's Circus. A heavy drinker, he was killed in 1872 while giving a sensational exhibition called "lion hunting," an act introduced by Macomo, in which the trainer chased animals about a cage armed with a pistol and sword. Macarthy, who had already lost an arm in an earlier accident with his cats, fell during the chase, relinquishing all control of the lions, and was torn apart.

These bloody occurrences impelled a London journalist to urge using wild animals for exhibition purposes only when they could be properly cared for by experienced keepers. When circus owners retorted that even zoo keepers were often killed because accidents were inevitable, he replied that a caravan open on all sides, illuminated by flaring gas, surrounded by a noisy audience, housing wild beasts who were irritated by the heat and clamor and forced into performing tricks by a man armed

In January of 1850, the seventeen year old "Lion Queen," Helen Bright, was killed by a tiger in George Wombwell's menagerie. The previously well-behaved animal knocked her down and seized her by the throat after she struck it with a whip.

with a whip and a branding iron was not to be compared with a zoo.[66] Even an ex-lion king wrote in an 1872 article that wild animal acts deserved no praise. He blamed the majority of accidents on drinking. "Tamers," he wrote, usually began their careers, "bold and sober," but once torn, "their nerve would fail—wouldn't yours, sir, if you had half the flesh peeled off your side, or the side of your head torn off?" The "tamer" soon sought alcohol to steady himself, and "plenty of people are always ready to treat the daring fellow that plays with the lions as if they were kittens, and so he gets reckless, lets the beast . . . get dodging around behind him . . . or hits a beast . . . and rouses the sleeping devil, or makes a stagger and goes down, and they set upon him." The writer admitted that his wife's anxiety that "every night I would be brought out to her a mangled corpse," was not the only thing that moved him to retire. He also began to suffer from delerium tremens. Pointing out that the Lord Chancellor had already abolished the use of lion queens, he called for a halt to all wild animal acts. Trainers, he declared, risked their lives several times a day "for no useful object whatsoever."[67]

American audiences were no less bloodthirsty in the thrills they sought than their English counterparts. Even though accidents were shockingly frequent, American tamers sometimes faked injuries to satisfy bloodthirsty crowds. The British enjoyed lion-baiting, but Texans could not be outdone. In 1878, they staged bull and lion fights. Two thousand people gathered in San Antonio to see the fight between "Old Tige," the bull and "Old George," the lion. Ten-year-old Tige had killed five other bulls in single combat and also defeated a lioness the week before. Texans cheered the bull's victory over "Old George." In a future fight they planned to match Tige against three noted Mexican bullfighters and they hoped he would go hard on the "greasers." A lion-tiger fight was to follow. The New York Times concluded that "Texans are quite high flavored in their sports, and care little how many bulls, lions and Mexicans are whipped."[68]

"Lion tamers" in America suffered the same grievous wounds that English "lion kings" received from their charges, but authors approached their subjects without the reform zeal found in England. An 1888 article described William H. Winner, a former lion tamer with Barnum & Bailey, relegated to being a menagerie keeper. "Billy" believed new circus novelties had forced him from a starring role and now for common laborer's pay he still risked his life every hour tending the wild animals. He had the flesh "torn from him in shreds time and again."[69] A blow from a lion's paw had taken a piece out of his skull as large as the palm of his hand. Through the indentation in his head "the pulsations of the brain could be clearly felt."[70] A hyena had bitten two fingers off his right hand. A puma had disfigured him when it took off all but the end of his nose, leaving only a "leetle nibben."[71] The teeth of a panther had met through his neck, while its claws had torn the flesh in strips from his thighs and sides. "Billy" put his head in the lion's mouth in his act, and twice the cat had bitten through his face and head removing a large part of the jawbone. His shoulder and leg were broken by wildcats and his ribs crushed by an elephant. "His whole body bore the marks of more than forty terrible wounds, yet he lives today, to all intents and purposes a well man."[72] The author stressed two points about Winner which would be reported in later stories concerning animal trainers: sentimentality for his mother and a fatalistic attitude of predestiny.

"Billy" said there were no secrets to lion "taming"; there was only brute force. "Teach them to fear you and they will mind you," said the man who had been given up for dead twice. The power of the human eye was exaggerated: "Look a lion straight in the eye and if you keep it up half a minute the chances are he will bite that powerful eye right out of your head and take whatever else he could while doing it." The tools of the trade were nerve, a club, and a rawhide whip as "thick as your wrist."[73]

William Cameron Coup, the great circus innovator and developer, wrote in his memoirs that the danger involved in handling wild animals was "well-nigh incapable of exaggeration."[74] "The awe inspired in the breast of the average country man by the 'daring act' of the lion tamer is well founded," he wrote.[75] Coup said he never lost admiration for the grit of a person willing to enter the cage of a wild animal. Every professional trainer he knew bore the marks of encounters with his fierce pupils. "The whole fraternity is physically ragged and tattered—torn and mutilated by the teeth of beasts they have trained."[76] Coup found it surprising that men would deliberately choose such a profession after looking at veteran performers, for they could see before them a "ghastly and discouraging array of ragged ears, of split noses, of shredded limbs and lacerated trunks."[77] Trainers laughed and scoffed at the idea of danger or dread, he remarked, even though

Circus Pioneer: William Cameron Coup.

animals were notorious for their rapid changes of mood, sudden shifts in behavior that sent many circus people to early graves. Eternal vigilance was necessary, he commented, for any relaxation gave animals all the opportunity they needed to strike killing blows at their trainers. Even the stupidest beast could catch a lack of alertness in the man far more quickly than the keenest animal trainer could catch a change in temperament in the animal. A trainer had to be sober, in full command of all his faculties, and not subject to any distracting influences. The slightest dropping of his guard could be fatal to him. Still, despite the dangers, Coup believed there was no sport more splendid and royal than that of a man placing his life in imminent peril for the purpose of subjecting a wild beast, far his superior in strength, swiftness, and fighting power, completely to his will. "It is truly a sport for a king!"[78]

Trainers obeyed one universal rule in working their animals, according to Coup. First show the beast what it was supposed to do and then make him do it. They preferred animals who were ready for a fight to sulky, sullen brutes that kept them perpetually suspicious. Another rule that had to be followed, Coup wrote, was to punish any animal who inflicted injury on the trainer. Punishment should be given, if possible, by the injured person himself. Coup felt it was professional treachery for a trainer, even if half-killed, to overlook this chastisement after he recovered, because almost certainly a rebellious animal, if left unpunished, would kill the next man who entered his cage. Not to show the brute who was master was the act of a coward and a sure way to bring disaster upon any other person trusting himself in the "power of an animal that has downed its master."[79] If the trainer was killed or permanently disabled, the duty of beating the culprit fell to a new man. Coup justified the use of hot irons to cow infuriated cats only in cases of extreme peril to a downed trainer. When an animal could not be subdued, a humane showman should retire the beast rather than subject more trainers to a continuing risk. In conclusion, he believed there was nothing essentially cruel about working the great carnivores, though much firmness had to be shown. He thought there was far greater cruelty in the training of horses.[80]

Even Jack London, who later vehemently condemned wild animal acts, wrote sympathetically

Jack London.

about trainers in a 1903 article. Describing a Leopard Man he had seen as a dreamy, gentle-spoken, melancholy fellow, with narrow hips, narrow shoulders, and looking anemic, London thought he was paid commensurate with the thrills he produced. He found no romance in "his courageous career or deeds of daring," but only "a gray sameness and infinite boredom." With a faraway look he showed his scars, the most recent one in his shoulder where a tigress had gone down to the bone. "His right arm from the elbow down, looked as though it had gone through a threshing machine, what of the ravage wrought by claws and fangs. But it was nothing he said, only the old wounds bothered him when rainy weather came on."[81]

Wild animal acts in America in the late nineteenth century were still relatively crude affairs. Known as "hurrah" acts, wild animal performances here consisted largely of lions being made to jump and run around, hop over one another and generally simulate much excitement.[82] George Conklin, whose long career began shortly after the Civil War, has described a "hurrah" act he performed many times. Dressed in spangled tights, he would enter a den across the top of which was painted "Conklin is our master," and begin by extending his leg and having the lions jump over it. Then a leopard would put her front paws on the side bars of the cage, and Conklin would lift her by the hind legs, holding her while lions jumped back and forth over her. Next he would lie across three reclining cats with his hand and his elbow resting on the head of one of the lions. Conklin followed this feat by sticking his head in the lion's mouth, and then, using a strip of meat, he played tug-of-war with the great cat. The grand climax consisted of working the cats up into a mock fury, firing two or three blanks, and dodging out of the cage.[83] Like Van Amburgh, Conklin boasted that he avoided feeding his cats for several days, if he wanted his act to be really sensational. But he also attributed his lack of serious injuries to careful study of his animals, avoidance of rough handling of the cubs, patience, and the winning of confidence by not overly punishing the cats. In fact, Conklin thought it best if someone other than the trainer did the chastising. In breaking the animals he used a collar, chain, muzzle, and boxing-type gloves. His favorite weapon during this stage was a common broom. He stressed the

Typical dog act at the turn of the century that probably spurred Jack London's ire. — *Tom Henricks.*

importance of not overworking the beasts and noticing their changing moods. There was no room for fear on the part of the trainer and above all he must not be a "boozer." Conklin believed he was the first to utilize hyenas who were previously considered untrainable. He found bears the worst animals to work with and tigers and jaguars the most treacherous.[84] He is supposedly the one who first made use of a chair or stool as a subduer of the big cats, but it was an inadvertent discovery. During a circus parade when the line of march became blocked Conklin decided to leave the cage in which he was sitting with several animals, but when he attempted to exit, he found his way barred by a young, only partly broken tiger. Commands, whips, and blanks failed to budge him. At wit's end, Conklin reached for a stool nearby and pointed the four legs at the tiger. With a spit and a snarl, the tiger made for the farthest corner of the cage, his tail between his legs. It was too great a discovery to overlook. Conklin coaxed the tiger to return to the exit where he pointed the stool at it a second time. It had the same effect as before, and thus the chair became a standard part of training equipment. Animals fear what they cannot understand. There was nothing harmful in Conklin's chair, but the tiger was unable to concentrate on all four legs at one time.[85]

Although fear would always remain a factor in the training arena, thoughtful men late in the nineteenth century decided that exhibition tactics were unfair to both animals and trainers. After driving animals into near hysteria, the "tamer" had little control over his beasts which vastly increased

Carl Hagenbeck.

his chances of not emerging from the cage in one piece. The creatures were in a constant state of unnecessary tension from starvings and beatings which were not only cruel but costly. In an effort to retain wild animal acts while at the same time minimizing danger to trainers and cruelty to animals, Carl Hagenbeck introduced a variation in which wild beasts would demonstrate their beauty and cleverness, spearheading a revolution in circus performances.[86]

Born in 1844, the son of a Hamburg fishmonger, Hagenbeck first became interested in the wild animal business when his father bought a group of seals from a fishing boat captain. A naturalist at heart, with a genuine affection and sympathy for wild beasts, Hagenbeck pioneered the correct handling of animals, placing strong emphasis on their general condition.[87]

Hagenbeck began a Hamburg-based animal catching-importing-trading business which soon became a phenomenal success. From 1866 to 1887 his firm sold over 300 elephants, 150 giraffes, 60 antelope, 180 camels, 120 dromedaries, 150 reindeer, 17 Asian rhinos, and 4,000 assorted carnivores.[88] Barnum made his first big purchase of beasts in 1872 from Hagenbeck and offered the German a partnership, which he declined. Rivalry in the burgeoning American circus industry of the 1880s resulted in "elephant wars," with huge orders for pachyderms from opposing showmen Phineas T. Barnum and Adam Forepaugh.

Whenever the animal trade lagged, Hagenbeck organized ethnographic exhibitions that featured such groups as Lapps, Nubians, Eskimos, American Indians, and Hottentots. But these exhibits were combined with animal per-

Hagenbeck coming!

This is how it all started at Spielbudenplatz 19, in St. Pauli, in 1848. The young Carl Hagenbeck helps his father uncrate a monkey that has just been delivered by a seaman. – *Albert Rix.*

formances. In 1879, Hagenbeck's brother-in-law, William Rice, known as the "Tiger King," staged an elaborate performance in Berlin involving "disciplined carnivora" and a "variety of more or less savage men and women." One display consisted of a "handsome young negress in a thrilling scene of action" with three full grown Bengal tigers. The show ended tragically, however, when one of his big cats attacked Rice and although he was attended by the "Emperor's body surgeon and a leading anatomist," he died in great agony. The Negress, "Black Helen," who was really Helen Johnson of New Jersey, suffered an attack too, and was hospitalized in a "precarious condition." Officials closed the exhibit and prohibited any further "wild beast taming within Berlin."[89]

Hagenbeck himself trained wild beasts for the circus. For years he was distressed about the cruel, stupid, and ultimately ineffectual training methods in use. Moreover, no one could blame

lions and tigers that had been terrified for attacking and tearing their tormentors to pieces. "Brutes," he said, "after all are beings akin to ourselves. They will repay cruelty with hatred and kindness with trust."[90] Believing that there was no reason to drive every spark of intelligence out of an animal and every reason to develop all the talent creatures possessed, Hagenbeck encouraged a system of careful individual attention. In 1887, he established a circus in Hamburg and found an unemployed trainer named Deyerling who was willing to try the new system. Hagenbeck demonstrated his methods using dogs and cats and exerting no force except in cases of gross disobedience.

The first experiments with large carnivores were carried out over a two-year period with twenty-one lions. Hagenbeck advocated careful selection of animals since he understood that each one had its own unique disposition and only a few possessed sufficient concentration, ability, or docility

Hagenbeck in the lion's den.

to perform. Only four of the lions had the necessary talent for training under his system, but their success was phenomenal. They did an assortment of tricks that was capped by pulling a chariot triumphantly around the cage. Hagenbeck's troupe made its first appearance in Paris in 1889 and their subsequent European tour proved exceedingly profitable.[91]

Hagenbeck believed he had demonstrated that wild animals were not nearly so savage as popularly imagined but were instead affectionate creatures. He himself made many friends among lions and tigers. But he learned that the big cats were very dangerous when in season, and if trainers did not remove surly, jealous males from the troupe during these periods, they would probably be mauled as rivals.[92] Hagenbeck insisted that his trainers be intelligent and have a love of animals. Patience and sympathy resulted in remarkable performances. Thus, the trainer was no longer a taskmaster with the beast his slave. Instead, the relationship became one of teacher and pupil. Hagenbeck demonstrated the obsolescence of acts such as those of the English "lion king," Thomas Batty, which he had seen as a boy in Hamburg. Batty's

exhibit—in which he frightened six lions and drove them around the cage, terrifying them into leaping over barriers pushed in from the outside, then, standing near the exit, firing several shots from a carbine and leaping out of the cage—was a thing of the past.

The cardinal rule in Hagenbeck's method was to expel from his troupe any animals which did not possess sufficient intelligence or were too clumsy to become successful performers. Indiscriminate recruitment of animals meant failure. If their behavior or temperament changed, they were to be removed from the act. Combining species in the same cage required patient, painstaking work and study of each individual animal to prevent disastrous fights. Every step was carefully planned and arranged with nothing left to chance. The trainer was to have genuine affection for his animals and believe his most valuable tool was not a whip, but a leather pouch filled with meat chunks. He had to understand that the appearance of ferocity on the part of the big cats was merely show and that snarling and growling was merely designed to add to the excitement of the act. But even Hagenbeck acknowledged that at the heart of all wild animals, even though "deep down perhaps," there existed the "remnant of their primitive ferocity" which might burst out in fury at any time. This demanded courage and the constant vigilance of trainers.[93]

Hagenbeck's brother, Wilhelm, also pioneered these new training methods. Among his important achievements was teaching a young lion to perform equestrian tricks. He also assembled a notable group of seventy polar bears who performed various novel stunts. Carl, himself, demonstrated that there was virtually no animal resistant to training in some degree through steady patience and intelligent handling, and he demonstrated this when he exhibited an act that included two tigers, two lions, two black panthers, two leopards, three Angora goats, two Somali sheep, an Indian dwarf zebu, a Shetland pony, and two poodles.[94]

In 1891, Carl Hagenbeck began readying exhibits for the World's Fair, to be held in Chicago in 1893.[95] Twice he lost his troupes to illness, first to glanders and then to cholera, but despite these

difficulties his acts were a sensation when he displayed them on the Midway Plaisance at the fair. Using a big cage arena that he had invented in 1887, his trainers had space for larger groups of animals and more props with which to work.[96]

The following year Hagenbeck took his wild animal show to New York where it appeared at Madison Square Garden. The *New York Times*, reporting the event, observed that animal trainers and men associated with wild beasts in captivity gradually "grow by force of their association to resemble their savage pupils in bodily and facial characteristics." It offered in evidence Professor Darling, the lion trainer, who it thought had a distinctively leonine appearance with his tawny beard and hair, firm nose, and fixed stern eyes. Even his walk was a slow, catlike tread. Although he disliked being reminded of the resemblance, he daily acquired more and more of the "outward aspects of the lion." Herr Mehrman and his black bear also had the same way of walking and of throwing their heads and looking about. Since Herr Mehrman also

Hagenbeck trainer Heinrich Mehrmann presenting a mixed group of animals.

worked with tigers, his face had taken on their appearance. William Philadelphia, another lion trainer with the show, who was almost killed by one of his charges, was proud of his resemblance to the big cats, and he consciously tried to make gestures similar to those of his lions. The *Times* concluded that trainers could not make an easy recovery from the mental impression caused by the intense study of a particular beast.[97]

During the summer, Hagenbeck's acts moved to Manhattan Beach where they were called "wonderful exhibitions of animal intelligence and the mastery of human courage over brute ferocity." Reportedly, the savage beasts behaved as docilely as kittens.[98] Acts included Princess Helena, a lioness that rode on horseback, other lions that pulled chariots with still more lions riding in them, tigers that balanced on a rolling ball, Siberian bears that jumped hurdles and wrestled with their trainer, and bears that walked a tightrope. All the animals were pronounced sleek and exceptionally well-groomed.[99]

In September, the show returned to Madison Square Garden with sixty new animals added to the troupe. The event of the week was the return of the popular William Philadelphia. "Those who said this plucky little fellow's nerve was gone when Black Prince nearly finished him last year will change their opinion when they see his present exhibition, that of a tigress riding horseback, which for nerve and daring has seldom been equalled."[100] Ten years later another World's Fair, in St. Louis in 1904, again featured Hagenbeck's animals. The *Scientific American* commented that no great exposition could be complete without a Hagenbeck display. At the fair, in a large open air panorama, wild animals normally hostile to each other congregated in facsimiles of their dens, lairs, mountain fastnesses, and gorges.[101]

During a thirty-year period Hagenbeck had trained over seven hundred large animals, in addition to teaching the majority of trainers in America and Europe his methods. His most interesting group, one of two Nubian lions, one lion-tiger crossbreed, three Bengal tigers, two Indian leopards, two South American pumas, two polar bears, and four boar-hounds, took four years to train and the rejection of forty-four animals before the final sixteen were selected. He did not look for large profits from his animal acts but instead re-

The entrance to Hagenbeck's zoo in Stellingen (1907).

"Dinner time at the training quarters" (Hagenbeck's 1902).

"Taking the Hurdles between Lions and Tigers" (Hagenbeck's 1902).

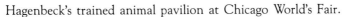

Hagenbeck's trained animal pavilion at Chicago World's Fair.

Poster for Hagenbeck's World's Fair Exhibition. —*Fred D. Pfening, Jr.*

garded them as a good medium for advertising his training methods. His principal income came from selling wild animals to zoos, menageries, and private parks.[102]

Equipped with patience, tact, good judgment, and a love for animals, anyone could become a wild animal trainer. That, at least, was what Hagenbeck believed. His American agent, however, thought trainers, like poets, were born. He saw hundreds try at the school in Hamburg and quickly give up. Others progressed no farther than cleaning cages, the very first step of apprenticeship. The next step was much more difficult. It demanded the ability to convince animals that the trainer was the master who compelled obedience. Braggarts watching Hagenbeck's exhibitions declared they were willing to go in with the big acts but after signing a written release with "ghastly blanks for particulars of death or mutilation," they never reached the cage. This, he felt, was for the best; even Hagenbeck's finest trainers might let down their guard and be mauled or killed.[103]

"A group trained after eighteen months of teaching" (Hagenbeck's 1902).

Col. Francis Ferari and his leopards. — *Fred D. Pfening, Jr.*

The revolution in animal training techniques and showmanship did not include Hagenbeck and his students alone. When Colonel Francis A. Ferari and Captain Joseph G. Ferari—the Ferari brothers—and Frank Bostock, English fun-fair showmen, brought their equipment and animals to America in 1894, they also brought ideas about animal training with them that were similar to Hagenbeck's. The partners first set up on a Flatbush Avenue lot in Brooklyn and then moved to the booming seaside resort of Coney Island. The Feraris, British citizens despite being the descendants of generations of Italian show people, had won their military titles from battles with wild animals. Frank Bostock, a third generation animal man, was a descendant of George Wombwell, the first English menagerie owner. Contemporary writers described him as a suave, polished, handsomely formed, virile man who looked "good in a uniform in a cage of lions," and Francis Ferari as a "Spanish don with the commanding air of a sea captain."[104] These men were destined to become founding fathers of the American carnival industry when they took their animal shows on the road as the Bostock-Ferari Mighty Midway. But their acts gained their greatest publicity at Coney Island.

At first the Englishmen refused to use the "narsty" ballyhoo popularized by the Americans, but soon they were forced to adopt this "ignoble means of attracting attention."[105] A Captain Maitland, dressed in plaids, and twirling his mustachios

Frank C. Bostock.

at one end of the front entrance, ballied Bostock's show as Queen Victoria's favorite. Then, announcing the price of admission and pointing to the steps leading to the crossover, he had people toss their quarters into a large wooden bowl resting beside him on a small table. Two uniformed guards escorted the crowd past the wooden bowl. As the seats filled, the aroused animals roared and bellowed, which attracted more eager people. Maitland then introduced two of the trainers and signaled the band to play. In the absence of good ventilation there was a fast turnover and a repetition of the bally.[106] Another method of attracting potential customers was to "drag" the townspeople down to the animal show. A trainer stood near the entrance of the park with a large chunk of meat on a big fork. People who hoped to see the animals fed followed him along the midway.[107]

Bostock, who had been taught by his family to love and value his beasts, was supposedly kind and considerate to every animal he met.[108] He believed that just as some men had been blessed with the ability to rule other men, others were gifted with a power over beasts. Man, he admitted, could generally master any animal, but to control it without harm or violence is a far different matter. "It is a subtle, magnetic force, a superficial expression of an inner quality which I think anyone might be proud to possess. In many years of dealings with men and beasts, I have learned fully to trust a man who is fully trusted by the beasts committed to his keeping."[109] Trainers wanted to work for him since he provided the best animals, good salaries, and a

high standard of living conditions. Like Hagenbeck, Bostock's trainers gave Americans a new opinion of wild animal men. They were not mysterious people stalking about in high boots possessed of a "remarkable power of the eye" that cowed lions and tigers. Animals were willing to perform for them because of the patience, kindness, and superior intelligence of their trainers, not out of fear of "torturing points and red-hot irons." Only a genuine fondness for animals made a man a great trainer. It gave him sympathy for them, and with that, understanding, and finally mastery. Typical of the new breed of trainer was Madame Bianca, a French trainer with Bostock's show, who despaired so deeply over leopards she lost in a menagerie fire that she retired altogether from the profession.

But liking the great cats was no guarantee of protection for trainers. The cats might not like them, might fear them, might even hate them. Animal men learned that revolvers and even armor were of little or no assistance against attacks. The only real protection was inspiring the animals with such awe that they never dared attack the trainer. Since an all-out onslaught would almost always be fatal to the man because of the animal's vastly superior strength, cats had to be kept so fearful of man's power that they would never attempt anything. Once a beast saw fear in the trainer, discipline was destroyed. If a trainer ran from the arena or was rescued by assistants, it played on his nerves to such an extent that he lost all mastery. The beauty of an animal could also be dangerous

Bostock trainer. — *Fred D. Pfening, Jr.*

Another Bostock trainer: Mlle. Aurora and her polar bears.

since many trainers took desperate and unbelievable risks because of a fascination for a particular beast.[110] No matter how polished the acts became and how docile the animals appeared, it was still only a veneer, for the wild fierce nature could break out any time.[111] Men also began to understand the intense jealousy, meanness, and cruelties that existed among animals, although the constant danger and hairbreadth escapes were usually known only to those behind the scenes.[112]

The runway provided the most frightening peril to the Coney Island trainers. That narrow, boarded lane encircling the den that led the performing animals to the ring was a terrifying place, a low, dimly lit passage, that curved constantly so that visibility was a scant twenty feet. As he peered ahead, the trainer could easily imagine that he heard the soft tread of a lion or that he saw the glow of the greenish eyes of a tiger, and the slightest noise might mean the bolt of a cage had

Frank Bostock and his eight lions.

slipped or a board given way. On May 14, 1911, with a large weekend audience, the lion Black Prince attacked trainer Vincent Rivero in the runway. His scalp ripped from the back of his head to his right eyebrow and his left shoulder bitten, Rivero walked through the audience to the office, while people gasped in horror. The newspaper called it "the usual Sunday accident in the animal arena."[113]

Even more difficult to teach effectively than the animals were trainers themselves although they were chosen with great care. Severe tests given apprentices to try their courage and coolness in emergencies included leaving an animal intentionally loose in the runway when the new man least expected it. The trainer needed a dominating personality that showed both his authority and his own complete self-mastery. Good personal habits in a "life of constant nerve strain and much physical suffering" were of utmost importance. Trainers had to have absolute personal integrity. They were to smoke and drink very little, if at all. Bostock thought wild animals instinctively knew when men were addicted to bad habits. The beast, he wrote, despised people who drink or lead loose lives with "all the contempt of his animal nature and recognizes neither their authority nor superiority." Big cats respected graceful, refined and pleasing personalities. The more magnetic, polished, and accomplished the trainer was, the greater would be his success. The least carelessness, the least indifference, even an unusual movement, could spell death. Unwearying patience and good judgement were also cardinal virtues, and one of the main reasons, Bostock declared, that Germans and Englishmen made excellent performers. But quickness of temper and a desire for revenge would immediately eliminate a potential trainer.[114] The mortality rate of cat men shows that the "trained lion is a product of science, but the tame lion is a chimera of the optimistic imagination, a forecast of the millenium."[115] The moment a big cat realized his dominance he was likely to use his terrible teeth or still more horrible claws, Bostock warned. "The moment an animal realizes his power his training is at an end," and his "long slumbering ferocity breaks out with redoubled vigor."[116] Whether an attack was accidental or intentional a trainer was never to make the slightest sign of pain or annoyance. He had to realize in the course of a career that he would be clawed and torn many

times. When a beast actually sprang, however, it had to be either cowed into submission quickly or the trainer had to try to get out of the cage. As long as the man was on his feet, he had a chance of controlling the animals; knocked down, all his power gone, his only chance of survival was raising himself back up.

Agility, nerve, and knowledge of animal nature were important. The trainer had to have a superb physique, clear eyes, hard sinewy muscles, well grown limbs, well developed body, clean healthy skin, good blood circulation, excellent mental capabilities, and no physical blemishes. Bostock felt none of his trainers epitomized these ideals more than tall, handsome, magnetic-eyed Jack Bonavita, a man who had developed an act with twenty-seven male African lions, an assembly on a scale never before thought possible.[117]

Bonavita, a "mild monomaniac on the subject of courage," claimed he got more confidence every time he faced an angry lion and survived the battle. Whenever warned of possible danger, he pointed out that his name, "Bonavita," meant

Captain Jack Bonavita.

Captain Bonavita carrying a lion weighing 500 pounds.

"good life," as if that had some sort of talismanic quality.[118] But he experienced difficulties in getting animals to understand what he wanted. Perhaps this most difficult aspect of training, coupled with his complete lack of fear, is what led to his several serious injuries. He always strove to finish his act no matter how severe his wounds—in "the very finest lion-tamer spirit"—as it was mistakenly called—and he always went on for another show.[119]

Despite having fifty bad accidents, Bonavita insisted that "A man does not refuse to go to battle because he has been hurt."[120] In the end his courage resulted in his death. While putting a group of polar bears through their paces for a motion picture production in Los Angeles in 1917, he was fatally wounded. But then "Bonavita" was only adoptive after all. His real name was John F. Gentner.

Polar bear used at the Pan American Exposition for drawing children's carriage.

Jack Bonavita and his lions (Bostock's).

Jack Bonavita and his lions (Bostock's). — *Fred D. Pfening, Jr.*

Bonavita started his circus career as an acrobat, but when he grew too large and heavy he took over a puma act, then soon changed to lions, which became his real love. The subjugation and training of the great felines became the dominant type of wild animal act, and in his heyday Bonavita thrilled audiences everywhere with his heroics. The circus-going public believed then as now in the ferocious reputation of the big cats and it demanded that "lion tamers" face the greatest possible peril. Bonavita certainly did that when he made his first appearance at the Pan American Exhibit in 1901. His entrance with twenty-seven lions so impressed the audience that the silence was intense. The gates at the back of the arena opened, and slowly, majestically, twenty-seven big cats walked out and at Bonavita's unspoken order — for he never spoke to his animals — each one took his place. President Theodore Roosevelt, who saw one of these performances, vowed he had never seen or heard anything like it and called Bonavita a hero. But when he introduced some new animals to his act, he wound up in the midst of twenty-seven battling lions. Remaining calm and self-possessed, but with every nerve and muscle at their highest tension, he got out by jumping over the backs of the fighting animals, receiving a rip in his

Bonavita after the loss of his arm. He considered the most
hazardous part of his performance the act of driving the
great herd of lions into the arena.

shoulder. After the cats fought it out, he reentered
the arena and drove them to their cages.[121]

A calm, sensitive man, Bonavita was under tremendous strain, relaxing in the company of his
Great Dane, Pluto, and his cat, Tramp. Courteous
and reserved, he rarely talked about himself—only
about his lions.[122] He believed more could be
achieved with them through kindness than harshness, though he was not foolish enough to believe
there was such a thing as a lion's devotion.[123] He

had no reason to, especially after a 1901 disaster at
Coney Island.

The Coney Island wild animal show was located
in Dreamland, a lavish $3,500,000 park of broad
promenades, plazas, lagoons and a 375-foot replica
of a Spanish tower. One million incandescent light
bulbs lit the enclosure that could accommodate
250,000 people.[124] Running the peanut and pop-
corn concession was Marie Dressler, who twenty-
five years later would become Hollywood's most

This was the most critical moment in Claire Heliot's act with twelve lions.

Claire Heliot with her favorite lion.

Bonavita approved the idea but his doctors insisted that the only way they would release him was on the condition that he would never return to the hospital. Bonavita's appearance proved a sensation at the park. The public refused to leave him alone, even in his hotel. His condition worsened, but when doctors at Coney Island Hospital refused to readmit him, he was taken to Brooklyn Hospital, where his arm was amputated. It took him nearly a year to recover before he returned to the arena, even more the romantic hero than ever before.[126]

Bostock Animal Act: Mme. Morelli.

Mme. Luise Morelli of Bostock's and her pet leopard, Cartush.

sought after actress, friend of presidents, and darling of high society. She was romantically attracted to Jack Bonavita and never missed any of his performances. But at one of them his lion, Baltimore, attacked Bonavita, catching the trainer's arm in its great mouth and crunching it until every bone in his hand and wrist were broken. Taken to the Coney Island Hospital where Marie Dressler visited him every day (bringing him watermelon, his favorite treat), Bonavita had two of his fingers amputated.[125] The newspapers gave the story much attention and played up the chance of serious infection. Samuel Gumpertz, the park manager, posted daily bulletins in front of Dreamland stating Bonavita's temperature, condition, and prospects for recovery. As an added ballyhoo, Gumpertz planned to display the hero himself in a wheelchair alongside the cage where his lions were performing under the direction of an understudy.

Dreamland, Coney Island, New York.

In 1911, two weeks after the lion, Black Prince, had attacked Vincent Rivero in the runway, a devastating fire swept Dreamland, gutting the beautiful park. The animals in the Bostock-Ferari menagerie sensed the fire first and put up a tremendous howling. Ferari, Bonavita, and the other trainers rushed to the arena to try to quiet the frightened beasts. They hoped the leaping flames at the other side of the park would be contained by the lagoon. As the fire intensified, they let the animals into the arena, walked them around and around, and hoped to calm them by making it look like a training session. The trainers then started getting the terrified creatures into shipping crates, as they worked against time in a desperate rescue attempt. But everything seemed against them. Firemen cut the electricity and the arena was plunged into darkness, eerily lighted only by the glow of the fire. The animals began fighting among themselves, but for some reason did not attack the men. The trainers and keepers managed to box five lionesses and four leopards, before being forced back by the falling Dreamland tower. Ferari ordered them back to shoot as many animals as they could to save them from a fiery death, but the heat was so intense that even he had to give up. A lion thought to be Black Prince escaped, mane blazing, into a mass of spectators. After a

Dreamland, Coney Island, New York.

Bostock arena in Dreamland. — *Tom Henricks*

Bonavita's fight with seven lions in the runway.

Bianca rescues Bostock from Brutus.

Rajah's attack upon Bonavita in the runway.

The tiger Rajah kicked by the quagga.

Putting the tiger Rajah again upon the elephant's back.

"How the lioness was captured on the open prairie." This shows an excellent example of "sidewalling" in capturing an escaped animal.

frenzied chase, he was cornered and riddled with bullets atop a ride called "The Rocky Road to Dublin." Dead from the wounds, his skull split by a fireman's ax, the lion was seized by souvenir hunters who pulled out his teeth and tried to cut off his head.[127] The next day Ferari announced his reopening with the surviving animals in a portable arena under canvas, but the fire had destroyed almost all of one of the finest animal collections in America.[128]

Despite the good publicity generated by Hagenbeck and Bostock, differing opinions about the "rightness" of wild animal acts began to appear in books and periodicals. Bostock acknowledged that he felt guilty for jailing these forest, desert, and jungle creatures, but that after wrestling with his conscience he had decided that he caused them no discomforts equal to the tragedies, hunger, and thirst they would experience in the wilds. There was no cruelty in their training, he argued, and

In demonstrating training techniques, *St. Nicholas* magazine showed the step-by-step process. Here the "Lion destroys the chair."

The motion pictures provided another need for trained wild animals, as shown in this movie shot in Fort Lee, New Jersey, in 1914.

JOHN T. BENSON, Proprietor

John T. Benson advertised himself as "Society's Wild Animal Educator. The only man who successfully subdued that terrible lion Satan. Purveyor of wild animals to his excellency Theodore Roosevelt, Timothy L. Woodruff, New York and Newport's Four Hundred, The State of New York, and all Institutions of Natural History. The man who stocked the Adirondacks." (Insert is logo of Benson's Wild Animal Farm in the 1940s. The farm still exists.)— *Fred D. Pfening, Jr.*

any punishment they received was no more than what was "exercised occasionally in the correction of an evilly disposed child." Although he insisted animals were willing and even eager pupils, criticism increased.[129]

A 1900 article questioning the morality of "shows of trick animals" asked if animals were placed on earth merely to amuse man. Although it argued that wild animal acts criminally risked human life, far greater criticism was leveled at the shows' pandering to the worst in people. They were "degrading spectacles . . . of horrible suffering to both man and brute." "A morbid sensationalism is at the root of the whole growth," it snorted; people like "the smell of battle," but, it added, "without any of its danger." It was "danger at a distance"—a fake, a surrogate for real life.[130] But it was often far too real for the trainer, as Harvey Sutherland commented in a 1902 edition of *Current Literature.* People, he wrote, liked the idea of a trainer going "directly from the circus to the morgue."[131] This bloodthirstiness was bitingly satirized by George Peck in 1906:

An average audience never gets its money's worth unless someone is hurt doing some daring act. Pa suggested that they have some one pretend to be hurt in every act, and have them picked up and carried out on stretchers with doctors wearing red crosses on their arms in attendance, giving medicine and restoratives. The show tried it at Bucyrus, O., and had seven men and two women injured so they had to be carried out, and the audience went wild, and almost mobbed the dressing-room, to see the doctor operate on the injured. It was such a great success that next week we are going to put in an automobile ambulance and have an operating table in the dressingroom with a gauze screen so the audiences can see us cut off legs like they do in a hospital. Maybe we shall put in a dissecting room if the people seem to demand it.[132]

Early female trainer in small circus circa 1910. — *Fred D. Pfening, Jr.*

Cruelty toward animals, however, was the most widespread point of the criticism of wild animal acts. Since beasts obeyed only what they feared, it stood to reason that extreme cruelty had to be used to instill fear. Sutherland, for example, declared that the motto of any animal training school should be "No lickun, no larnun." The lion, he wrote angrily, might be the king of beasts, but after his claws were clipped and his jaws muzzled, after he was repeatedly knocked out of his senses with a club, yanked by his collar and chain, stung by a rawhide whip, and had blanks fired at him, there was not much left of the king.[133] Others, admitting that cruel and barbarous training practices might be used by second and third rate "fakes," pointed out that such people outnumbered skilled practitioners in every profession.[134] S. L. Bensuan, in the *English Illustrated Magazine*, took another

Cage wagon of era. — *Fred D. Pfening, Jr.*

Early wild animal act. — *Fred D. Pfening, Jr.*

tack. This Britisher contended that "the average foreigner has no soft place in his heart for brute creation. . . . Consequently it is sufficient to say the majority of animals are trained abroad."[135] Some rare men may have been done an injustice by the article, Bensuan conceded, but on the whole "the profession of performing animal trainer is a brutal and offensive one, and one in which the sins of the many cannot be redeemed by the behavior of a few."[136] Another critic believed that southern Europeans were not inherently cruel to animals, but instead were influenced by the doctrines of the older Jesuites, who taught that man was not an animal, but the miniature of a higher being, with dominion over the "dumb creatures," and had every right to assert such dominion without mercy or moderation. The rising concern for animals was largely a phenomenon of cities and factory

Setup of arenas for the 1923 performance of Ringling Bros.–Barnum & Bailey Circus at Madison Square Garden. — *Fred D. Pfening, Jr.*

1915 poster. — *Fred D. Pfening, Jr.*

1922 poster. — *Fred D. Pfening, Jr.*

1923 poster. — *Fred D. Pfening, Jr.*

1922 poster. — *Fred D. Pfening, Jr.*

districts and was seldom shared by farmers or other rural folk. Social changes stimulated humane feelings and heightened sympathy. The suffering beast was an acceptable object of benevolence since it "profaned no social taboos and upset no economic applecarts." It was an attractive outlet for humanitarian impulses.[137] Darwin had also produced another terror: the animal in man. This fear was evidenced in *Dr. Jekyll and Mr. Hyde* and Wells' *The Island of Dr. Moreau*. One soothing answer was to use animals as role models and emphasize their natural wisdom. Reformers tried hard to obliterate the image of nature as "red in tooth and claw," and replace it with the concept that animals naturally possessed sympathy, compassion and love. James Turner

concludes that kindness to animals and compassion for every living creature was the surest refutation of the human being's bestial savagery.[138] But critics were puzzled by the apparently endless patience of animal trainers, which seemed to contrast sharply with the brute application of physical pain. Even Sutherland decided that being a lion trainer had much to do with patience.[139] *Harper's Weekly* agreed in a 1911 article which reported that the only secrets of the "lion tamer" were endless patience in administering repetitive lessons with the avoidance of needless cruelty.[140] But a year later it offered a different view when another article focused on the cruelties of the animal training school at Woodside, Long Island, picturing the lion as a "pitiful figure, lord of all the jungle

"This trick, where the lioness seizes the end of a piece of meat which the trainer holds in his mouth, is one of terrible danger. On one occasion the lioness, failing to catch her end of the meat, sprang at the trainer, tore his throat, and nearly killed him." (Mundy's Animal Show, Luna Park, Coney Island, 1911).

"Although this act is apparently rather tame compared with other parts of the performance, it is in reality the trainer's most dangerous moment. Twice he has been badly clawed by the lioness, through failing to put his arms quickly enough about her neck."

An extremely dangerous lion act, in which the lion is made to walk backward along a narrow plank. Being at an elevation above his trainer, he has an excellent opportunity to spring down upon her

"An extremely dangerous lion act, in which the lion is made to walk backward along a narrow plank. Being at an elevation above his trainer, he has an excellent opportunity to spring down upon her."

"A very difficult and dangerous act, requiring an extremely well-trained horse. The most critical moment is when the horse is made to stand still. The chances are then ten to one that the lion will spring at his trainer."

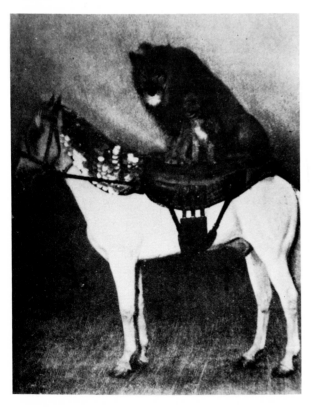

hunched upon a little stand, like a dunce in school."[141] The strongest condemnations of animal training would blend these two characteristics of patience and cruelty by depicting the wild animal trainer as a cold-blooded fiend.

In "The Gentle Art of Training Wild Beasts," a bitter, cutting satire, Maurice Brown Kirby ridiculed the notion of an affectionate tie between trainers and their animals. The only use an animal trainer had for the word "kindness," Kirby wrote, was when he discussed professional methods with an interviewer. The bond between man and animal was a good strong stick: the fiercer the beast, the bigger and stronger the stick. The first thing to break in an animal was his spirit, and that had to be done with a club. Animals, he wrote, are not "taught, they are pushed and shoved and mauled and whipped and dragged and choked and tortured into tricks." As the most patient trainer he had ever met once told him: "When they won't give way to pain, they won't be broke." In a horrible description of a full-grown bear that "refused" to be broke, Kirby graphically explained how "ripping the ring" meant to control the animal by rings fastened to its nostrils and ears until there was nothing left "to make fast to." He detailed the methodical, brutal breaking of a tiger by a "handsome, extravagantly reckless" trainer, "a passed

Maurice Brown Kirby used these photos to illustrate his caustic 1908 article "The Gentle Art of Training Wild Beasts." This was entitled "Operating on a tiger's broken leg."

"Bears in shifting dens, ready to travel to permanent quarters."

Kirby used this illustration to show that "The Lashed Whip is Conspicuous among the Means Employed in Training Tigers."

"A detail of training is the firing of blank cartridges into a beast's nostrils."

Kirby believed that "The repeated infliction of pain is the force that has 'tamed' these leopards."

master in the art of thrilling an audience" and appealing to women's "morbid love of daredeviltry." "The beast was there to be trained and he was there to train him. Ethics are out of the place in an arena. So is sympathy. The animal has neither. Why should the trainer be affected by them?"[142]

The fiction of this era represented generally held beliefs about circus life. For example, one of the basic appeals of the circus was its suspected wicked worldiness, so that although many circus employees were in fact rural boys seeking adventure and travel, the circus gave them foreign-sounding names and used exotic advertising to cloak the show with an air of sophistication. But the old puritanical strictures also clung to the circus. It was a refuge of scalawags, n'eer-do-wells, idlers, child thieves, and contemptible foreigners. In the fiction of the dime novels, staunch bastions of the work ethic, the circus often appeared in an unfavorable light. Boy heroes normally left the circus after a series of trials and tribulations to begin a

successful career in a more acceptable profession, or else were discovered by long-lost upper-class relatives who returned the lads to the higher echelons of society. Often the hero married the still innocent and redeemable daughter of a circus owner. Many of the show people were depicted as pitiful and not overly bright, but with a heart of solid gold. In this category typically were clowns and elderly workmen.

Dime novels frequently used animal trainers as their title characters: "Lion Charly," "The Boy Beast Tamer," "Samson, Jr. The Wild Beast Tamer," "Lion Luke, The Boy Animal Trainer," "Monte, The Animal King," "Shasta Sam and his Seven Tame Lions," "Dick Merriwell, Lion Tamer," or "Fred Fearnot and the Wild Beast Tamer."[143] These novels were certainly not written to condemn wild animal acts, but trainers were often portrayed as strange, somewhat less than human creatures. Occasionally they were described as southern Europeans and served as villains in the stories. But whether hero or villain the dime novel trainer was vividly stereotyped as brutal, vindictive, conceited and often cowardly. In one fictional work, readers learned that "the whip and a blast from Frank's gun usually got [the lion] on a pedestal. But not tonight. He kept on charging with the whip cracking in his face and when Frank yanked his gun and pulled the trigger, there was no flash and roar of gun powder. The smash of a mighty paw hurled him across the cage, he landed on his back unconscious."[144] Frank is a hero, but in another piece the trainer is obviously villainous:

> The swarthy man with well-oiled locks and a waxed moustache . . . stood in the midst of them, dressed in spangled tights, a whip in one hand and a pistol in the other. His dark eyes shot out rapid glances to right and left, above, below, in front and even behind, it seemed, as with imperious gesture, snap of whip or sharp word of command he put the fierce beasts through their rounds of tricks . . . with low growls and sullen looks of rage the great creatures went through their humiliating programme . . . animals . . . trained to do his will . . . by the power of these piercing eyes.[145]

In another excerpt the belief of the importance of the hypnotic eye, along with the conceit and brutality of the trainer is emphasized:

> The wild beast tamer's name was Wentworth and he was a splendid looking fellow physically but his bump of self-esteem was simply enormous and he looked upon everyone as his inferior. . . . I can take a whip and go into that cage and do anything that Wentworth can. It is his eyes that

Col. Edgar Daniel Boone and Miss Carlotta were the first to present trained animals in an American circus in 1891 on the Adam Forepaugh Circus. — *Fred D. Pfening, Jr.*

Margerita Gollmar, 1916. — *Fred D. Pfening, Jr.*

Nineteenth-century trainer.

Drawn by A. B. Frost

THE LION-TAMER

those beasts are afraid of . . . there is not an animal in that cage who can stand before my eyes. . . . Fred looked the animal in the face and gave him a sharp cut with the rawhide. The leopard quickly retreated. He saw no fear in the eyes of the new trainer . . . it was plainly seen that they were only waiting to catch his eye off theirs to spring at him and tear him to pieces.[146]

The last two quotes demonstrate the cowardly brutality of trainers:

The tiger fell back against the bars limp and half dead. Crack! Crack! Crack! Cruelly Budd West lashed the beast. It was scarcely necessary. . . . the animal trainer was a thorough coward and as mean and selfish as he was cowardly.[147]

Feeling he must redeem himself and drive the lion into the cage, he crept, with stealthy movements near to the beast, whose eyes were fixed on the boy. Then with a quick spring, he thrust the point of the hot rod into one of the lion's ears. A

Illustrations from the 1901 *St. Nicholas* article on the occupation of "Wild Beast Tamer." *Above*: "The tamer's triumph reading his newspaper in the lion's den." *Below*: "Coming to close quarters."

"Beginning the training."

roar of surprise and pain rolled from the lion's throat. He turned savagely on Leonto, with such wide open and vindictive jaws that the lion tamer's hours on earth seemed numbered. But Leonto had all the agility of the professional athlete. He evaded the lion's rush and then the blows of the lion whip fell in a stinging shower. "Into the cage there," Leonto commanded, his voice hoarse and savage. "You Scipio! Into that cage!" The pain cowed the lion and he retreated before the fierce onslaught.[148]

One novel in particular almost sounded the death knell for wild animal acts. Jack London's *Michael, Brother of Jerry*, published in 1917, was a devastating attack that aroused a reaction no previous condemnation of wild animal acts ever had. Skillfully weaving together the traditional criticism of animal shows as degrading to humans and cruel to animals, London did his best "to blur the distinction between animal and human."[149] He wrote: "We who are so very human are very animal . . . you must not deny your relatives, the other animals. Their history is your history, and if you kick them to the bottom of the abyss to the bottom of the abyss you go yourself."[150]

Written as a companion piece to *Jerry of the Islands*, an earlier story whose title character is a dog, *Michael, Brother of Jerry* follows the experiences of a dog named Michael, who inadvertently falls into the clutches of a series of professional animal trainers and handlers. London explained in a preface that his insatiable curiosity had led him behind the scenes to learn how animal performances were developed. What he found, he wrote, was a "body of cruelty so horrible that I am confident no normal person exists, who once aware of it, could ever enjoy looking on at any trained animal turn." He was far from a "namby pamby," he wrote, and had seen "more than the average man's share of inhumanity and cruelty from the forecastle and prison, the slum and the desert, the execution chamber and the lazar house, the battlefield and the military hospital." He had beheld starvation, men and women whipped, people driven to madness, mutilations and horrible death, but nothing had appalled and shocked him more than the sight of happy, laughing, applauding audiences watching trained animals perform their turns. He could tolerate unconscious cruelty and undeliberate tor-

In 1900, *McClure's* magazine ran an article on "The Training of Lions, Tigers, and Other Great Cats" that was illustrated by Charles R. Knight of the American Museum of Natural History. They were called probably the most perfect drawings of lions ever produced. They were not simply pictures, but actual portraits. Pictured here: "The second great step in advance: The lion has learned to endure the touch of the human hand . . . he likes it, for few animals are indifferent to petting."

"The next instant, with open mouth and claws distended, he is sailing through the air, straight for the throat of the man, his 800 pounds of sinew and muscle inspired by the ferocity of fear and hate."

"Giving vent to outraged feelings in loud roars."

"Growling."

"He draws back, growls, and thrusting out a huge paw, pins the intruding object (a broomstick) to the floor."

CHAS R Knight

"Snarling, he drops on his haunches and claws at the barrier."

"He feels it rubbed, gently rubbed along his neck
and back . . . there is nothing a lion so loves as
grooming."

"Emerson."

ture, but "what turns my head and makes my gorge rise, is the cold-blooded, conscious, deliberate cruelty and torment that is manifest behind 99 of every 100 trained animal turns. Cruelty as a fine art had attained its perfect flower in the trained animal world." He demanded that all men, women, and children acquaint themselves with animal training methods, join or form humane societies, and walk out whenever any animal act was staged. Those who read his book, he hoped, would "weep red tears and sweat bloody sweats" as they came to know what real cruelty and brutality were.[151]

The novel features an animal trainer named Harris Collins, at fifty-two a slender (he weighs only 112 pounds), gentle, sentimental man, and a doting husband and father. He is easily frightened by burglars, police, and by physical violence. (His greatest fear is that his large wife may someday crown him with a plate of hot soup.) But he shows no fear of wild animals of the most ferocious sort, and here London describes him as little less than a two-legged devil. Born in England—he has learned his trade from his father—he now runs a training school at Cedarwild, Long Island, where he rules an animal hell. No visitors, not even his own family, are ever allowed to watch him training, but other animal men who have seen Collins work, and who call him the king of trainers and the greatest man who has ever gone into a cage, all agree he has no soul.[152]

Whether London actually saw the brutal training procedures he said he did is open to serious question. His narrative concerning the breaking of wild animals and the slogans of trainers is virtually identical to what Maurice Brown Kirby had described in his article for *Everybody's Magazine* nine years earlier. In fact, London describes almost verbatim from Kirby the unsuccessful attempts to break a bear and the better results obtained with a lion, elephant, and tiger. The main differences lie in the names that are used for the animals and the human qualities attributed to them. Detailing the training of Ben Bolt, the tiger, London wrote it "went on interminably—for an hour—for men-animals had the patience of gods while he was only a jungle brute. Thus tigers are broken. And the verb means just what it means. A performing animal is **broken.** Something breaks in an animal of the wild ere such an animal submits to do tricks before a paying audience."[153]

Boyce Rensberger, science writer for the *New York Times*, has recently accused London of borrowing from fairy tales rather than first hand experience in his nature writing, and he argues that London's literary motto was "make it vivid. Truth doesn't matter so much, as long as it lives."[154] The charge seems to fit *Michael, Brother of Jerry.* The book is avowedly and blatantly propagandistic. But as a man who loved the outdoors and exulted in the human spirit, London believed to oppose wild animal acts was to take a stand for good in the eternal battle between good and evil.[155] Suffering from uremia and serious mental depression that had driven him to opium and other drugs at the time he wrote the novel, he labored in agony to finish it before he died.[156]

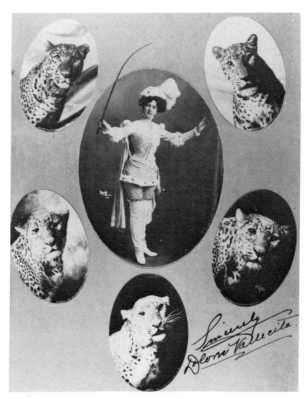

Dolores Vallecila. —*Fred D. Pfening, Jr.*

Early trainer riding in cage wagon during the street parade. —*Fred D. Pfening, Jr.*

Typical dime novel cover (1905).

Dime novel cover (1909).

He did finish it, and when it was published post-humously it converted more people than all his books dealing with socialism. Jack London Clubs began to be formed in the United States. Members rose from their seats whenever animal acts were exhibited and stalked out in silent protest against the cruelty practiced on the animals during training. By 1924, the clubs had a reported membership of four hundred thousand.[157]

London's writing had a powerful and far-reaching effect on animal lovers. When an English trainer was severely injured by a lion, the claws having punctured his lungs and an infection developing, he received letters that hoped his death would be protracted and agonizing. (It was, and after three weeks he died.)[158] Author John Galsworthy joined in the condemnation of wild animal acts, writing that it "was too ironical altogether that our love for animals should make us tolerate, and even enjoy, what our common sense, when we let it loose, tells us what must in the main spell misery for the creatures we proffer to love."[159] In England, long debates were held in Parliament to decide whether animal acts should be banned altogether or restricted by severe penalties for cruelty and constant vigilance by humane societies. Testimony was highly emotional, those for abolition arguing that "it takes some terrorism to make an elephant groan like a man in anguish, a bear shut its eyes and cover up its face, and a tiger whimper."[160] The Nation commented that although circus audiences were normally kindly and humane, the fun they derived from the show was "firmly based on a fundamental instinct of cruelty."[161]

Then in 1925 fell what seemed to be the final blow, when Ringling Bros.–Barnum & Bailey Circus announced that all acts containing the big cats had "been discarded because the management recognized that in many quarters there is a decided aversion to the presentation of trained wild animal acts which convey to many people the suggestion of cruelty in training and handling."[162] The transporting and transferring of performing wild animals often caused delays and was always dangerous. Parents had also objected to bringing young children to a show in which men or women entered a cage with ferocious beasts.[163] The New York Times rejoiced in the decision. It would give "mourners over the evils of this time . . . a little surcease of their sorrow." No longer would people be shocked at the sight of human beings entering the cages of savage beasts. Interest in these acts, always morbid, had been based on a desire, if not to see someone killed, then at least to be present "when the ever-threatened revolt of the huge beasts took place." The Times also deplored what it called a "lurking exultation" trainers felt in their mastery of animals far stronger and better equipped than themselves. Although circus men never admitted their training practices were cruel, it concluded that they at least had the sensitivity to recognize that there was a widespread belief that the acts were basically brutal.[164]

In reality, John Ringling never liked wild animal acts. Not until 1919 had he even allowed them in his circus. He felt the cage and runway detracted from the beautiful Grand Entry that began every circus performance, dismantling caused slowdowns in the program, and the equipment created obstructions in case of fire or a blowdown.[165] He felt "the lure of the circus" was the desire of every human being to be young again. Since people

John Ringling. – *Fred D. Pfening, Jr.*

Scenes from Bostock's midway featuring the "Hagenbeck" Wild Animal Show Co.—*Marion Organ Collection*

Scenes from Bostock's midway featuring the "Hagenbeck" Wild Animal Show Co. —*Marion Organ Collection.*

wanted to leave all care and worry at home, the show should strive to avoid anything unpleasant or that might bring sorrowful memories. "No act that might suggest accident or injury is permitted."[166] Only the public's interest in wild animal acts and the fact that his brother Charles Ringling liked them prompted John to use them in his program. Charles philosophized that "to me my circus is my menagerie. . . . I always think in terms of animals instead of sawdust and . . . other things that . . . make a circus." Whenever he wondered if he was the man he would like to be, he went to the menagerie and looked at his animals in the face, "for unless my animals like me, I am a failure." If animals did not like a man, there was something wrong with him, because an animal knew a man better than a man knew his own kind. They were quick with sympathy and resentment and understood man's moods instantly.[167] In 1922, the Ringling circus featured seven animal acts; in 1923, eight; and in 1924 it staged a true "circus spectacular" when four steel arenas worked at one time. The rising strength of the reformers, however, gave John Ringling an excuse to eliminate these acts in 1925.[168]

The urgings of newspapers and magazines that all circus owners follow Ringling's example went unheeded. The American Circus Corporation's cat barn on the rich bottomland of the Wabash was the scene of great activity during the twenties as were their winter quarters in West Baden, Indiana, and Montgomery, Alabama. At Culver City, California, the winter home of the Al G. Barnes show, acts were broken and trained for the famous wild animal circus. As carnivals, fairs, amusement parks, and expositions relied more on mechanical rides to amuse their patrons, wild animal acts became the domain of specialized circuses. The high point was reached during the "Jazz Age" when over fifty animal trainers plied their trade. This fierce competition forced the Americans to present exceptionally reckless and daring performances with a new feeling of excitement and spontaneity. The popularity of these daredevils caused the domination of the wild animal act over "pure" circus turns. They became the mainstay and feature in all American shows, including Ringling Bros.–Barnum & Bailey.

Future American Circus Corporation magnates Bert Bowers and Jerry Mugivan (Hot Springs, 1910).—*Fred D. Pfening, Jr.*

Chapter II

THE TRAINED WILD ANIMAL CIRCUS

Wild animal acts developed in the traveling menageries of the late 1830s, but by the 1870s these shows disappeared, absorbed by the circuses to which they had given respectability. Not considered "pure circus," they were usually relegated to sideshow status, where they took the form of wild or "untamable" routines in which a trainer attempted to enter the den of a snarling, ferocious beast. The cats performed no real tricks but were trained to offer a show of rousing resistance to the "tamer." By the turn of the century these demonstrations were found predominantly in fairs, expositions, amusement parks, and carnivals. Foreign performers, primarily German and English, using Carl Hagenbeck's newly invented training methods for far more sophisticated presentations and a greater number of animals, also introduced the portable steel arena he invented and so paved the way for wild animal acts to become an integral part of circuses once again.

The popularity of these displays stimulated enterprising American showmen to establish new trained wild animal circuses. The most successful pioneers in this field were Al G. Barnes on the West Coast and the Hoosier circus men, Ben Wallace, Jerry Mugivan, Bert Bowers, and Edward Ballard. Their shows grew in strength and eventually, by 1921, culminated in the powerful American Circus Corporation (ACC). This combine forced the previously untouchable Ringling Bros.-Barnum & Bailey Circus—which had united in 1919 under the management of the Ringling Brothers, who had bought Barnum & Bailey in 1907—into a position of buying them out or losing superiority.

In September of 1929, John Ringling, last of the famous brothers, bought out the ACC.

Ben Wallace.—*Albert Conover*

63

Edward Ballard.—*Albert Conover*

Jerry Mugivan.—*Albert Conover*

Bert Bowers.—*Albert Conover*

After purchasing it, Ringling leaned heavily on the efficient, well-liked Hagenbeck-Wallace Circus to produce enough profits to operate both shows during the Depression. The canny Peru, Indiana, showmen always believed the majority of the public in the "Roaring Twenties" still enjoyed wild animal acts despite the animus against them in intellectual circles. They developed a number of exciting American wild animal trainers, who specialized in the fighting act which combined humane breaking methods with a performance that resembled on a very large scale the old "untamable acts." Its success depended on the showmanship abilities of both the trainer and his animals. No one developed this style of presentation better than Hagenbeck-Wallace's young prodigy, Clyde Beatty. His name became synonymous with the wild animal act in the United States, and even John Ringling, who denounced these performances, relied on his spectacular daring during the

Cageboys at the Hagenbeck-Wallace winterquarters. —*Fred D. Pfening, Jr.*

Hagenbeck-Wallace winterquarters, Peru. —*Fred D. Pfening, Jr.*

Depression. But it was precisely Beatty's popularity that led to the formation of a new organization that broke the circus monopoly the Ringlings held. Framed in just a few months in 1934–35, the Cole Bros. Circus was a major railroad show that stimulated enthusiasm for circuses among writers, fans, historians, and collectors because it not only represented the cause of the underdog but revived the free street parade as well and offered an excellent performance to boot.

By the late 1930s, the wild animal act became the high point of all major circuses, a status it has never lost. Gradually, because of a lack of performers, the American fighting act has given way to the seemingly more controlled, one species, European style, dominated by German trainers. In these acts the trainer's complete mastery over the animals is emphasized through complicated tricks and often elaborate props, rather than the ferocity of the cats and the daring of the trainer as in the fighting school.

In 1895, one of the innovators of the trained wild animal circus started a wagon show with the proceeds from the sale of his farm. Born Alpheus George Barnes Stonehouse in 1862 in Lobo, Ontario, his initial exhibition consisted of a pony, a phonograph, and an Edison Vitagraph. This soon developed into a traveling show under canvas,

Al G. Barnes letterhead. —*Harry Chipman*

Entrance to the Al G. Barnes winterquarters. —*Fred D. Pfening, Jr.*

consisting principally of performances by trained wild and domestic animals. At first this specialty circus played carnivals and fairs with Stonehouse himself as the primary trainer. In 1903, he joined a wild west show in which he presented an act featuring a mountain lion riding a pony. After traveling with other circuses, and shortening his name, the showman debuted his own Al G. Barnes Trained Wild Animal Circus as an independent venture in 1909. At first the menagerie was displayed in the main tent, but the circus grew steadily and by 1916 was a four-ring show.[1] When Barnes purchased three hundred acres of ranchland west of Culver City, California, for his winter quarters, the place became a popular tourist attraction. Visitors could look at the many animals there and watch in perfect amazement whenever Barnes would hitch two elk to a cart for a drive to nearby Venice.[2]

He was described as a soft-voiced, handsome man, courteous, kind and sympathetic, who loved animals and would not tolerate cruelty in their training or handling.[3] He devised his own acts and gained a reputation for originality and for radical yet practical innovations, such as the use of spotlights in the circus performance. Only when an act was more attractive, more entertaining, and more highly developed than anything of its kind was Barnes satisfied.[4] During the early wagon show days he personally trained all the performing animals and worked them himself in their acts, but as

Al G. Barnes.—*Dyer M. Reynolds*

Al G. Barnes and Lotus.—*Fred D. Pfening, Jr.*

the circus grew, he delegated more and more duties to other trainers. Strongly disagreeing with the common assumption that trainers abused wild animals, he believed that only ignorant, impatient amateurs used harsh methods. Any of his handlers who were caught mistreating an animal were discharged with no second chance given. But he knew the dangerous, volatile natures of wild creatures—a fearful beast, he once said, could not be taught and emphasized that the foolhardy never made successful trainers.

Al G. Barnes's careful choice of trainers helped to produce an extremely popular circus. His chief trainer and menagerie superintendent for more than twenty years was a Hungarian immigrant named Louis Roth, who had served his apprenticeship at Louis Ruhe's Long Island wild animal farm. Later working with Frank C. Bostock, Roth had demonstrated his training ability by teaching some unusual riding combinations: a tiger and an elephant, a leopard and a zebra, three adult lions and a horse, and the trainer—Roth himself—and a lion. With the Rawlings Circus, he presented a mixed group of lions and tigers, an untamable lioness, and a wrestling lion. In 1909, after answering an ad in *Billboard*, the ambitious Roth took a position with the Barnes show. During his long tenure there he instructed the majority of the show's performers. At the peak of the circus's popularity, he was supervising seven trainers. He stood by during each of their turns, ready to take

Louis Roth, with Al G. Barnes Circus. He joined this circus in 1909 after learning his trade with Bostock's. — *Fred D. Pfening, Jr.*

Louis Roth, the teacher of Mabel Stark and a longtime Al G. Barnes star in his own right (1917). — *Fred D. Pfening, Jr.*

charge if necessary. Roth also worked two feature acts himself; since accidents occurred frequently, he regularly substituted for incapacitated performers. One two-week period saw him presenting nine different acts. The show's thirteen animal acts included such unusual displays as a dozen performing pumas and a dancing girl in a den of ten lions. One of Roth's acts consisted of twenty-one tigers and another broke Jack Bonavita's record lion presentation of twenty-seven by one.[5]

In 1912, Roth acquired his most famous pupil in the person of a woman, Mabel Stark, who was destined to become America's most famous female wild animal trainer. To be sure, women had appeared in dens and arenas prior to Stark, and in fact more than sixty years earlier the ill-fated "lion queens" had performed in England. In 1887, William Cameron Coup had offered ten thousand dollars "for an equal to Mademoiselle Rinehart, the Only Female Lion Tamer, who enters a massive den of living wild lions and leopards and performs them like kittens."[6] Again in 1903, an unidentified woman performer had remarked publicly

that females were more proficient than males as trainers since they possessed greater patience and because their "mother instinct" enabled them to command the obedience of animals.[7] Madame Morelli, the little Frenchwoman who starred in Bostock's show and made "a half-score of leopards, panthers and jaguars do things which nature never intended them to do," was known for her performances in evening dress. She was said to be able to whip "considerably more than her own weight in wild cats."[8]

A contemporary of Mme. Morelli was Claire Heliot, who began her lion training career in 1897. She was German but spoke to her cats in French, believing that in her communications with them she was solving mysteries as old as the Garden of Eden. This modern Eve claimed that her twelve lions were the kindest and most intelligent animals in the world and that their love would be her payment for her considerate treatment of them. Even if she were to be accidently knocked to the ground, she alleged, she would still be safe.[9] According to the *New York Times*, she governed her lions as the

Mabel Stark. — *R. E. Conover*

Mabel Stark. *Circus World Museum, Baraboo, Wisconsin.*

Mabel Stark. *Circus World Museum, Baraboo, Wisconsin.*

Ione Carl (John Robinson Circus, 1923). — *Fred D. Pfening, Jr.*

Wife of the cookhouse man, she wrestled a tiger and worked eight tigers in 1926. — *Tom Henricks*

"best of women govern the human brute by trusting them blindly," and not by force. Heliot, herself, believed courage was a form of self-hypnosis: "We refuse to be afraid, we trust to an avatar of luck and we survive because the sands of destiny are not run out." At the end of her act she tested these theories by carrying a 360-pound lion on her shoulders.[10]

Circus owners during the first quarter of the twentieth century found there was no better showmanship than having a woman command the jungle beasts. These women, usually the wives of menagerie men or trainers, had started by helping their husbands with the animals and then had finally asked to enter the training arena with them. Once they started, wives often took their husbands' place according to prolific circus author Courtney Ryley Cooper. Animals would obey their new trainer with an implicit sort of faith since she usually was less nervous and fidgety and more completely oblivious of the dangers than her husband.[11] Cooper believed that a woman could

Lucia Zora, who was billed as the bravest woman in the world (Sells-Floto).

Margaret Thompson at the Sells-Floto winterquarters in Denver, Colorado. — *Fred D. Pfening, Jr.*

often tame a wild beast when a man failed because the "gentleness of womankind" was best able to soothe the fear that caused animals to attack. A woman trainer was not "a person born without fear" as the advertisements claimed, but she was wise enough to win confidence from the cats. Her act won her greater applause than what other female performers were able to command because it required more concentration.[12]

Women who became trainers by this route during this era included Mrs. Fred Alispaw, wife of the menagerie supervisor of Sells-Floto, who was billed as "Zora, the Bravest Woman in the World." This former Russian ballerina worked elephants, lions, tigers, and leopards. Another was Margaret Thompson, who married veteran animal trainer "Dutch" Ricardo. He entered the training cage, put the animals through their paces and then sent his wife in to do exactly the same thing. The technique worked and soon she acquired her own center ring act which concluded with her singing

Mabel Stark—1934.

while a tiger leaped back and forth over her head. Thompson's closest call came when a lion attacked and gashed both sides of her neck, missing the jugular vein by a quarter of an inch. When questioned about this near disaster, she smilingly said, "It isn't when they miss that matters, it is when they don't."[13]

By the early 1920s virtually every circus large enough to have wild animal acts featured one or more female trainers. The reasons behind the willingness of all these women to enter the steel arena is certainly a matter of conjecture. Connie Clausen, who traveled with a circus for a short time, suggested that since the circus woman traditionally behaved very submissively to her husband it did not "count a whit that she had just hung five lines of wash (scrubbed clean by hand in a bucket of ice-cold water); that she was back in the act three hours after the twins were born, and nursed them between "spec" and "finale." When he came on the scene . . . her muscles went into storage and her courage into mothballs" and with "every breath she assured him how much smarter, stronger, harder-working and better-looking he

was than she. [The wives] put their brains to sleep lest their ideas conflict with HIS."[14]

But Mabel Stark was different. Neither exotically foreign or married to an animal man, she sought her own identity and a special niche in circus history. Tigers became her one, overwhelming obsession. Even among the danger-hardened people of the circus, her bravery, nerve, and indomitable will power were a source of comment. She said there was no reason for fear unless it was your time and then it was useless to be afraid. Stark preferred to be killed by her cats she said, rather than "by an automobile or pneumonia or some other stupid disease."[15] Unless she could go into the cage, she once wrote, life itself was not worth living. At the age of seventy-eight, after fifty-seven years of active performing where she was nearly completely incapacitated as a result of the many horrible maulings she had suffered during her long career, she still entered the arena daily with a group of tigers.[16] That was in 1967, but that same year, she was forced into retirement. Four months afterward she died from an overdosage of barbiturates, her life no longer worth living.

Mabel Stark.—*Fred D. Pfening, Jr.*

She was born in Toronto, Canada, in 1889, but grew up an orphan in Princeton, Kentucky. She studied to be a nurse, but on graduating from nursing school she promptly collapsed under a nervous breakdown. Traveling to California to recuperate, she went one day to the Selig Zoo in Los Angeles, where she saw a tiger and instantly fell in love with it. She forgot the nursing career she had planned and applied for a position with the Al G. Barnes Circus. She pestered, agitated, and begged Louis Roth for the opportunity to go in the cage with a few tigers, which she always called "the royal lords of all animal creation."[17] Hoping to get rid of her, the circus press agent cleared the way for her to enter the arena, not really caring if she were killed or not. He had her sign a release, and she went in. Incredibly, she survived. Roth, who had thought she would surely be killed, took her on as his pupil. The year was 1911.

Stark detested all her first assignments. She disliked horses, goats, and even lions. But in 1914 she worked an act with Sampson, called the aviation lion, and another with a group of male lions riding a stallion, and finally she performed with a small troupe of tigers. By 1916, she was presenting the show's major tiger act.

For Mabel Stark, tigers were the most magnificent expression of animal life. She felt they could be subdued, temporarily, but they could never be conquered, except by love. In the big cage, the

Mabel Stark and two cubs.

A Mabel Stark tiger greets a newsman. — *Fred D. Pfening, Jr.*

most important attributes a trainer could have were courage and patience, as well as nimble feet, and nimbler wits. She found no thrill equal to that of matching wits with the big cats. Their rousing defiance did not frighten her since she believed her will was stronger than their rippling muscles. That did not mean that her tigers never attacked her. Far from it; but no matter what injuries she ever received from one of her tigers, she always blamed herself completely.[18] And she received many injuries. In fact, she proudly boasted that every inch of her body was scratched or bitten into battle scars. A famous circus story has it that a young woman once approached Mabel Stark while she was resting in her dressing tent after a strenuous performance. The young woman jokingly suggested that she would like to learn to tame cats too, so she could handle her mother-in-law, and she asked what it took to be a great tiger trainer. "This," said Mabel, and she thrust out her legs from under her dressing gown. They were covered from ankle to thigh with scars.[19]

In 1922, Mabel Stark left the Barnes show to join the Ringling circus. She opened in Madison Square Garden in an end ring, but immediately caused a sensation that brought her headlines. "Circus Girl Cows Tiger and Panther—Thrilling Scene in Garden as Young Trainer Faces Fierce Feline Group," roared the *New York Times*. The *Times* correspondent described her as a slim girl in a blue suit who laughed while she fought with five tigers and a black panther. Impressed by her bravery, he noted that, unlike male European trainers, who carried a whip, a pistol, and a three-pronged iron training fork, Mabel relied mainly on a whip and a simple five-foot pole, only an inch-and-a half in diameter. "Nobody else dares drive animals as she does it," he wrote. "She didn't stop smiling in a half contemptuous manner for a moment yesterday, even though for a time it seemed that Frank Stockton's *The Lady or the Tiger* would be reinacted without any doubt as to the ending." He related the incident: Nig, the black panther, defied the trainer for nearly five minutes during which he refused to obey any of her commands. The audience turned silently and breathlessly focused on ring one, anxious to see how the woman in the blue suit would handle the situation. She tried a resounding crack with her stick over his head but when that had no effect, she smilingly fired a blank pistol up close and, as the reporter told it, "cowed" the animal until "He slunk over to the perch." Then she contemptuously drove all her animals back and forth over a steeplechase hurdle, finally coolly turning her back on the animals to acknowledge the booming rounds of applause meant only for her. Of the six wild animal acts featured with the "Big One" that year, Mabel Stark's end ring was clearly the greatest success.[20]

The New York *World* gave full-page coverage to the same story the *Times* had reported, and even the *Nation* printed a short commentary about it. When reporters learned that this energetic, brave woman had once studied to be a nurse, they pressed her for interviews, and the *Times* ran a story about her in which she was quoted as saying that she had never suffered from nervousness since she had left nursing. No animal trainer could, she said, and be a success.[21]

The publicity was just what Mabel Stark had wanted. A featured, center ring star with the Barnes show, she was not happy with her end-ring

Allen Chaffee's 1923 book, "Tony and the Big Top" was obviously inspired by Mabel Stark's exciting appearance at Madison Square Garden with her black jaguar. The fictional heroine wins the center ring after the veteran male trainer is injured.

status with Ringling at all, and as she later said in her autobiography, she would have regained her position if she had "had to make Nigger stand on his head." John Ringling, angered at first by the incident that caused a delay in his show, relished the free publicity and the enthusiastic crowd reaction. When the road season began, Mabel was back in the center ring.[22]

She starred in the Ringling center ring with eight striped beauties again in 1923, but two years later the big show banned wild animal acts. The Tiger Woman was relegated to the cowboy and cowgirl number.[23] The tigers, transferred to the menagerie, "roared in an effort to retain their stardom," and a wistful Mabel Stark consoled herself with the thought "that the elimination of the more dangerous acts was for the best."[24]

She was probably right. After a sojourn in Europe, she joined the American Circus Corporation's John Robinson show in 1928 to perform her

wild animal act again. It was during that season that the small, lithe, high cheek-boned performer received her worst mauling. In a muddy arena in Bangor, Maine, she lost her footing. No sooner had she fallen than one of her tigers ripped her left thigh, almost severing her leg. The other tigers joined in the attack and by the time fellow trainer Terrell Jacobs fought off the cats, she had a lacerated, mashed face, a deep hole in her shoulder, torn deltoid muscles, and a hole in her neck.[25] At a local hospital, she directed physicians in the proper way to treat tooth and claw wounds so that no fatal infection would set in, ordering that they pour raw carbolic acid directly into the rips and tears. In a matter of weeks, swathed in bandages and walking with a cane, she returned to the show.[26]

About five years later a tiger gave her a blow to her head so powerful that she worked for a year "in a grey cloud of pain" until a brain tumor was de-

tected and successfully removed.[27]

Her subsequent career was just as dangerous, but never as dramatic as her early years. She performed with Sells-Floto in 1929 and then rejoined the Barnes show, now Ringling-owned, until it went off the road in 1935. She toured with some small circuses in the 1940s, showed her tigers in Japan in the '50s and then returned to the Jungle Compound at Thousand Oaks, California, for the remainder of her career. Recently she has become a heroine to the women's movement. Completely independent, she selected, purchased, broke, and trained her own tigers. She proved that size and strength were not important in handling the big cats. But certainly equally significant is her place in circus history. She once said she would give the circus everything since it had given her all that she wanted. She justified wild animal acts for the challenge and tingling excitement they provided. If a good show meant keeping dangerous, unpredictable, explosive renegades in an act, then they had to stay. The chance to dominate tigers pushed crippling, disfiguring injuries into insignificance. She was a major factor in the success of the trained wild animal circuses, especially in the Al G. Barnes show.

Mabel Stark, Terrell Jacobs, and Bert Nelson—star trainers with the Al G. Barnes Circus (1936).—*Harry Chipman*

Louis Roth, Paul L. Hoefler, and Louis Goebel, who operated a famous wild animal farm at Thousand Oaks, California.

Polar bear cage being unloaded (Sparks, 1927). —*Fred D. Pfening, Jr.*

On November 23, 1905, newspapers announced that a major new enterprise was about to make its debut before the public. Originating in the German Exhibition of the 1904 St. Louis World's Fair (which subsequently toured much of the eastern portion of the United States when the fair closed), it was to be a trained animal show featuring regular circus acts. Permanently based in Cincinnati, it was named the Hagenbeck Animal Show and Circus, and it got under way with a good deal of optimism and éclat.[28] By the end of the year, however, the newcomer was in deep trouble. American circuses offered such fierce competition that at the end of 1906 the heavily indebted show faced bankruptcy. To salvage something from the situation, its inexperienced managers John Havlin and Frank Tate tried to form a partnership with the Ringlings. Ringling was interested in using the show's name, but since Carl Hagenbeck had never even left Germany to participate actively in the circus (although one of his sons, Lawrence, did tour with it), Havlin and Tate could not furnish Ringling with clear title to the Hagenbeck name he wanted, so the deal collapsed.

The importance of the name lay in the widespread belief among circus men that Germans were superior in the field of training wild animals. Most circuses at one time or another added a German name to their titles or gave teutonic-sounding names to their trainers. For example, Gollmar Brothers in 1901 billed their show as Gollmar

Bros. & Schuman's United Monster Shows. The advertising even included an illustration of the imaginary Herr Schuman.[29] But no title was considered more valuable than that of the internationally famous Hagenbeck.

Shortly after the Ringling merger fell through, an impresario from Peru, Indiana, entered the picture. This was Ben Wallace, an extraordinary, largely self-made man who had come with his parents and eight brothers and sisters to the little Indiana town from Pennsylvania in 1863, when he was fifteen. His father became custodian of the poor farm but when a fatal attack of malaria struck him down in 1864, Ben assumed the family responsibilities. Hiring himself as a substitute to fight in the Civil War, he banked $995 of the $1,000 he received, reported to Indianapolis, and joined his regiment, the Thirteenth Volunteer Infantry. But the war ended before the outfit ever left the capital, and Wallace returned to Peru. There he opened a livery stable, married, and when his wife died in 1870, married a second time, to the local hotel keeper's daughter, who taught the illiterate young man to read and write.

Meanwhile his business steadily prospered. By 1881, he boasted of owning the largest livery in Indiana. Yet its very success led Wallace to abandon it. As a popular stopover able to accommodate large numbers of animals, Wallace's stable frequently attracted traveling entertainment troupes, and when Wallace came into the possession of the

Great Wallace Show's winterquarters in Peru, Indiana (1895). — *Fred D. Pfening, Jr.*

American Circus Corporation winterquarters in the early 1930s.

Ticket wagon of the
H-W circus in the
thirties. — *William Koford*

animals and circus trappings of one of these com-
panies in payment of a feed bill, he decided to sell
his livery and enter the circus business full-time.
Forming a partnership with experienced showmen
James Anderson and Al G. Fields, Wallace put together a show—the Wallace & Co. Great Menagerie,
International Museum, Alliance of Novelties,
Mardi Gras and Street Carnival (later shortened
to the Great Wallace Shows)—and on April 26,
1884, he left Peru and took his show on tour.

The circus profited. It grew in size, and soon
Wallace bought out his partners. By 1886, the
show was large enough to switch to rails. Wallace
purchased 38 acres near Peru to use as winterquarters, but the burgeoning circus demanded more
space, and in 1891 he bought 227 acres along the
Wabash River from Chief Gabriel Godfroy of the
Miami Indians. Always clever in business, he
would end his tour in Texas, where he would sell
his baggage stock and buy mules, then winter
them in Peru, selling them for big profits there,
which he would use to purchase better horses. Before he retired, Wallace owned almost 2,700 acres
of the richest bottomland in Indiana, herds of
Angus and Hereford cattle, thirteen houses on
"Wallace Row," the Wallace Theater, the Colonial
Apartment Building and the Wabash Valley Bank
in addition to the circus, railroad yards, and a
farm, famous for its many buildings painted in
"Wallace yellow." Miami County prospered along
with this jovial friendly teetotaler, who was known

locally as "Uncle Ben," "Governor," or "Colonel
Wallace."

Occasionally, however, Wallace would ask to be
referred to as "Colonel Johnson, Mr. Wallace's
assistant," a dodge he found wise to employ because of his show's deep involvement in "grift," the
blanket term used to describe such circus activities
as shortchanging rackets, gambling, and "indecent" dances. The earliest forms of grift had been
stealing clothes from lines and pickpocketing, but
by the first quarter of this century, it meant gambling games in the sideshow, "cooch dancers" with
a "blowoff," and the "connection" racket in which
ticket sellers in the connection between the big top
and menagerie shortchanged the customers as
they rushed for reserved seats. The dancers and
gambling games usually had to be fixed with local
authorities. Patrons willing to be "taken" were ac-
commodated in many different ways, but customers could also see an attractive, well-equipped
circus with an excellent performance—and while
in Peru, Wallace warned his men always to "shoot
square." (Even there, however, a certain over-
zealous, civic-mindedness led them into trouble.
Once, they stole a statue of an elk from one of the
tour's towns so that it could be placed in front of
Peru's Elk Hall.) When the heat got too strong,
Wallace found it prudent to disguise himself as a
roustabout—or conceal himself in a monkey cage
while his men raced under cover of night through
back alleys and yards to reach the train. From

Winterquarter visitors gaze at part of the huge H-W menagerie. — *Ken Whipple*

Visitors gather to enter the Peru winterquarters. — *Ken Whipple*

1892 to 1894 even the circus was renamed Cook & Whitby. But no matter what the title, the "possum bellies" brimmed with profits when the show reached Peru every fall.[30]

For such an entrepreneur, the failure of the Hagenbeck Animal Show offered yet another opportunity for aggrandizement, and when the Hagenbeck-Ringling deal fell apart, it was Wallace who devised what turned out to be a successful plan to obtain control of the Hagenbeck circus and name. In 1907, he and his partners Jerry Mugivan and John Talbott loaned Tate and Havlin fifteen thousand dollars to clear up existing debts. In return, Wallace was given exclusive control of the new show until the loan was repaid. In return for managing the rail circus, Wallace, Mugi-van, and Talbott were to receive all profits from the "privileges" (sideshows, concessions, and grift). The deal concluded, the circus was repaired and refitted at Wallace's Peru winterquarters. Hagenbeck, who had been kept unaware of these developments, first learned of the new Hagenbeck-Wallace show through an item in *Billboard*, and he immediately protested that his name and reputation had been greatly injured by its use in connection with the Wallace name and he sought legal restraint on its use. But when Havlin and Tate defaulted on their loans, Wallace became virtual owner of the circus and a court ruled that when he bought the circus, he bought the name too. He exploited it all along the show's route displaying posters with side-by-side likenesses of Hagenbeck and Wallace. Thus for the nominal sum of forty-five thousand dollars, he acquired the most sought after name in the wild animal business.[31]

The strength of the new combination forced Ringling to put the Forepaugh-Sells Circus they had acquired in 1906 back on the road as competition in 1910. Billing wars grew so fierce that the following year circus men met in Chicago to try to draw up a code of ethics.[32] Then in the spring of 1913, the Wabash and Mississinewa rivers rose quickly and unexpectedly, flooding the Wallace winterquarters. The baggage horses were on high ground and were saved, but eight elephants,

twenty-one lions and tigers, and eight performing horses perished. The devastating flood persuaded the aging Wallace to retire. Observing that after traveling all forty-eight states, the soundest investment was still Wabash Valley black bottomland, on July 1, 1913, "Colonel" Wallace shocked Peru by selling his circus.

The buyer was the Indiana Corporation, an Indianapolis-based firm headed by Edward Ballard and five other investors. Ballard was another of those remarkable men, who like Ben Wallace had risen from poverty to fabulous wealth through a combination of opportunism and effort. He was

The resort area of French Lick, Indiana.

The inner courtyard of the West Baden Springs Hotel where circus acts often performed.

New West Baden Springs Hotel, West Baden, Ind., Carlsbad of America.

The West Baden Springs Hotel of Edward Ballard.

born Charles Edward Ballard in September, 1874, just outside the hilly little southwestern Indiana town of West Baden, which with adjoining French Lick comprised a major health spa and resort area. His father, embittered and impoverished after being forced to assume a debt he had cosigned for a friend, was unable to provide for his family and young Ed quit school after the fourth grade to work as a pinboy in a bowling alley. Later he carried mail on horseback and later still worked as a porter in a saloon. Thrifty and ambitious, he saved enough by the time he was twenty-one to open his own saloon in which the most lucrative part was card games and roulette in an upstairs room. In 1895, Ballard agreed to run a new casino in a local hotel. He had to borrow six thousand dollars to equip it but in two years he had repaid the loan and begun to make a profit. He bought land and took in loans and mortgages but refused to profit on these investments, preferring, he said, to use his wealth to help old friends. Things became temporarily tight in 1905 as a result of a campaign against gambling in the Indiana resorts that the Hearst newspapers waged. Three years later the voters elected a new governor, friendly to Democrat Tom Taggart, Indianapolis political boss and owner of the French Lick Hotel, and official opposition to gambling operations stopped. In 1915,

Ballard took over the Brown Hotel Casino and established a gambling code for it: no liquor sold to gamblers and no local residents or employees allowed to wager. During these same years, Ballard began to diversify when he joined the Indiana Corporation.

Ballard took over complete control of this corporation in 1915, although he retained Wallace's circus-wise nephew, C. E. Corey, and that same year he moved the Hagenbeck-Wallace Circus—of which he was now sole owner—to West Baden. Ten thousand people flocked to the circus that September when it came to winter in West Baden for the first time, and Ballard was hailed as a hero and one of the town's greatest benefactors.[33]

Ballard continued to be active in the resort business. In 1916, he bought the magnificent West Baden Springs Hotel. So splendid it was called the "Eighth Wonder of the World," the hotel featured a domed and balconied lobby where guests entered and registered, and a "Pompeian Court," paved with over twelve million marble mosaics, where a fountain played among palm trees and ferns cascaded down from wrought-iron balconies.[34] A unique structure built in 1902, it rose to a height of six stories and contained 708 rooms. Its great dome, 200 feet in diameter and 130 feet high, surpassed in breadth the St. Peter's cathedral

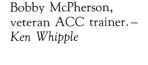

Bobby McPherson,
veteran ACC trainer. –
Ken Whipple

dome after which it was supposedly modeled.[35]

Joining his resort business with his circus interests, Ballard had circus performances presented in the Atrium. After dinner guests went to the court or occupied windows of the floors above. Then by way of a runway built from the ring to outside the building, five huge lions and the trainer, Schweyer, would come in. An observer at one of these shows wrote: "[Schweyer] put the beasts through several stunts with absolute fearlessness, although one of the lions, Brutus, threatened to tear him to pieces several times." Following this came an equestrian performance and then there was an act involving five elephants which concluded the entertainment.[36]

The area boomed in that "fast moving, fast spending and fast living era." Although Ballard was a Republican, his friendship with Taggart eased the expensive rivalry between hotels. The Kentucky Derby weekend drew enormous numbers of guests. But all year long playboys, politicians, athletes, and show people visited West Baden. Among the notables who came were the governors of Indiana and Illinois, the mayor of Chicago, Tammany Hall leaders, John J. Pershing, J. M. Studebaker, Irving Berlin, and even Al Capone, who patrolled the grounds in his Lincoln with its fenders of steel and doors with combination locks. The St. Louis Browns, Chicago Cubs, Pittsburgh Pirates, Philadelphia Phillies, St. Louis

Bobby McPherson. —*Fred D. Pfening, Jr.*

Hagenbeck was a German, even though he had never been connected with the show and, what's more, had died in 1913. But worse than this, on June 22, 1918, an empty westbound troop train plowed into the second section of the H-W train near Ivanhoe, Indiana, and four wooden coach loads of sleeping troupers were ground into oblivion by the steel cars. In all, eighty-six people were killed in the tragedy. But the tough show survived these threats to its existence, and in 1919 it became the basis of the new American Circus Corporation of Ballard, Mugivan, and Bowers.

Jerry Mugivan, known as the "Turk," and Bert Bowers, "The Little Man," began their circus careers as ticket sellers with the small Sanger and Lentz Show in 1893. They left show business for several years to retail railroad tickets but they returned to it when they joined the Sells and Gray Circus as assistant legal adjustors. From there they went to Ben Wallace's Great Wallace Circus where they ran the lucrative "privileges" and dining car.

Rudolph Mathies, star Ringling tiger trainer in the early 20s and again in 1947.—*Fred D. Pfening, Jr.*

Cardinals, and Cincinnati Reds all trained there, and so did the fighters John J. (Gentleman Jim) Corbett, Thomas J. Sharkey, John L. Sullivan and Gene Tunney. The spectacular circus performances in the court during the winter helped attract more conventions.[37]

Ballard lived in a beautiful colonial home built of handmade bricks. It contained marble fireplaces imported from France, fountains and statuary from Italy, and black walnut paneling from Germany. Twelve acres of landscaped gardens, ponds, and shade trees surrounded the mansion. Immediately behind it were the circus winterquarters and across the road from the front of the house was a large open field in which the show exhibited. For nine years this would be the home of Hagenbeck-Wallace.[38]

Ballard's chief difficulties in the World War I era arose from the anti-German sentiment of the time and the willingness of the Ringlings to exploit it. Ringling "rat sheets" emphasized the fact that

Fred Delmar and his Fighting Lions in 1921. Clyde Beatty was offered a chance to work this act but chose to remain with John Robinson. Louis Fertel took over the cats and was killed. — *Harry Chipman*

After an abortive attempt to manage a hopeless Kansas City amusement park, the two partners found some circus equipment in storage. They bought it along with twenty-eight head of draft stock, and took it all to the old burned-out winter-quarters of the Howe's show in Centropolis, Missouri, in 1904. They named the new circus Great Van Amburgh Shows; it boasted a menagerie consisting of one lioness, a grey wolf, a black wolf, one cage of monkeys, and a cage of cockatoos.

Their tour commenced on April 23, 1904, and despite blowdowns, washouts, and brakeless wagons, they made the season. The citizens of Cedar Rapids, Nebraska, amused by the sparse menagerie, left the circus a big tin elephant sign on which was painted, "Donated to Mr. Van Amburgh by the Cedar Rapids Zoo." Stung by the insult, Mugivan and Bowers purchased a real elephant, four or five cages of miscellaneous animals, some dogs, a trained hog, and a big snake. The following year, they bought their first railroad car. A year later, they owned eleven.

Then in 1907 the two invested in the Hagenbeck-Wallace venture while still adding to their own circus. Since they were grift operators, their shows went through a series of name changes: Van Amburgh to Howe's and the newly acquired Dode Fisk Circus to Sanger's Great European. Mugivan and Bowers had long coveted the well-respected and nearly ninety-year-old John Robinson title. The closest they could come was buying Danny Robinson's "Famous Robinson" show, a title they utilized in place of Sanger's. But in 1916 they finally got the real John Robinson name. Thus, at the time of the formation of the American Circus Corporation in 1919, the triumvirate of Ballard, Mugivan, and Bowers owned John Robinson and Hagenbeck-Wallace on thirty cars, and Howe's Great London on fifteen cars. The next year they purchased their largest show, Sells-Floto, from *Denver Post* publishers Tammen and Bonfils, and in the deal they obtained the Buffalo Bill title. The growing ACC then bought six hundred acres from the Wallace estate to establish their winterquarters.[39]

"Dutch" Ricardo, veteran Sells-Floto trainer. — *Fred D. Pfening, Jr.*

Herman Ziegler breaking a lion at the famous Goebel's Lion Farm in Los Angeles, 1936. — *Fred D. Pfening, Jr.*

In the next ten years, the ACC would come to own what was probably the largest collection of animals in the world. The "Circus City Zoological Garden" contained 6 giraffes, 3 hippos, 30 camels, 40 elephants, 125 lions and tigers, 500 blooded horses, 200 dogs and ponies, and ostriches, llamas, zebras, monkeys, pumas, black panthers, and polar, Russian, and Himalayan bears. Eleven hundred tons of timothy and alfalfa were harvested annually and a slaughter house was maintained to provide feed for the menagerie.[40]

The American Circus Corporation in 1920 also bought the Yankee Robinson show. After taking its equipment to winterquarters, they combined it with the best of the Howe's show and formed a top-notch twenty-five-car circus for manager Danny Odom to take on the road. The Howe's Great London and Van Amburgh Trained Wild

Louis Roth, like the other Al G. Barnes California-based trainers, often engaged in motion picture work. Here a 1930s epic is filmed with Roth as the double. — *Harry Chipman*

Animal Circus sported new all-steel flatcars and bright orange paint with dark brown lettering and white trim. The menagerie included seven elephants, along with camels, a sacred cow, zebras, a young male hippo (destined to grow into one of the largest ever in captivity), leopards, pumas, lions, tigers, polar bears, monkeys, and a glass-enclosed snake den. The show had an outstanding mile-long parade capped by a very handsome bandwagon. Louis Roth, hired from the Al G. Barnes Circus, directed the wild animal acts. Although the steel arena was up during the entire performance, regular circus acts gave excellent balance to the show. The animal acts included dancing lions, a puma and leopard act, tigers riding an elephant, and Roth's two featured acts—six Bengal tigers and four riding lions.

The strategy for the 1921 season was to make an eleven hundred-mile jump to Albuquerque, New Mexico, and then challenge the strength of the Al G. Barnes Wild Animal Circus in its own western

Louis Roth's wife Nellie with an act of her own. — *Harry Chipman*

Louis Roth with two large male lions sports his medals. — *Harry Chipman*

territory. This trip was marred by a trouble-making employee who had been "red-lighted"—tossed off the train—when he returned and poisoned the lions. Stronger than Mugivan may have expected, Barnes provided more competition than the ACC show anticipated. "The Turk" never again deliberately sent a show against Barnes and determined to buy the rival circus out when the opportunity arose. Howe's moved into the profitable Pacific Northwest and Canada where wild animal acts were especially popular. But as the ACC show traveled east to Minnesota and Illinois, it met surprisingly strong opposition from the Barnes circus which had ranged out of its normal western territory. By August, Howe's had moved far enough east to evade Barnes and prepared to begin its southern tour on the twenty-seventh. They planned to end the season with a homerun into winterquarters at Vandveer Park in Montgomery, Alabama, after a 17,437-mile season.[41]

Circuses generally believed their profits had to be made before the Fourth of July for a successful season. But the late August stops in southern Ohio proved both profitable and fateful. Turnaway crowds greeted the circus at Hillsboro and the next day in Washington Court House the menagerie superintendent hesitantly hired a short, curly headed boy from Bainbridge as a cage-cleaner. There was no better place than the bold ACC for this wiry, eager, and recklessly ambitious boy called Buster who within ten years would be the acknowledged master of wild animal trainers in the entire nation. As a columnist would write,

> trainers in the past have been brave men who have laughed at the idea of the cautious life as they faced a dozen lions and tigers or fifteen lions in a thirty-foot enclosure while the crowds day after day and night after night held their breaths lest the expected catastrophe occur while they were watching. But compared to the present king of all trainers these men were struggling through a comparatively mediocre novitiate waiting for Clyde Beatty to step into the big cage and put on a show that according to his less daring predecessors, was not only impossible, but would be absolutely suicidal in the first attempt.[42]

No one in the ACC in 1921 could foresee that, however, and Beatty joined the outfit in one of the most meager positions in the circus.

The following season, 1922, again entailed the ACC's use of exciting strategy and managerial skills to get the abundantly available entertainment dollar. In the east, Hagenbeck-Wallace and Sells-Floto gave little breathing room to Ringling, as the Indiana showmen got into territories ahead of the opposition, played towns at the same time, if necessary, and even swept up the crumbs after rival shows left an area. The Howe's circus remained identical to the 1921 version except in name. The ACC leased the Gollmar title for it from cousins of the Ringlings. Its emphasis con-

Theodore Schroeder and his sensational polar bear routine. He first appeared with RBB&B in 1921. Later he became the director of the Detroit Zoo for thirteen years.—*Fred D. Pfening, Jr.*

Theodore Schroeder at the Peru winterquarters in 1928. He was with the John Robinson Circus that year. —*Fred D. Pfening, Jr.*

Chubby Guilfoyle and Franz Woska on Sparks in 1927. On May 25, 1928, Guilfoyle lost an arm to a lion in Syracuse but continued to work for many more years. —*Fred D. Pfening, Jr.*

tinued to be wild animal acts, although Louis Roth had returned to Barnes. Now it featured a new lioness routine and an aerial balloon lion act in which the big cat was raised high in the tent on a platform while a colorful display of fireworks shot off all around it.[43]

In 1922, Charles Ringling and the New York Civic League launched a great campaign against grift. *Billboard* encouraged the movement and gave free space in its pages. They hoped to get showmen in the outdoor amusement industry to pledge to operate griftless in 1923.[44] The ACC claimed the Ringling stand and the criticism leveled against the Hoosiers was hypocritical. They charged that Ringling ticket sellers themselves practiced short-changing and that their extremely high concession prices were virtual highway robbery. The circuses the ACC had acquired had all utilized grift before becoming part of the holding company. The owners insisted the unsavory practices had not been strengthened on any of the acquisitions. Grift was a self-perpetuating evil, which reportedly began as a defensive measure to offset unrealistic license fees in some communities. Local officials knowing the reputation of the ACC-owned shows expected payoff money for the privilege of playing their town whether grift was present or not. If the grift had been dropped, trumped up charges and fines wold be leveled against the show. Even a "Sunday School" operation like Ringling had to make payoffs in cash and free passes. The San Antonio and Dallas police departments demanded thousands of free passes or they made arrests on the flimsiest excuses. In one instance, they fined

hundreds of circus laborers for indecent exposure when on a hot summer day they stripped to the waist.

Manager Danny Odom reportedly was very tough, but also efficient and fair. Like all the ACC's executives, he stubbornly resisted dropping the much criticized grift. Even Jerry Mugivan, who in many ways welcomed the exposure of grift and corrupt city officials, rebelled against the crusade, mainly because "do-gooder" Charles Ringling led it.[45] Then in October that year, the ACC's stand changed abruptly when an Earle, Arkansas, deputy sheriff shot and killed Billy Miles, Gollmar's legal adjustor, in a dispute over payoff money.[46]

Mugivan and Bowers decided to concentrate their efforts on three shows in 1923. They wanted to retire from active management and also have their holdings all winter in Peru. The Gollmar equipment was moved north from Alabama and combined with the best of the Robinson Circus, whose title would be retained. For its one-hundredth annual tour, John Robinson became strictly a wild animal show, "the largest of all such entertainments now before the public."[47]

Star of the show was Peter Taylor and his mixed group of lions and tigers. Taylor, advertised as a native of Birmingham, England, and a big game hunter, supposedly had been plying his trade in the jungles of Africa and South America for the previous ten years, except for one, during which he had trained animals in England.[48] A deft showman, he had brought the fighting act style of presentation to a new level of sophistication. *Colliers*

Pete Taylor in the 1923 spec of the John Robinson Circus.—*Fred D. Pfening, Jr.*

Pete Taylor, outstanding mixed fighting act trainer. Clyde Beatty would take over his act and owed his technique and style to Taylor's teaching.

hit out on cue and usually one animal was taught to simulate an actual attack, with emphasis placed on the cats' natural lightning quick movements. No animal act is more difficult to execute effectively, since the trainer and his beasts must be excellent actors.[50]

All three of the American Circus Corporation's shows continued their emphasis on wild animal acts in 1924. The Ringling ban on these acts the next year had no effect on Mugivan, Bowers, and Ballard's circuses except to make them available to animals and trainers let go by the Big One. They may have abandoned their grift reluctantly, but they never intended to go along with this crusade. Instead, their writers and publicists produced many nationally distributed articles and books favorable to wild animal acts. Courtney Ryley Cooper, Sells-Floto publicist, wrote numerous pieces about circus animals that stressed the kindness of trainers and the happiness and intelligence of wild beasts in captivity. *Under the Big Top* (1923) portrayed animals who paced their cages out of a need to exercise, not an urge to escape. An escaped beast, he wrote, was terrified until safe in its cage. It had no desire to attack man unless the panic and irrational behavior of the crowd drove the animal to defend itself. If females were not

Beatty (left) with famous circus author and publicist, Courtney Ryley Cooper, and the greatest aerialist of the day, Alfredo Condono.—*Peru Circus City Festival, Inc. Museum*

described this style in a 1909 article as "the big untamable act. . . . [In] such an act the tamer seems to be in no wise content with the natural ferocity of his animals. . . . [He] concludes his exhibition by deliberately and as it were, suicidally goading his beasts to the limit of animal endurance. They turn (or ought to turn upon him) every shuddery moment. And in the very eye blink, when he whips into safety through the spring bar door, SMASH, it is (or ought to be) covered four feet deep with big cats raring to get at him."[49] The early "tamers" during the middle 1880s invented this style and tried to produce a more spectacular act by enticing the animals to roar, leap, and strike out. Accidents often occurred when either trainer or cats overplayed their roles. The descendant of this turn, the fighting act, accented the wildness of the beasts. The big cats were trained to snarl and

overworked and were treated carefully and intelligently, they would reward the show with healthy cubs.[51]

In *Lions 'N' Tigers 'N' Everything* (1924) Cooper wrote that trainers were not chosen for brutality, cunning, or even bravery. They knew how to pull decayed teeth, perform minor operations, diagnose and treat diseases, and respect the temperament, individuality, and emotions of each animal. Their goal was first to conquer a beast's fear and then to befriend the animal. Each had simultaneously to teach an animal it had nothing to fear, instill routines in its mind, and make it aware it would be rewarded. A wild animal man and his assistants had to see to it that their charges were well fed, suffered no indigestion, and enjoyed adequate ventilation.[52] He was a person of constant experiments and irrepressible inquiry, since a mistake in judgement often meant a trip to the hospital.[53]

The drastic changes in wild animal acts over the past fifty years was a major theme in Cooper's next book, *Circus Day* (1925). In the past, he wrote, animals had not been credited with any emotions, and they had habitually been ill-treated. But if animals were cheap, then trainers were cheaper. Audiences wanted gore and thrills. The more often the performance ended with the trainer carried away on a stretcher, the better the crowd liked it. "Every member of an animal act was bleeding when it came out of the arena."[54] By the twenties audiences still sought thrills, but now animals could be trained without an ounce of cruelty yet with even more exciting results. "Conditions change—where suffering—now is peace—where forcing now communion and understanding." Today's caged animal, according to Cooper, was better looking than before, often weighed more than his forerunners, and was free of worms and disease.[55]

Olga Celeste appeared with Ringling in 1922 and worked in the center ring when seven acts were presented simultaneously. She also was one of the pioneers in training wild animals for movie work.—*Harry Chipman*

Olga Celeste.

"John went to the circus yesterday."

A LIVING REFUTATION OF MISLEADING PROPAGANDA

There has been much propaganda broadcasted regarding the cruelty exercised against wild beasts in training them for public exhibition.

This agitation is being conducted by well meaning and kind people, but they have not investigated the subject thoroughly.

The most positive and effective refutation of their assertion is to be found in the menagerie of the Hagenbeck-Wallace Circus, which show is this season carrying more trained wild beasts than any two shows enroute. A comparison of the condition, the appearance and actions of the beasts used in the wild animal acts with those used merely for exhibition purposes will prove at once that the trained beasts are far superior to the others in condition, in contentment and health. Americans who have traveled amid jungles and seen wild beasts in their native state all agree that those in captivity are much stronger, and in much better condition than those of the jungles. This stands to reason —it would be a miracle if it were otherwise.

The wild animal acts seen daily with the Hagenbeck-Wallace Circus are developed in the winter quarters at Peru, Indiana, where the fearless but patient trainers work all winter long, training wild beasts. They follow the process of elimination— upon finding that a beast is difficult to teach from sheer stubbornness or lack of sense, the animal is not abused or mistreated but is sold for exhibition purposes and another more likely animal substituted in its place. All training is done at Peru in public, at no time is the public barred—for the trainers do not do anything of which they would be ashamed for outsiders to see.

Those who are condemning the training of wild animals are actually defeating the very purpose for which they are contending—namely the bettering and the protecting of wild beasts.

—(Editor Magazine and Daily Review).

Statement from the 1928 Hagenbeck-Wallace Program.

Opposite page: The wild animal trainer has proved an excellent subject for cartoonists. – *Ringling Bros. and Barnum & Bailey Circus Magazine*

Peter Taylor wrote in *Billboard* in 1925 that Humane Society claims that wild animal acts were cruel were not based on facts. Insisting experts loved and understood animals and that they would be useless as trainers if they employed cruel practices, he pointed out that only the foolhardy, those who did not understand or fear animals, used abusive practices. A wise circus never utilized inexperienced, inept trainers, but only those who could both handle animals and also understand their natures and give them proper care. The "secrets" of any trainer's success were his ability to gain an animal's confidence through clear communication, his unwillingness to let an animal injure itself, and his good disciplinary methods and kindness. Cracking the whip over a beast to chastise it for refusing to obey an order or for crouching to attack was not cruel but discipline. Taylor believed the life of a performing animal was good. It lived longer, enjoyed its existence more than a zoo animal, and had far better health than a wild creature.[56]

Writing in the *American Magazine* in 1925, another animal man related that when a performer was injured in an accident with trained wild animals, the beast was very rarely at fault. Trained animals were creatures of habit and once they had learned their job, they did not vary. Only the trainer might eventually do something careless or stupid to injure himself and at the same time ruin

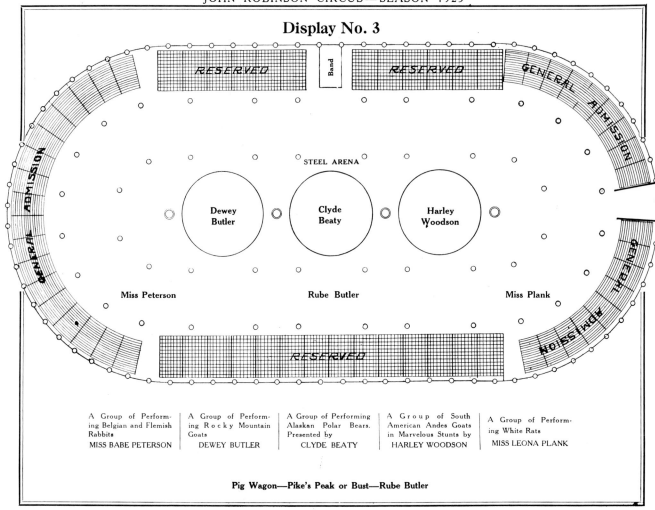

JOHN ROBINSON CIRCUS—SEASON 1923

Display No. 3

Band

RESERVED   RESERVED

GENERAL ADMISSION

GENERAL ADMISSION

STEEL ARENA

Dewey Butler

Clyde Beaty

Harley Woodson

Miss Peterson   Rube Butler   Miss Plank

GENERAL ADMISSION

RESERVED

| A Group of Performing Belgian and Flemish Rabbits MISS BABE PETERSON | A Group of Performing Rocky Mountain Goats DEWEY BUTLER | A Group of Performing Alaskan Polar Bears. Presented by CLYDE BEATY | A Group of South American Andes Goats in Marvelous Stunts by HARLEY WOODSON | A Group of Performing White Rats MISS LEONA PLANK |

Pig Wagon—Pike's Peak or Bust—Rube Butler

The John Robinson Circus of 1923 featured every type of wild animal act; in fact, the steel arena was never dismantled during the entire performance. Display 3 featured Clyde Beatty in the center ring with a group of polar bears.

the confidence the animal had for him. The prime requisite for a good trainer was excellent self-control and an amiable disposition.[57] Al Priddy, circus public relations man, agreed. Animal people, he wrote, had to possess a high degree of personal integrity as well as intelligence and natural kindness, for wild creatures are "wonderful judges of people and quickly weed out the unfit, by the grim process of elimination." His terse observation—"treat the animals with kindness and fairness and they will do everything in their power to please you"—summed up his outlook. When they were well treated, wild beasts became real troupers who loved the travel, the excitement of milling crowds, and even the music associated with circuses. In fact, when they were left behind they

tended to brood, to drop in weight, and apparently lose interest in life itself.[58]

Protests such as these tended to balance the current unfavorable publicity given wild animal acts. Although the Ringling ban continued, other circuses' concentration on these acts led *Billboard* to report that a metamorphosis had occurred in the circus program. It observed that well-known acts that featured human performers which had long been the distinctive characteristic of American shows had been replaced by trained wild animal exhibitions and gorgeously beautiful pageants. " 'Cutting down the nut' [operating expenses] has made the trained wild animal circuses prevalent." The trade paper complained that patrons now "see **little else** but trained wild animal acts any more."

John Helliot at the Peru winterquarters. — *Fred D. Pfening, Jr.*

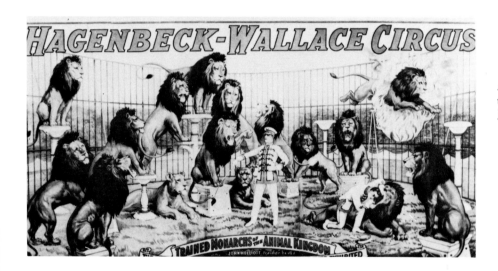

A 1922 H-W poster featuring John Helliot. — *Fred D. Pfening, Jr.*

1922 H-W poster. — *Fred D. Pfening, Jr.*

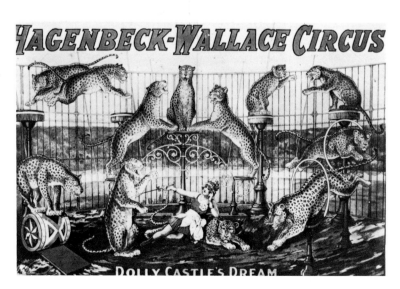

Franz Woska, featured trainer with Sparks in 1926, '27, and '28. Woska became menagerie superintendent for RBB&B. — *Fred D. Pfening, Jr.*

The trend, it noted, had begun after World War I when feature acts threatened to join carnivals and expositions if their salaries were not raised, when railroads upped their rates, and at the same time a labor shortage ballooned circus expenses. The popularity of the innovative Barnes show, plus its greatly reduced operating expenses, attracted the attention of showmen. When the American Circus Corporation successfully followed suit, it demonstrated these crowd-pleasing programs were the solution.[59]

In 1925, Hagenbeck-Wallace became the ACC flagship and it also featured wild animal acts heavily. But on July 2 of that year, what initially appeared a severe blow occurred when Pete Taylor was lost to the show. What happened to the Hagenbeck-Wallace star is steeped in legend and there are many versions. In one account, he was rushing into the arena to break up a lion/tiger fight, when he fell and struck his head against the steel bars. The resulting injury to his neck kept him from performing. According to another story, Taylor just left the show for romantic reasons. The most popular version has it that Taylor suffered from "arena shock," a breakdown peculiar to animal trainers in which, although their courage remains strong, they experience nightmares of attacking lions and tigers, cold sweats, and a loss of confidence.[60] They look for excuses to get out of performing, and by that time the collapse is complete, and they can never dominate an animal

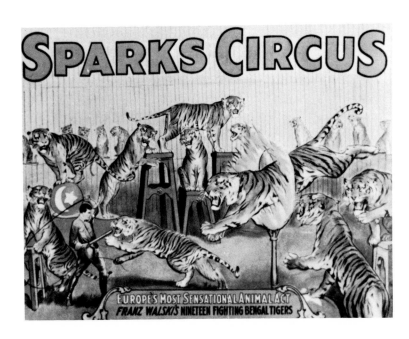

A 1920s Sparks poster featuring Woska. — *Fred D. Pfening, Jr.*

Circus Animal Seriously Wounds Courageous Young Man in Charge Here.

Clyde Beatty, renowned wild animal trainer and the pride of the Hagenbeck-Wallace circus, was seriously injured at 2 o'clock Friday afternoon at the circus grounds in the south part of the city when a large tigress sprang upon him during a rehearsal, knocking him to the ground and severely clawing him about the arms and chest.

A true showman in every sense, Beatty insisted, even while on the operating table at the Good Samaritan Hospital, that he would "go on with the show" and that he would put his 34 beasts through their performance as scheduled at the Saturday showing of the circus.

The accident occurred during the stirring scene in which Beatty forces thirty-four tigers and lionesses, working together in the arena, into a tableau formation. One of the tigresses became ugly and refused to take her place and Beatty advanced on the animal with whip, chair and blank pistol in hand. He had turned slightly after forcing the tigress to her place when the animal leaped upon him, dug her long claws deep into his arms and bore him to the ground.

The attack was the signal for several of the other beasts to leap upon him and he suffered several long and deep gashes in his forearms. His assistants cleared the arena of the beasts and removed him at once to the hospital, where it was found that he was not dangerously hurt, barring possible infection and that his spirit was high. He insisted that he would be in his place for the two performances Saturday.

This was not the first time in which Beatty has been attacked by his "pets". He bears numerous scars where he has been clawed and bitten by lions and tigers. As late as Thursday night he stated that he was subject to attacks by the beasts at any time, but that they were most dangerous in the springtime of the year, when they are not accustomed to the new surroundings and when their spirits are naturally high.

Manager Odom, who is in charge of the circus' appearance here, stated following the accident that it would not adversely affect the shows Saturday in any degree. He also wished to make it clear that while the animal act involves considerable danger to the trainer there is absolutely no danger to anyone else.

That Beatty is the most popular individual connected with the circus was admitted by several of the circus officials. Little more than a boy, his courage and personality have made him popular wherever he goes.

April 25, 1930

Great Crowd of Spectators Highly Pleased with Splendid Program

ANIMAL ACTS FEATURED

Clyde Beatty, Injured Trainer Gets Acclaim of Big Audience

With sunshine beaming from a warming sky after the week of chilling weather the Hagenbeck-Wallace circus strutted its pageantry and thrilled with "specs" on Saturday afternoon in a way that did it rich credit as one of the

finest circus organizations on the road.

Among the scores of circuses that have visited Kokomo none has ever been here with a cleaner or more up-to-date equipment, or with a higher type of personnel. The circus people, who after all are just ordinary folks for the most part, have acquited themselves with high credit in their brief residence of four days in Kokomo . . . .

Two wild animal acts were featured in the program, either one of them a thriller. The crowd was enthusiastic in its acclaim of Clyde Beatty, who was present at the performance, although swathed in bandages as a result of his thrilling encounter with an enraged tiger Friday afternoon. Beatty left the hospital on Friday evening after thirty stitches had been taken in his arms and insisted on taking his place in the show, even against the advice of his fellow performers. Beatty was emphatic in his statement that he would do his regular turn at the Saturday evening showing and that the big cats would go

through their performance as if there had been no accident. Circus officials stated that the popular young trainer was seriously hurt and that they had pleaded with him in vain to permit a substitute act.

Although seriously handicapped by his wounds, which had stiffened his fingers, Beatty entered the arena, and with whip, chair and gun in hand reasserted his mastery over the thirty-four brutes which sat snarling around him. No more striking example of sheer nerve has ever been witnessed in a circus performance and the crowd indicated its enthusiasm in its wild applause as the wounded man completed his entire performance.

Beatty has been recognized as the greatest American animal trainer. None other has ever worked a large number of tigers and lions together before, and even old and experienced trainers have expressed their wonder that Beatty has survived the scores of performances in which he has already appeared.

April 26, 1930

Articles such as these from the Kokomo *Tribune* set the tone for future articles about Clyde Beatty.

again. Whatever happened, manager Danny Odom was left without a feature act and when Clyde Beatty asked for a chance to work the ten lion, four tiger presentation, he had no choice but reluctantly to turn it over to the skinny, reckless youth. But it was probably the best choice he could have made. Beatty had been Taylor's assistant trainer, and an eager student of the nuances of the fighting style wild animal presentation. For endless hours, Taylor had schooled his assistant in cueing animals with style and flair. Beatty had had a small preliminary polar bear act with the Robinson show, and it had been a difficult routine for an inexperienced boy, for the "stolid, terse muzzle, the small practically hidden eyes, the thick, short fur overgrowing the features

give the trainer no window to the bear's emotions such as he has in a lion's great eyes. A tiger's white whiskers, as flexible as they are, are worth a good deal toward saving the trainer from harm, and the expressive lip, the subtle definitive index of roars are worth much more—not to mention the tail and the curl of the toes, and though he may occasionally chop his jaws before attacking, emitting a low breathy growl, often he won't."[61]

But no matter how dangerous and intelligent, bears are always perceived as clownish and "cute" by audiences. Even though Beatty would work the largest polar bear act ever seen in America, a beautiful display eerily lighted by blue spots, he knew bears could never bring him the prominence he sought. Early in his career Beatty understood that

THE WILD ANIMAL TRAINER IN AMERICA

Chubby Guilfoyle was another ACC trainer and tutor of Clyde Beatty (John Robinson, 1923).

the psychology of handling an audience was just as important as skill in working animals.[62]

On July 3, in New Britain, Connecticut, Beatty became the center ring star of the show, a role he would never relinquish for forty years. In that time he gave thirty thousand performances before forty million people, traveled more than one million miles, handled over a thousand lions and tigers—and made almost one hundred trips to the hospital during his career.[63] His life made the exploits of dime novel heroes pale by comparison. From a three-dollar-a-week cageboy, he became the handler of a record number of lions and tigers, the possessor of his own private zoo, and ultimately owner of the last tented railroad circus in America. The coauthor of three books, he starred in half a dozen movies, was the subject of countless articles, comic books, and "Little Books," and for a time had his own radio program. It has been rightly said that he was the "only American circus product of this century to attain true super-hero status."[64] Unlike such other extremely popular American circus figures as P. T. Barnum, Buffalo

Bill, or Tom Mix, Beatty's legend was born and developed wholly in the circus, and he stayed with it until his death.

Beal called him a supershowman who made every move in the arena a picture. "Flashy, courageous to the point of being foolhardy . . . one of the greatest actor-handlers that ever entered the arena . . . [he] shoots off a thrill a second. . . . Unique among animal trainers in that he has become the idol of the country's youth, he has a constantly growing audience which looks upon him as its particular hero."[65] Different from the suave English and the austere Germans, different too from the overwhelming grim and stoic Mabel Stark, Beatty became the symbol and representation of every small town child who ever wanted to run away and join the circus. His peers on the ACC shows called him "green," enthusiastic, and extremely exuberant and lacking the rather blase professionalism that marked other performers after being "with it" for almost ten years. His rise to

Beatty's first acts featured bears. He admired the animals for their intelligence, personality, and quick ability to learn, but knew that the cats would give him the fame that he sought.

With H-W from 1925 to 1934, Beatty became an increasingly important feature.

In 1922, the teenage Beatty was with Gollmar Bros. and led a young hippo around the hippo-drome track. — *Fred D. Pfening, Jr.*

In 1924, Beatty worked several acts with John Robinson. — *Fred D. Pfening, Jr.*

Clyde Beatty.

fame coincided with the decline in popularity of the wild west show and increased enthusiasm for the cowboy hero. The Miller Brothers's 101 Ranch representation of ranchers bringing civilization and progress to the West was no longer as much admired as the cowboys, who had presumably learned to live with nature rather than destroy it. The cowboy—innocent, loyal, and sturdy of character—could stand fatigue and pain and could face violence and tragedy with inflexible resolve and good humor. Tom Mix, for example, who was the ultimate cowboy stereotype, was a symbol of purity, morality, prowess, and courage.[66] These same desirable characteristics were attributed to Beatty in the circus world. A *New York Times* movie review called him the "Frank Merriwell of the big top, the shy lover, the scourge of the black-hearted, the one man jungle safari . . . a bashful young man who finds sanctuary from the terrors of the everyday world with his frisky pets in the big cage . . . he saves everybody in sight, from everything in sight."[67] During the first seven years of his career, writers and publicists even gave him a trusty sidekick, Nero, a big, black-maned Nubian lion, that protected his master from the stealthy, treacherous attacks of the striped devils in the act. Although Beatty claimed Nero's actions were those of an arena boss protecting his domain,

Beatty (right) with Allen King. King, a breaker of cats and often featured performer himself, worked Beatty's act when the young trainer was injured by Nero.— *Fred D. Pfening, Jr.*

Beatty first adopted the military costume favored by his predecessor, Pete Taylor. —*Dave Price*

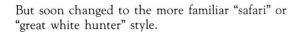

But soon changed to the more familiar "safari" or "great white hunter" style.

He was often pictured with his favorite lion Prince, later called Nero. —*Fred D. Pfening, Jr.*

the story enhanced the appeal of the performance at a time when Tarzan and his animal helpers also were garnering audience enthusiasm.

Beatty's act represented the "purest version of the all-American fighting act, but with exceptional style which comes from a marvelous rapport of the man with his beasts that few others have achieved." He claimed he never used unnecessary force or shouted at his cats, and he insisted an "animal's dignity has to be respected; you shouldn't humiliate any animal, but especially not a wild one."[68] Still, the act involved a wilder kind of animal training than that of the effete, polished European style. An exciting, primitive spirit pervaded it. (His mother once fainted when she saw him perform, and she wished the act was "cuter and less exciting," but his Chillicothe relatives announced, "them lines and taggers sure look purty sitting all around that big cage."[69]) Beatty despised being called a "lion tamer," always insisting the big cats were never tame. His beasts were portrayed as dangerous jungle killers, and in his publicity, he emphasized the spoiled, sneaky nature of hand-raised cats as opposed to the stronger, more ferocious and smarter imported animals. Bobby McPherson, veteran ACC tiger trainer, said Beatty was already the nerviest and most successful trainer he had ever known. "That kid [Beatty was twenty-two] has a real act and real nerve and if you don't believe those animals are really wild, just step inside."[70]

Beatty's fighting style was always popular with photographers. — *Harry Chipman*

Beatty's first big new story appeared in the *Detroit News*, February 16, 1926, when he starred with his newly acquired cat act in the big Detroit indoor winter circus. It was a full-page article entitled: "He Enjoys Being in a Cage with 15 Lions and Three Tigers—Chewed Up Eight Times, But Trainer Who Thrilled Detroit Loves His Job," and it established a theme for future stories. It traced his career back to the time when, as a boy, he never tired of seeing wild animals at the Cincinnati Zoo. He simply could not get them off his mind, and he ran away with a circus to solve the problem. It quoted the young animal man saying that "the first 'chewing up' is the making or breaking of an animal trainer. . . . Unless his nerve remains unshaken he might rather turn to washing dishes than try to enter a cage again. But if he can go back without fear he will be an animal trainer until he gets too old or the lions get him—which Beatty nonchalantly admits might happen any

day." Only six weeks earlier, the *News* reported Beatty had been attacked in Texarkana, Arkansas, by Utah, a treacherous lion born in captivity. Although badly clawed on the body and arm, he was saved from more serious injury by Nero, previously an unruly lion, but now "almost a pet." But Beatty, according to the story, tried never to think of the danger before entering the arena. "If I stopped to think—I probably never would go in." And he went in, he said, because: "It is the most thrilling work in the world and I would not give it up for anything. When will I quit? I'll stick it out until they get me. Of course, they will chew me up some day. It may be today or tomorrow. They always get you sooner or later, but I am ready and willing to take the chance."[71]

During the next few years with Hagenbeck-Wallace, Beatty worked to build up his act. He mixed natural enemies, lions and tigers, on a larger scale than anyone had ever dared. He increased the

Beatty gained enormous popularity in Detroit. Here he is seen with long-time Detroit Shrine Circus chairman, "Eddie" Stinson, the airplane manufacturer. — *Peru Circus City Festival, Inc. Museum*

Wild animal training barn at Peru. It was here that the cats were broken and rehearsed. The famous attack by Nero on Clyde Beatty also occurred in this building. — *Ken Whipple*

conflict by mixing the sexes, which virtually guaranteed a true fighting act. His old teacher Pete Taylor had told him that to attain stardom as a wild animal trainer in an era when more than fifty were performing in America, he would need unusual dedication, ability, and bravado. One species one-sex acts with a small number of cats were not enough to excite an audience satiated with such routine performances. "The one-sex, one-species cat acts of the past no longer mean a great deal to audiences. There is little conflict, and the animals perform perfunctorily and without much spirit. They do their stuff, but they do it in such routine fashion that the spectators should be pardoned for yawning now and then."[72] Beatty

wanted an act so dangerous that he never had to worry about being replaced. To create the riskiest act possible, he added more cats every year. By 1927, he was working thirty lions and tigers in a thirty-two-foot arena and in 1929 he added two more![73]

Meanwhile the American Circus Corporation became the dominant force in the circus world with the acquisition of Al G. Barnes and Sparks. They now owned every major railroad show in the United States with the exception of Ringling. The fast, trim, lean-to-the-bone, thirty car shows could harass the Big One, which had been allowed to grow cumbersome, overburdened, and stodgy by old complacent bosses, but what the ACC wanted was an established attraction that would finally drive Ringling against the wall.

Beatty was a star on the rise in 1929 but the ACC really gained an edge when Ed Ballard lured Tom Mix away from the Miller Bros. 101 Ranch Wild West Show with which he had already contracted. Mix brought Sells-Floto a popular drawing card at the peak of his audience appeal. In recognition of his enormous popularity circus equipment was relettered to read: "Sells-Floto Circus and Tom Mix Himself." Although like his predecessor on the Tammen and Bonfils-owned Floto circus, Buffalo Bill, Mix had personal and drinking problems, children loved him. They flocked to see him and his "wonder horse" Tony,

and if he gave an occasionally sloppy performance it was kindly attributed, not to his drinking, but to injuries he had acquired doing his own movie stunts. But Mix did not come cheap. He demanded—and got—private car accommodations for two horses, a Rolls-Royce, and an entourage of seven people, plus the highest salary ever paid a circus performer. "I am not afraid of work," declared Mix three years later at his breach of contract trial, "but I must have my comfort."[74]

The Sells-Floto gamble paid off. In 1929, for the first time, an ACC show outdrew Ringling and brought home greater profits. Late that summer John Ringling was forced to surrender his last stronghold. The *New York Times* headlines said it

This H-W baggage wagon had the distinction of doubling as Clyde Beatty's dressing room while he starred with that show.—*William Koford*

Cage wagons for Beatty's cats fill the flats of the H-W train.—*William Koford*

H-W cage wagons are
towed to the lot. –
William Koford

In the 1930s, the H-W
street parade attracted
thousands.

all:

> RINGLING CIRCUS BREAKS WITH GAR-
> DEN. SHOWMAN REJECTS NEW LEASE,
> REFUSING TO ALLOW BOXING BOUTS TO
> INTERFERE EACH WEEK ... GARDEN
> HEAD ... MAKES DEAL WITH ANOTHER
> CIRCUS ... COMBINATION CONSISTING
> OF THE SELLS-FLOTO CIRCUS, THE
> HAGENBECK-WALLACE ANIMAL SHOW.[75]

The battle between the Ringling organization and
the ACC appeared to have reached its climax.

Then on Monday, September 9, 1929, an extra
of the *Peru Daily Tribune* hit the streets that
screamed in the boldest type available: **PERU
CIRCUSES SOLD Deal to Ringling Involves
Millions.** John Ringling, unable to compete, had
resorted to his last option. Borrowing $1,714,000
from the Providence Company of New York he
offered cash to Ballard, Mugivan, and Bowers for
their five shows and they accepted. (According to
local legend, John Ringling and Jerry Mugivan
flipped a coin in the bar of the Bearss Hotel in

H-W setup featuring the huge five-pole menagerie tent on the right.

Beatty in the late 1920s (1928 Detroit). — *Fred D. Pfening, Jr.*

Peru, to decide who would have the right to buy the other out. Ringling won.) The Ringling monopoly was virtually complete; by 1938 the Big One was the only one of these six shows left on the road.[76]

Well before then all the principals involved in the sale were dead. Jerry Mugivan, known as a rough Irishman with a heart of gold, called the "Big Boss" by all his troupers, died first on January 23, 1930, in Detroit, following an operation. Bert Bowers also died of an illness, but Ed Ballard met a more violent end. On November 7, 1936, in Hot Springs, Arkansas, he was shot by a former business associate, Detroit gambler "Silver Bob" Alexander, who then killed himself. As for John Ringling, his extravagant purchase and the subsequent Depression caused him to forfeit payments in 1932 and lose control of the show. He died brokenhearted in 1936 after having sacrificed everything to keep the Ringling name supreme in the circus world.

But in 1930, John Ringling could boast of no less than six railroad circuses moving on 235 cars. Ringling ruled a tented empire. The ACC had driven Ringling to the wall in large part because of the great popularity of its wild animal acts. Ringling, who disliked such acts, was now their director. Would he give in to audience desires, and retain them? The question mark on their future was plain. In 1930, in fact, only three shows went out

that season with arena acts, H-W, Barnes, and Sparks. Ringling, who placed his own show in Madison Square Garden, had none.

Even as Ringling pondered the future, Clyde Beatty heightened his own fame and the popularity of wild animal acts in an incident that set newspaper pressrooms buzzing. At a public dress rehearsal H-W staged at Kokomo, Indiana, on April 24, 1930, a tigress named Trudy attacked Beatty, then performing with thirty-two cats, knocked him to the ground, "ripped his right side open from shoulder to waist with sweeping claws," and bit his left arm. Then Prince [in later stories referred to as Nero], "sprang across the prostrate form of the trainer and tore a large wound in the tiger and a blow from a paw sent the animal spinning across the arena. Beatty, still conscious, arose and drove the cageful of animals from the arena into the runway, staggered outside the cage and collapsed. . . . A true showman in every sense Beatty insisted . . . even while on the operating table that he would put his 32 beasts through their performance as scheduled for the opening."[77]

This adventure gained Beatty national publicity as every newspaper ran the story of the young, fearless trainer rescued by his loyal lion. *Field and Stream* devoted an entire article to Beatty as did *Literary Digest*. Both described him as a "personable young fellow" and called the high point of his act the stare-down of Nero after he backed the

Beatty's act in the early thirties.

Beatty's act in the early
thirties. — *Tom Henricks*

trainer against the bars, disarmed him with a sweep of his mighty paw, and roared in fury. Beatty stopped the charge by suddenly taking a step toward him, leaning forward until his face was within a foot of his and staring him into submission. Nero, with a baleful look, gradually stopped roaring, snarled, shook his head in baffled rage, and backed away to return to his pedestal.[78] It was a masterful performance that lent credence to the oldest of wild animal training superstitions, the hypnotic eye.

John Ringling, facing a Depression and a daily operating "nut" of $11,000 could not bring himself to admit that Hagenbeck-Wallace, with only $3,200 in daily expenses, not only had a superior show but was grossing enough to keep both itself and

Beatty's famous stare-down of Nero. —*Fred D. Pfening, Jr.*

Last Week I Heard

By WALTER W. PULLER

So, Nero, that great 'big, kind-hearted, human-souled, perfectly trained and oh, so innocent (you believe it, I never did) lion finally got Clyde Beatty, a friend of mine for years? Never was I one of those "I told you so" boys, but it sure looks to me like the betrayal of a trusted friend. This cat (Clyde called him that) Nero sure turned out to be a fine feline Judas—a royal double crosser! A sort of a king of beasts turned deuce.

"Here's a real pal," Clyde often told me, as he reached into a cage and petted Nero on the muzzle. "He's saved me half a dozen times and he's the only one in the gang of 36 that I can trust. I brought him up from a cub and he's just like a human being. He knows everything I say to him."

Then Clyde would pet Nero some more and reach into the cage to tug at the thick, tawny mane. Nero sorta muzzled up to his trainer's hand and seemed to appreciate his presence. Once or twice I attempted to pet (attempted, I said—and at a distance) and there was shown the finest little set of fangs it has been our privilege to view. That was enough. That and the roar. We left the petting to Clyde.

But here it is Sunday. Last week I had a fine letter from Clyde, reminding me that he would put his cats into the arena at the State Fair Coliseum this afternoon in preparation for the Shrine Circus. "Meet me at the hotel," Clyde wrote, "Then I'll show you some real cats. I got three new ones and boy, are they tough?" I had the day marked on the calendar: "Meet Clyde Beatty." Now I'll have to go up to the Coliseum and watch three sub-stitute trainers endeavor to whip those lions and tigers into shape so they can go on with them Monday. I hope they are successful.

Whenever a theater or circus yarn is sent out it immediately sounds like a lot of publicity to a lot of people. But Clyde is now secluded in a Peru hospital and may be dead even as this appears. He is in a badly mangled condition and no one can see him just because that double-crosser of a Nero whom Clyde had befriended from baby days, jumped him, when the 26-year-old trainer had his back turned. Nero chewed Clyde's leg and clawed his back and left an infection which specialists have been battling for a week. There's a trusted friend for you.

"Haven't you an idea that these lions and tigers are going to get you some time for the final count?" we had often asked Clyde.

"Well, if they do, I'll be passing out in the game I love, anyway," he replied with a grin. He is a full-fledged fatalist, as are most circus performers. "Besides while a tiger is getting me and I'm gong down with my boots on," he chided, "an automobile might get you and wouldn't you be ashamed of yourself?" Well, maybe he's right.

Thousands upon thousands who have seen young Beatty rush into the arena, with a chair, a blank cartridge pistol and a whip, to cow 38 lions and tigers, will miss him this year at the Shrine circus. Clyde is small of stature, is quiet and modest, has a powerful arm and a fearless heart and made millions throughout the land gasp, then hold their breath until his final spectacular exit from the barred arena. His act was unpar-alled in the circus world. Beatty is personally known to hundreds of Detroiters who are pulling for his recovery. And that goes for me ten thousand times!

Stories such as highly dramatic one from the Detroit *News* provided invaluable publicity from the Nero attack.

January 31, 1932

Ringling on the road. Managed by ACC-trained
Jess Adkins, successor to the retired Danny Odom,
H-W's most amazing feature was a 410-foot-long,
nine-pole menagerie tent.[79] Yet Ringling could not
avoid realities. The circus king needed a powerful
feature for his 1931 Madison Square Garden
stand, if that at least was to be a success, and he
had one he could no longer ignore.

On April 2, 1931, the Garden audience was omi-
nously warned by the ringmaster's dramatic statement: "Everyone is forbidden to move around or
talk during the next act." Gradually the house
lights dimmed and then went off as brilliant spots
illuminated the steel arena in the center ring.
Now:

> The Greatest Wild Animal Presentation Ever
> Witnessed. Ringling Bros.–Barnum & Bailey Cir-
> cus takes Pleasure to Present the Youngest and
> Most Fearless Trainer in the World. A Mere
> Youth that Battles with Death at Every Perform-
> ance with Royal Bengal, Siberian, Sumatra Tigers
> in the Same Cage with Black-maned Forest Lions
> and Lionesses. Forty Royal Beasts of the Jungle.
> The Great and Only Person to Master these
> Jungle Beasts, Mr. Clyde Beatty.[80]

Then came Beatty, fighting his way into the cage
already filled with milling big cats, and drenched
with sweat, he battled the snarling, growling, roaring beasts for eighteen minutes. The wild animal
act ban was over.

John Ringling at the peak of his power.—*Herbert
Duval III*

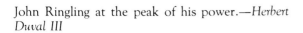

"Formal" picture shot of Beatty during the 1931 Madison Square Garden appearance. —*Peru Circus City Festival, Inc. Museum*

The *New York Times* which had heartily endorsed the ban, was obviously disgusted at the reinstatement of an act that thoroughly dramatized the wild, vicious, dangerous nature of the big cats. The day after Beatty's debut at the Garden it reported in studied understatement and even ridicule that the animals were "carefree," definitely less than forty in number, and so bored they yawned. The circus, it snapped, seemed to think New York was "yearning for lions, tigers, pistols and whips."[81] Twenty days later, the *Times* denounced Beatty's act more directly. Pleading that humane societies protect performing lions and tigers, it ran a letter complaining that Beatty's act was one "of the most cruel exhibitions I have ever encountered." The correspondent charged that Beatty clubbed his animals so loudly that the blows could be heard a half block away. For over half an hour, the writer continued, the beasts were punished, one at a time, causing even his children to cry.[82] The next day, Ringling spokesmen and Beatty assured the SPCA that the act was completely changed and "all objectionable parts" had been removed.[83] The statement was apparently not convincing to the wife of the managing editor of the *Times*, since she avoided the circus entirely for as long as Beatty

Beatty in his Madison Square Garden appearance.

Lines outside Madison Square Garden.

was with it. Luckily for Beatty other newspaper reporters and columnists did not agree with the sentiments of the *Times*. The Ohioan charmed them with his dynamic, supercharged act that contrasted strikingly with his naive, small-town-boy personality. New Yorkers called his electrifying performance the greatest thrill since Lindbergh. One paper devoted a full page to a study of his eyes because of their supposed hypnotic qualities. Raymond Ditmars, curator of mammals for the New York Zoological Society (the Bronx Zoo) debunked the charges that Beatty used any "cruel practices." "Contrary to the beliefs of some sentimentalists, cruelty is not an efficient circus method. The great cats, for instance, can be urged so far and no further and under a cruel master would refuse to perform," Ditmars insisted. He claimed he found some of the finest animal specimens in circus menageries. "The movement of circus life is a boon to captive animals, for on the whole they are in excellent condition."[84]

When Ernest Hemingway took an interest in Beatty and made a shrewd, observant study of the animal trainer's work, he surprised him by his awareness of certain aspects of training which, while experienced circus men took for granted, only professional animal trainers knew the significance of—for example, the importance of footwork necessary to accommodate animals as fast as lions and tigers. Although speed was essential, knowl-

edge of the animals' behavior counted for more, because it meant the ability to move instinctively in the right direction. Hemingway observed that the act was at its best when Beatty fought the cats at close range. This controlled resistance was encouraged in the animals. Hemingway pointed out similarities between bullfighting and the cat act. As in the Spanish pastime, if an animal wandered off the audience was lost. Beatty later said that the visit (and presentation of an autographed copy of *Death in the Afternoon*) made a lasting impression on him, but he did not feel he fitted in Hemingway's category of those unable to resist the temptation of flirting with death because of the thrill of it. He believed any risks he took were out of foolish recklessness or the desire to please an audience, not an attempt to see how close he could come to death without being killed.[85]

After his indoor New York and Boston dates, Ringling fulfilled an earlier promise and returned Beatty to H-W for the outdoor season. Since the Adkins-managed show came home to Peru a big winner, Ringling planned to follow the same format for the 1932 season. Beatty, a tireless worker, drilled his cats daily in winterquarters and by late January put the final touches on the act before the winter indoor dates in Detroit, Toledo, and Cleveland. But disaster was about to strike.

When Carl Lorenz Hagenbeck saw Beatty's act he commented: "Those cats will get Beatty. The

More of Beatty's act in the thirties. —
Tom Henricks

More of Beatty's act in the thirties.

act is too dangerous."[86] Beatty broke all the famous German family's training rules: he mixed animals with great hatred toward one another; he kept lionesses in the act who provoked the males into fights that disrupted the performance; he retained rebellious cats (Beatty believed there was no cat he could not handle), and he even kept proven killers if their strength and beauty excited him. For instance, describing the murderous lion, "Detroit," Beatty wrote:

Detroit . . . intoxicated me with his obvious superiority to other animals. . . . to me tigers have always seemed more attractive than lions. There is a dancer's grace in their stealthy step and slinking stride, and the long curving arc of their striped bodies is a pretty picture. However, Detroit's beauty, if it can be called that, was the

beauty of anger and defiance—the way he wrinkled up his nose in hate, twisted open his mouth and lips in a grotesque snarl and narrowed his blazing eyes, the way he swung his right front paw with knock-out force. Maybe I'm cockeyed, but I thought he was something to see.[87]

The day was Saturday, January 23, 1932, in Peru, Indiana. Beatty still preferred the six-hundred-pound Nero, whom he called the "most sporting and philosophic" animal he knew. The lion dominated the other cats and sent challengers spinning without a second glance as he refused to give "punks" too much attention.[88] When Beatty took Nero into the arena alone, he followed the trainer around like a dog and even let him ride on his back, but if other cats were in the arena, Nero looked at him as the one creature that stood in his

Beatty entering the arena.

Beatty always traveled on the road with a dog. This
particular one was named Timber.

way to total rule. Beatty's foolhardy admiration for the big cat caused him to relax his guard that unseasonably warm afternoon. He was standing in the arena near two of the "arena boss's" favorite lionesses when Nero abruptly veered away from an intended hurdle jump, charged the trainer, and knocked him to the ground. "Flat on my back in the arena with a lion over me . . . [was] the worst moment I have ever known."[89] Nero first made for Beatty's face, but with desperate strength he shoved him away.

> With a murderous roar, he backed up slightly, then delivered the horrible bite I had been fearing. Sliding his enormous head along the top of my body, he suddenly sank his two long upper tusks into the top of my right leg about three inches above the knee. Those great fangs knifed through the flesh. . . . Instantly, as he held part of the leg in his upper tusks, he brought his big lower teeth up from below. Then he closed his teeth, the tusks pierced deeper and deeper, in through the flesh. . . . Not at any previous time in my animal training career had I suffered such a bite and now it seemed that something in me was dying. I was faint all over and getting nauseous. Surely the pain of it would knock me out.[90]

Beatty was interested in aviation, but the circus management felt it was too dangerous a hobby.

Then just as suddenly as it began, Nero eyed the two lionesses, bounded away, and returned to his cage with no difficulty.

Circus employees rushed the trainer into Peru, where a doctor cauterized the punctures and sent him by ambulance to the hospital. Although the ragged wounds caused great pain, the biggest danger came from possible infection. The worst fears of the doctors materialized when Beatty's temperature began to rise. By Monday the hospital listed him in critical condition. His mother and sisters were called from Bainbridge and they were the only visitors allowed at his bedside. Jess Adkins panicked. The young cat man was the top attraction of the circus world, on his survival might depend the entire success not only of H-W but Ringling as well. From Chicago, another animal trainer, Allen King, rushed a serum that had sometimes proved successful in similar cases, but no improvement occurred after the antitoxin was administered. Specialists from all over the country were consulted; sixty blood specimens were sent to the University of Indiana Medical School. The circus doctor conferred with a noted Chicago diagnostician, the Surgeon General of the United States, Johns Hopkins Hospital, the head of the Bureau of Animal Industry, and Dr. William Mann, director

of the National Zoological Gardens of Washington. It was finally decided that Beatty suffered from a disease caused by the *pasturella* germ usually only found in animals. There were only a dozen recorded cases in the whole world (all of which had proved fatal), and none in the United States.[91] Nero had probably eaten some infected meat and although unaffected himself, passed on the illness. While newspapers called it "jungle fever," doctors hoped to try and arrest it with a new antitoxin developed by the Eli Lilly Company. Beatty, who remained in critical condition and sank into a nightly coma, was described as strained and weakened from his 104-degree temperature, and reportedly deeply depressed after he learned that Allen King had taken his animal act to the Detroit engagement.[92] *Billboard's* gloomy announcement that his chances for recovery were doubtful was supported by Jess Adkins's news that the "infection in his leg does not seem to abate or even show a tendency to be arrested and is burrowing itself deeper into the muscles of his leg in

Beatty in the Peru winterquarters training barn. — *Fred D. Pfening, Jr.*

spite of adequate drainage."[93] Before trying the new antitoxin, attending physicians decided an operation on Beatty's leg might reveal the basis of the infection. They removed a large pus sac attached to the bone and Beatty soon began to improve. Writers attributed his ability to recover from what was usually a fatal disease to the fact that "his whole system was clean" from never using intoxicating liquor or tobacco.[94]

Ten weeks elapsed before Beatty reentered the arena, more a hero than ever. The "jungle fever" episode gained national attention. "Invariably the newspapers praise him and express the hope he will be well again and soon return to his wild animal troupe he loves so well." Typical letters from circus fans thanked Jess Adkins and the doctor for saving Beatty. Walter Winchell, who had written caustically only two months before when Beatty's wife divorced him that the trainer could handle

forty cats but not one woman, was roundly criticized. His fans believed their "all-American boy" could do no wrong.[95] Even Nero was exculpated of wrong doing and idolized. One newspaper claimed that Beatty had fallen over his chair and the lion had attempted to save him from unseen danger.[96] Another article believed that Nero had temporarily lost his senses, but then had darted through the gate like a flash and run back to his cage where he cowered in a corner and sulked as if ashamed of himself.[97] John Ringling delayed the Madison Square Garden opening until his star's return. Weak and limping, Beatty became the first circus performer honored by his name in lights on the Garden marquee.

In view of his rising fame and popularity, Beatty agreed to write his autobiography with Edward Anthony, publisher of *Colliers* and *Women's Home Companion*. In 1929, Anthony had taken a then

Beatty with Nero. — *Circus World Museum*

unknown big game trapper, Frank Buck, and turned him into a celebrity with the best seller, *Bring 'em Back Alive*. Years later the author described Buck as an over-hearty, born storyteller, who punctuated each of his rambling tales with immodest comments about the exciting times he had had. Anthony contrasted Beatty as a great showman who was "liked by practically everyone, including the press, because of his daring, modesty and dry sense of humor." Although Beatty himself had approached Anthony with the idea for a book, the writer was warned by a fellow newsman that Beatty had more "sheer guts" than anyone he knew, but his approach was matter of fact — that's my job. The reporter counseled Anthony first to become acquainted with Beatty's exploits, then get him started, and since the trainer is a perfectionist, he would tell the whole story. A student at heart, Beatty would welcome the chance "to tell why things happen as well as what happened." Dexter Fellows, publicity chief of Ringling Bros., warned Anthony that the proposed biography "better be a thriller or no one connected with this circus will ever speak to you again." Century bought the book, *The Big Cage*, on the strength of one chapter and an outline. One more chapter sold the story to Universal Pictures.[98]

Beatty with Nero. — *Circus World Museum*

Frontispiece for *The Big Cage* (1933).

The shy, innocent side of Beatty became part of his legend, and it was reiterated by other writers. James R. Patterson, a publicist with Hagenbeck-Wallace, described how the underpaid Beatty (he was making $75 a week) readily agreed to interviews with the press, but refused a radio talk. "I can't talk to an audience," he was quoted as saying "With one man it's okay, but with a crowd my hands shake, I sweat and my voice won't work." Patterson, well-acquainted with the trainer's answers to interviews, fooled the listening audience by playing Beatty on the radio program.[99] Humorist Irvin S. Cobb related a story in which his daughter held a buffet supper for some circus

Beatty and his cats. The trainer's greatest forte was his dynamic style and showmanship. — *Circus World Museum*

people and New York literary celebrities. Gene Tunney, the former heavyweight champion, and "one of the show folks spent a bedazzled half-hour harkening while Gene told of his ring victories and then this enthralled listener burst into a group in the next room crying out: 'Gee, it must be great to have as much nerve as that Tunney fellow's got!' The author of this tribute was youthful Clyde Beatty, whose job, twice daily, was to go into a steel-barred cage and master a snarling, rebellious collection of forty full-grown lions and half-tamed tigers."[100] Only five feet six inches and 145 pounds, Beatty fought cats that stood seven feet on their hind legs and weighed from 300 to 600 pounds. "I'm a little middleweight against the equal of two heavyweights," whose razor-sharp claws, he later admitted, possessed a swifter, more deadly swing than any pugilist.[101]

Beatty understood the forty cat act gave him only a fifty-fifty chance of survival and anytime he felt his ego swell, he reminded himself that each succeeding crowd coming to see him "thought that eventually I was going to be killed, and that they might be in on it. Some of them probably thought that seeing me get killed would be some kind of distinction, like attending an execution."[102] Unlike other trainers, who always claimed nervelessness was a requisite for success with wild animals, Beatty admitted that the arena "is and must be ruled by mass fear. I have said that I am scared

The injured Beatty is dragged from the arena in *The Big Cage.*

Beatty simulated the Nero attack in *The Big Cage.*

constantly. Well so are the cats. There are forty of them, weighing nearly 20,000 pounds. . . . Me, I weigh 145 pounds. Yet funny as it may seem, they are scared of me, but, being a human being, I am better able to camouflage my fear with bluff, and keep them thinking I'm tough."[103] He never showed fear in the ring. "If you ever give an inch with animals it would be all over," he wrote, and added: "But sometimes, it seems when I relax my nerves give way." His wife confirmed that after a "perilous scene with an animal Clyde will quiver all night long. His nerves are not of iron."[104]

The Big Cage earned a two-page favorable review in the *New York Times*, and the movie version was scheduled to open at the Radio City Music Hall. John Ringling allowed the film to be made and he leased Universal the forty-eight big cats in Beatty's act for $3,000 per week. The circus received $36,000 for the twelve-week period, instead of paying out

Beatty costarred in the Universal movie with Mickey Rooney.—*Tom Henricks*

Beatty with Mickey Rooney and Andy Devine (third from left, back row) and the rest of the cast of *The Big Cage.—Peru Circus City Festival, Inc. Museum*

Beatty later starred in serials like Republic's *Darkest Africa* (1936).

the usual feed bill of $17,000.[105] But it was just then in 1933 that Ringling's financial problems and financial disputes overwhelmed him and the old circus king lost control of his empire forever. It fell to Samuel Gumpertz, one-time manager of Dreamland and the exploiter of lion king Jack Bonavita. When he became general manager of the Greatest Show on Earth, he refused to let Beatty make personal appearances at Radio City, believing the trainer would be overexposed. Since the theater management had only accepted the picture on the understanding that the star himself would introduce it, the agreement was broken. Hostility grew between Gumpertz and Beatty.

Beatty suffered another blow when Nero was poisoned on the train after the Ringling indoor dates. The lion had performed brilliantly both in the circus and in Hollywood since the attack, and was the feature of many articles. Beatty said, "On the Saturday night we closed he had never been better, and if not strictly his friend, I was his No. 1 fan, next to himself." When he found the "fallen monarch" dead, "the sadness gnawed at me and I could not overcome it. I . . . was too big to cry. . . . It is a painful thing to see a lion as great as Nero come to his end, . . . struck down in his prime." Although he hired a lawyer to investigate the death, the killer was never found.[106]

Beatty in *Darkest Africa*.

Twelve-year-old Manuel King was featured with Clyde Beatty in *Darkest Africa*.

A student of Chubby Guilfoyle, Manuel King, the son of "Snake" King, the owner of a Texas wild animal farm, was billed as the youngest trainer of all time and appeared at Atlantic City's Million Dollar Pier in 1935. — *Fred D. Pfening, Jr.*

Manuel King.—*Fred D. Pfening, Jr.*

walked out on the show, but returned when he remembered the circus owed him money for animals he had purchased. Gumpertz, angered by the delay in the opening, ordered all Beatty's publicity cut, and he announced that the following year a female trainer would handle seventy-five cats on the show. Although H-W took in $450,000 in profits during 1934, the manager received only $100 per week and Beatty only between $50 and $100, according to different authorities. But Beatty admitted his low salary was his own fault. He considered it a privilege to work the big cats, in fact, a

Beatty and his cats. The trainer's greatest forte was his dynamic style and showmanship.—*Circus World Museum*

That winter of 1933–34 Gumpertz relented and allowed Beatty to make another movie, this time a serial, *The Lost Jungle.* In these films, Beatty allowed directors to talk him into particularly foolish and reckless stunts. In *The Big Cage* an all-out fight staged between a lion and tiger had resulted in the death of the striped cat. In his second serial, *Darkest Africa,* directors convinced Beatty he could wrestle a strange tiger in a pit, barehanded. Universal offered him a full-time contract, but he had no great respect for movie people. "They're always willing to let me risk my neck when I go in the cage. But just let one of those babies let out a sneeze and try to find a director within a hundred yards of you." He returned to the circus, convinced it was safer there.[107]

When Beatty came back to New York for Ringling's 1934 spring engagement, Gumpertz refused to give him rehearsal time. Irritated, the trainer

Allen King would star in Standard Oil's Live Power exhibit at the 1932 Chicago World's Fair. In 1935, he co-starred with Beatty on the new Cole show.

Beatty married a H-W chorus girl, Harriett Evans, in 1933.

dream come true. One writer even speculated he would work for nothing more than "three squares" and a dry place to sleep.

Nevertheless, he was ripe for Jess Adkins and Zack Terrell's plans to start their own railroad show the following season, and when they formed the Indiana Circus Corporation (ICC) with the aid of notable Hoosier businessmen and politicians, their prospectus announced that "Mr. Clyde Beatty, greatest wild animal trainer of all time, is under contract." It continued:

Mr. Allen King, Star of the Stanard Oil Live Power Show at the World's Fair Chicago . . . is also under contract. . . . It is estimated seven mil-

His movie experience gave Beatty even a smoother style. —*Ken Whipple*

Opposite page: 1936 Cole Bros. herald advertising the Chicago stadium stand.

Clyde and Harriett Beatty on the Cole Bros. lot.—
Don Smith

lion people attended the Live Power Show in Chicago during the past season of 1934, so that Allen King is as well, or better known in the Central States than any other circus star that has ever appeared in this territory while Clyde Beatty is a nationally known star in the Circus World. In this combination we have the greatest outstanding circus stars in America today.[108]

Winterquarters were set up just north of Peru in Rochester, Indiana, and the seemingly impossible task of building a major railroad circus over just one winter began. The Ringling organization refused to sell even a "tent stake" to the fledgling circus, although a few Peru residents did confiscate some of the abundant surplus equipment for the new show. Most of the equipment, however, came from the Hall circus farm in Lancaster, Missouri, a depository of defunct shows. Ringling also refused to sell any of the titles it had obtained in the 1929 ACC deal, so that the new circus was forced to use the still available Cole title. The formation of the new thirty-five car Cole Bros. show in a matter of months is now considered one of the great epics in circus history. On April 20, 1935, the brand new circus opened in the Chicago Coliseum. It broke the Ringling monopoly of railroad shows and became the first circus on rails since 1931 that was not part of the empire.

No one had faced greater difficulties than Beatty, since his act was Ringling owned. Forced to start from scratch and build an entirely new act in time for the 1935 winter dates, he utilized cast off animals of other trainers and excess zoo lions and tigers. It was an amazing accomplishment that further enhanced his image. But he also became the target of an onslaught of bad publicity from the Ringling camp that continues to this day. A *Business Week* release in April of 1935 was the first of many:

> The Gumpertz policy is to keep the name of the show superior to any act. He is credited with having built Clyde Beatty's lion and tiger baiting stunt into a spectacular success. Clyde walked out and joined a rival organization. Mr. Gumpertz was not in the least non-plussed. He still had the

Bert Nelson. Harry Chipman.

Bert Nelson with Norma (1937). In 1935, Nelson authored a *Saturday Evening Post* story entitled "Lion Taming's the Bunk." He claimed the so-called danger was just so much ballyhoo and that he could work anyone's act after viewing a single performance. — *Harry Chipman*

BERT NELSON

Nelson in 1935. He also doubled for Johnny Weismuller in *Tarzan and His Mate* (1933). — *Voyle Armstrong*

lions and tigers which Mr. Beatty was wont to annoy. So what did he do but get Maria Rasputin daughter of the Mad Monk and guaranteed authentic to take over the old Beatty routine. . . . The act is going big with the Hagenbeck-Wallace Show. It is said the audience likes the Mad Monk's daughter just as well as it did Clyde and the animals like her a good deal better.[109]

In fact the attempt to star Rasputin's daughter proved a fiasco when she revealed her fear of animals. Bert Nelson, animal trainer and Hollywood stand-in for Johnny Weismuller in the Tarzan films, took over Beatty's cats on Hagenbeck-Wallace. His performance was able but not crowd-pleasing.

When John Ringling North, nephew of John Ringling, gained control of the Big One in 1938, he emphasized the desirability of only having

European animal acts, a policy the show has largely followed to this day, over "your whip and pistol boys, pretending to stand in deadly danger while cowing the cats by sheer brutality and the alleged power of the human eye."[110] In his memoirs, the Ringling publicist Dexter Fellows remarked that Beatty was a consummate showman, but his act brought a "flood of objections from societies for the prevention of cruelty to animals, various Jack London Clubs, and a large number of individuals."[111] Charly Baumann, star tiger trainer of one of Ringling's present day units, explained in his 1975 autobiography that American trainers played up to their audience's thirst for blood by presenting their animals' worst behavior. "The most famous American trainer of all was of this wild school of training. . . . He went into the arena scaring hell out of the creatures around him and

Attempts to replace Beatty after his departure from H-W led to humorous results. First, Rasputin's daughter was hired to mesmerize the animals into submission, and then the Mexican hypnotist, Blacaman. Both were heavily advertised but proved to be flops. — *Fred D. Pfening, Jr.*

Bert Nelson (Cardburt Nelson Snyder) began his career on Al G. Barnes in 1925 and became the featured trainer on Hagen-beck-Wallace–Fore-paugh-Sells in 1935, where he worked many of Beatty's cats after Clyde left to join Cole Bros. — *Fred D. Pfening, Jr.*

BEATTY PLAYS PING PONG TO KEEP AGILE

CLYDE BEATTY AND A MAN-SLAYING TIGER WHOM HE HANDLES BY COURAGE, BLUFF AND EXPERIENCE

"Dempsey, Sande, Bobby Jones and Walter Johnson were all game champions in their separate lines," says Hal Coffman, cartoonist for the N. Y. Evening Journal. "But the gamest champion and nerviest man I have ever known is Clyde Beatty.

"Day after day he faces sure death in just one slip or error of judgment."

The Cole Bros. Circus was playing its annual Spring engagement at the Hippodrome in New York. He sat in his dressing room and discussed life and death. Continuing Hal Coffman states:

"Clyde Beatty is a slight and handsome little fellow. In every line of business there is always one who stands head and shoulder above his contemporaries. In wild animal training Beatty is tops."

He had just come out of a cage filled with 37 of these gentle creatures. He had been running at top speed, parrying their huge swift claws with a chair, and yelling like a madman.

His wife, who seemed a little grateful to have him back, sat at his side.

"I still get a great kick out of every performance," said Beatty, who has been in the business 13 years and is now only 32. "This is one business where there's not much competition."

He talks casually and simply about his business, and he certainly looks as if it has agreed with him. But a look at his legs tells a different story. A revolting white scar on his right thigh testifies to the efficiency of a lion's teeth. He admitted reluctantly he has almost died several times from fever following these attacks.

"Courage and bluff and experience," he said, "are the great things in this business. If you back up they'll follow you. The thing to do is rush right at them."

This seemed a little foolhardy, but Beatty explained that the lion is something of a bully himself. He makes a lot of noise, but if you stand up to him and yell right back, your chances of beating him are better," he said.

Beatty at the moment is trying to produce something new in wild animals by breeding a male lion with a female

tiger. If successful, the issue would be called, says Beatty, a "liger." He explained they have bred a male tiger and a female lion in Germany and produced what they called a "tigon."

Trying desperately for a sporting angle to this grim business, the reporter asked what sport Mr. Beatty played to keep in shape for lion taming.

"Ping pong," he said simply.

Cole Bros. Circus with Clyde Beatty

is coming to..

....

....

for performances at 2 and 8 p. m. Ken Maynard, the screen's greatest Western star, along with 400 other performers will be seen. An immense street parade will be seen on the downtown streets at 11 a. m.

Release prepared by Cole Bros. publicity department.

the kids in the audience. He provoked his animals . . . Beatty himself created much of the danger and he was frequently mauled by his animals. In my opinion he was more a showman than a trainer. Many of his acts were trained for him by others, Beatty only played the trainer's role."[112] A 1978 article in *Sports Illustrated* about Ringling star

Gunther Gebel-Williams quoted Ringling Vice-President Allen Bloom: "The thing is that Gunther is so good and establishes such rapport with animals that they become docile and nobody believes they're real. Audiences love the threat of violence and blood, but if Beatty was still around wearing his pith helmet and firing those blanks, the

Clyde Beatty
Undisputably, World's Greatest Conqueror of Wild Beasts
By G. Cornwall Spencer

TWICE each day, Clyde Beatty faces death in its most hideous form.

Forty-three jungle-born bundles of nerves are with him in his iron-barred arena when he exhibits his spectacular wild animal act with the Cole Brothers Circus.

Forty-three lions and tigers! Each is treacherous, vicious, cunning! Each is a potential killer by instinct! Each holds only respect, but no fear, for its trainer and master!

At any moment, any one of the big "cats" may fly into a blind fury, clawing, slashing, roaring with rage—a murderous blood-lustful killer.

Beatty's lions and tigers have done it before and he KNOWS they will do it again!

Surgery has saved his face from being permanently scarred, but his body bears scores of horrible mementoes of his close, personal encounters with kill-bent beasts. His legs are a mass of scars from the razor-like claws and the murderous fangs of his charges!

At 32, Beatty has long been at the peak of his profession—the training of wild beasts to perform for thrill-seeking circus-goers.

He has reached heights not even dreamed of by former generations of animal trainers! He is unquestionably without peer in his line!

Yet, year by year, he strives to do more, to do bigger and better animal acts, to achieve the impossible.

When he taught a huge Bengal tiger to roll over on the sawdust like a house kitten and to chase its tail, Beatty was recognized as having reached unexcelled heights.

But Beatty still was not satisfied. He had done what no

Beatty became the subject of illustrators in Cole Bros. programs.

THRILLS GALORE
With the Greatest Wild Animal Trainer in the World

humane society would lock him up."[113]

In fact, humane societies did harass Beatty as soon as he went with the new Cole show. In Buffalo they threatened to treat him the "same way we do a peddler caught unmercifully beating his horse."[114] He was arrested for "agitating his animals with a whip" in Pittsburgh in 1936 and although he denied the charge, he still paid the fine.[115] Beatty always rejected charges of mistreating his animals and he readily invited the humane society agents either to pet his "kittens" or "come in the cage with me and get acquainted with my little friends." Even the *New York Times* editorial-ized on the ridiculous nature of the charges that he bullied his cats. Beatty's final run in with the law occurred in New York in 1937, when he was arrested following a performance.[116] The judge dismissed the charges as having no basis in fact, and humane societies never bothered him again during the remaining twenty-eight years of his career.

Cole Bros. hit its peak of popularity in 1937 when the circus shattered tradition and "became the first important tent show in a generation to challenge the Greatest Show on Earth not only by playing New York, hitherto practically a Ringling monopoly, but playing it before Ringling Bros. got

TIME

The Weekly Newsmagazine

CLYDE BEATTY & CAPTIVE

Volume XXIX   "Our c. ization places too high a valuation on the cute and the cunning."   Number 13
(See THEATRE)

In 1937, Beatty made the cover of *Time* when Cole Bros. played the New York Hippodrome.—*Courtesy Fred D. Pfening, Jr.*

there and playing it under a 'permanent top.'" That year *Time* pictured Beatty on its cover, undoubtedly the only circus star ever to gain this distinction, and described his act as in "another class altogether" compared to any other performances.

The world's most sensational one-man spectacle ... so thoroughly dramatized ... to get the last tingling thrill from the most distant customers ... The lunges, feints and sham attacks of his beasts help make it a magnificent feat of showmanship ... but ... lions hate tigers and tigers hate lions, and in this atmosphere of hate the unexpected is al-

In 1937, Cole Bros. opened in the New York Hippodrome.

ways on the verge of happening. . . . Lions and tigers cannot be instructed by pushing them around. Courage and showmanship avail a trainer little if he has not the almost telepathic knack of making his beasts understand what he wants.[117]

On October 27, 1937, the Cole Bros.–Clyde Beatty Circus played its final date before returning to winterquarters in Indiana. Circus fans traveled far, as if by premonition, to see this last performance. Writing about the date years later, one who

was there noted: "For one shining season the show had reached to great heights and those who were privileged to have seen it have never forgotten it and to this day will still declare there has never been anything quite like it thereafter."[118] The parade alone was a magnificent addition to a show that spanned the nation and earned rave reviews from New York to Hollywood. In its writeup *Billboard* said:

Below and opposite page: These 1937 Cole Bros. route book illustrations show one of the most successful circuses of all time. Unwittingly, they also marked the end of the "golden age" of the circus in America, which especially gives Emmett Kelly's cartoon a certain poignancy.

As usual Clyde Beatty and his lions and tigers occupy the center of interest and probably for the first time in his career the young showman closes the program. . . . This act bears out the fact that Messrs. Adkins and Terrell have still the biggest drawing card in the circus world. . . . Here is possibly the greatest circus attraction of this era. Instead of his appeal being diluted by perennial appearances Beatty does a reverse . . . by showing up as a considerably punchier item than in his first appearances with the Ringling show several years ago. His film and radio appearances help audience appreciation and have had their effect on him too. He has grown considerably in stature as a showman. He seems able to do anything with the cats except make them sing. The display could not have been anything but last because no attraction in this layout, could possibly follow and expect to hold audience attention.[119]

Stimulated by the 1937 season, Adkins and Terrell hoped to build another circus empire. They had already enlarged their winterquarters as early as August, 1937, and they announced they would put a second show on the road in 1938. Persuaded that two circuses would enable them to utilize their impressive managerial talents to better advantage, they reasoned that they could not only tap a wider market with two circuses but they would also have a backup circus working if one of them ran into trouble. So, in the spring, Cole Bros., which opened the season on thirty cars, was joined by a new circus, Robbins, which opened on fifteen. *Billboard* gave the Cole show an excellent review, commenting favorably about an unusual act featuring a lion and tiger riding an elephant, presented by Beatty's wife. Beatty himself "is doing the most spectacular act in his career as a wild animal trainer with possibly the largest number of cats ever used in an act of its kind. From the start it is filled with thrills and daring fearlessness. Beatty colors his work with dramatic showmanship and is master of the situation at all times. He has two rearing lions this year instead of one, and the roll-over tiger is still one of the highlights of the offering."[120] The successes Adkins and Terrell had enjoyed in 1937 had also encouraged other showmen to frame new circuses in 1938. In all, six railroad shows and five large motorized circuses set

Entrance to the Cole Bros. winterquarters at Rochester, Indiana. —*William Koford*

Lineup of cage wagons on the Cole Bros. train. —*George Hubler*

Not all the cat acts of the thirties were big and sensational. Many like Ernie Klauder's 1936 Seils-Sterling act were small. —*Fred D. Pfening, Jr.*

out with the highest expectations that spring. Then, on April 6, the Art Mix Circus folded in New Mexico. In four weeks it had attracted only two days of business. The new Tim McCoy Wild West Show closed in the spring in Washington, D.C., with a loss of $200,000. Soon it was evident that all the circuses were faced with a devastating combination of a very sudden and severe recession and foul weather. All the show owners were heavily mortgaged and they were all caught by surprise. Expecting good times, they had all expanded, not retrenched. Downie Bros., a major circus, shut down at the end of May. Union trouble that had begun a year earlier again flared up when the American Federation of Actors caused a walkout during Ringling's opening in New York. When the same union picketed Hagenbeck-Wallace, Robbins, and King, they crossed into Canada, but better business did not materialize there. Cole Bros. agreed to sign a union contract, but Ringling closed on June 25 after negotiations proved fruitless.

In 1938, Beatty was working his cats better than ever, but the Depression would deal a nearly fatal blow to American circuses.

The Ringling move completely demoralized the industry. Cole, whistling in the dark, advertised itself as "Now, the Greatest Show on Earth," but the end was near. On July 4, Seils-Sterling Circus went off the road. Cole battled torrential rains along with bad business, but the show continued to move with precision and employees remained exceptionally loyal. Still, the Cole investors could wait no longer. Fearing their show would be stranded, they ordered it back to Rochester. To prevent panic, the move was made in secret. On August 6, the surprised personnel found themselves back home.

Robbins, still on the road in August, was troubled by an oppressive heat wave. As the new show headed south, it was bolstered by six cars of Cole equipment and acts, including Beatty's. Business gradually began to improve for Robbins, and although news came that the Hagenbeck-Wallace and Tom Mix circuses had closed, Atlanta and Decatur brought capacity houses for it and the sudden end of the circus, when it came, was unexpected. When the performers woke up in the Nashville railroad yards, the announcement that the circus had closed and all employees let go was bitterly considered equivalent to a "redlighting." The Indiana Circus Corporation declared a debt of $418,338 without a single asset. The winter of 1938–39 was the most melancholy in circus history. It was the final year also for Al G. Barnes, the last of the old ACC shows. *Billboard* gravely remarked that things could not get worse, but then Jess Adkins, considered by some historians the last of the great circus managers and hopefully the teacher of a new generation of managers, died.[121]

Clyde Beatty faced a turning point. He had overcome the seemingly impossible task of building an entire new act when he left Ringling and staked his reputation with Cole. In return, the success of the new show had added to his image, but now Beatty decided to quit Cole, take his cats and three elephants in lieu of back pay owed to him, and strike out on his own. An optimist, like most circus men, Beatty incorporated the Clyde Beatty Circus Unit as a basis for a future show of his own. Cole Bros., despite a disastrous winterquarters fire, reorganized, but the loss of Beatty left a void that was never filled. In the public's mind the two were inseparable, and during the eleven years left of its existence the circus never featured another cat act.

Beatty helped prepare an act for his wife—a lion and a tiger riding an elephant.

Beatty and his wife also utilized their cats in an ad for the 1937 Studebaker.—*Ken Whipple*

Early spring visitors at the Peru winterquarters (1930s). — *Ken Whipple*

The fifty-year heyday of the American circus ended in 1938, but during this time the wild animal act became an established, in fact preeminent feature of major circuses. Ringling hired Peru trainer Terrell Jacobs in 1937 to break a group of black panthers captured by Frank Buck. Buck, along with Gargantua, were special features of the show. In 1938, after failing to break properly the proposed panther act, Jacobs appeared with a large mixed group of lions and tigers. Since 1940, Ringling has presented as its star attraction a long line of European trainers, culminating in 1971 with the purchase of Germany's entire Circus Williams to obtain the services of Gunther Gebel-Williams. Gebel-Williams, by far the most publicized trainer since Clyde Beatty, completely dominates the Red Unit with his tiger, elephant, leopard, giraffe, and horse acts. With long, bleached blond hair, a dazzling array of costumes, "sex-symbol" appeal, glib dialogue, and a reported "oneness" with his animals, Gebel-Williams has been the subject of numerous magazine and newspaper articles, interviews on almost every television "talk show," and even a network special. Nicknamed the "Lord of the Ring" he again proves the importance of the wild animal act to circus success.

The American fighting act has all but disappeared. The demise means the end of the lions and tigers of our own dreams and imaginations—flashing claws, glistening fangs in red gaping mouths, black bristling manes, tawny combatants wielding paws that can break the neck of a zebra with a single blow, menacing striped cats creeping forward in an exaggerated, stealthy prowl, green eyes gleaming with a fury about to erupt. The flimsily armed men battling these great cats, subjugating them by sheer will power, has gone the way of the Saturday morning movie cowboy. The precise, regimented European style acts remain—stainless steel props, shining mirrored balls, leapfrogging tigers, motorcycle-riding lions, chorus line big cats performing roll overs and hind leg walks for peroxided, sequined trainers.

1933 H-W circus program cover.

1934 H-W circus program cover (Beatty).

Poster advertising 1933 motion picture *The Big Cage*.

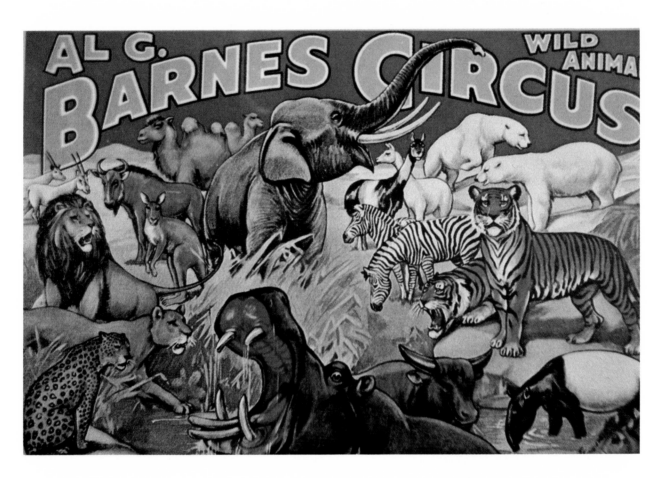

Al G. Barnes poster.

Gebel-Williams in a sure showstopper.

Monte Carlo tigers.

Henry Schroer presents an elephant-riding tiger on the Greatest
Show on Earth.

Harry Thomas and his tigers.

Alfred Court.

Chapter III

THE RECENT YEARS

The disastrous season of 1938 meant the end of the circus as a boisterous, reckless amusement run by aspiring kings of the tented world. The circus was tamed. Gone were the street parades, the opposition brigade fights, the immense teams of baggage horses, and the "hell-bent-for-leather" races that capped each performance. The Ringling organization was headed by John and Henry Ringling North, Yale-educated nephews of John Ringling. Influenced by Broadway musicals, the Norths transformed their show into a slick production that featured nontraditional music and heavy emphasis on spectacles, costumes, and showgirls. This trend continues under the recent owners, the Mattel Corporation, and circus producer, Irvin Feld. Utilization of aerial, acrobatic, and equestrian performers that rely on mechanical safety devices has further detracted from the spine-tingling bravado of the earlier circus. The wild animal act proved no exception to this change. In 1940, the Norths introduced the Frenchman, Alfred Court, and his entourage of animals and assistant trainers. The suave aristocrat set the style of performance that still dominates the two Ringling shows.

Other circuses continued to exist and the spirit of rivalry, although dampened, lingered among their owners. But no burgeoning empire arose to tackle the big One. Cole Bros. survived the 1938 season and the death of Jess Adkins, reorganized, and took to the road. But this show that originally featured two of the largest wild animal acts toured for eleven years without a single one. Clyde Beatty's career never diminished. He continued to

write books, appear in movies, and star in every circus with which he performed until his death in 1965. His style became synonymous with wild animal training to the American audience, and his name, virtually a generic term for "lion trainer," is considered one of the most valuable circus titles. But the competition of the 1920s that spawned his drive and ultimate success no longer existed. The tension, excitement, and imminent danger of a big fighting group hardly fits the polished image of the Ringling shows.

The takeover of Ringling Bros.–Barnum & Bailey Circus by the North brothers in the late 1930s has long been a controversial topic. Undoubtedly they saved the Big One, but in the process did they ruin the circus? In 1939, *The New Republic* said their

Beatty listens to Frank Buck, with onlookers Lou Costello and Bud Abbott. They co-starred in *Africa Screams.*

The Pallenberg bears also appeared on the 1939 Ringling show. — *Harry Chipman*

attempt to lower the operating "nut" meant cutting out the headline performers, keeping labor costs as low as the troupe would stand, and operating solely on the principle of "watch us make money." "Nothing," the magazine sadly concluded, "will kill the circus deader."[1]

But during the next two years criticism diminished. Hostilities in Europe provided "a full-blown windfall of Continental stars and spectacles, some of them hitherto unobtainable."[2] In 1941, *Time* went to the circus and came back glowing with praises: "it was like the lovely dream circus in Billy Rose's *Jumbo*," it reported, "only five times larger. To adults the effect was powerful, on the less mature it was staggering."[3]

Relying on Balanchine ballets, Stravinsky music, production numbers created in Paris by Follies Bergere designer Max Weldy, and by such Broadway producers as Norman Bel Geddes, the Ring-

ling show was streamlined and sophisticated. The new style demanded a new kind of animal act. At first the show starred Terrell Jacobs, a mixed fighting act trainer from Peru, Indiana, whom Henry Ringling North described as a "rough and ready character who had lost one eye to a lion [and used] the old fashioned, brutal, whip-and-pistol technique that I hate; but he was very, very brave."[4] Jacobs was scar covered, with more than two hundred tooth and claw marks in his body, including fifty-two on the back of his neck administered by a leopard. But it was no big cat that had cost him his eye. On that occasion he had tripped over a wire fence while chasing an escaped lion and a snapping branch blinded him. Jacobs apparently saw the handwriting on the wall while he performed with the Ringling show because he was quick to criticize the European trainers who would soon dominate the big circus. He sneered that the Euro-

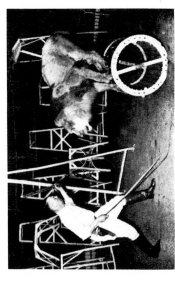

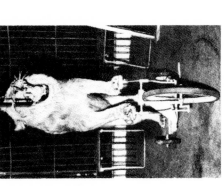

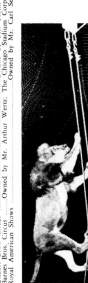

TRAINING and HANDLING
DOMESTICATED PETS
and

With Factual Stories on the Life of
TERRELL JACOBS
World's Greatest Subjugator of
SAVAGE JUNGLE BEASTS

Late in his career, Jacobs published this booklet.

peans used training forks in their work rather than rely on gentler methods and speedy agile footwork. The foreigners would jab these forks—each one consisted of a pair of long prongs bent outward at the end of a seventeen-foot pole with a short knife between the prongs—against the throat of a fierce cat to force him into submission. Jacobs claimed the ASPCA unfairly protested the use of blanks and whips by American trainers, when they were really only noisemakers.[5]

Early in the spring of 1940, the French trainer, Alfred Court, arrived in New York with an entourage of sixty animals and fourteen assistants.

Court, who had been a champion gymnast as a boy in school before running away to join a circus, had appeared first with the Ringling show in 1914 as an acrobat. Later he had become a juggler, ringmaster, and circus owner in Europe. At the age of thirty-five he had taken over a lion act from a drunken trainer and dedicated the rest of his circus career to the development of unusual wild animal turns. Now nearing sixty, Court owned five of the largest animal acts active in Europe and was quite wealthy. But to escape the war, he gratefully accepted John Ringling North's invitation to come to America.

Jacobs was featured with H-W during the tail-end of that circus's existence.—*Voyle Armstrong*

Jacobs and his wife Dolly. — *Voyle Armstrong*

Jacobs was a native of Peru, Indiana. Here he is pictured with his father. — *Voyle Armstrong*

Dolly and Terrell Jacobs. — *Voyle Armstrong*

Terrell Jacobs on the Al G. Barnes Circus. — *Voyle Armstrong*

Jacobs's letterhead while he was on the Barnes show.

In 1934, Jacobs starred with Al G. Barnes. — *Fred D. Pfening, Jr.*

Dolly Jacobs. — *Voyle Armstrong*

Jacobs worked the largest cat act of all time in America in the largest (50-foot) steel arena. The seventeen-minute act consisted of between thirty-eight and fifty-two animals (1939). — *Fred D. Pfening, Jr.*

Terrell and Dolly Jacobs. — *Fred D. Pfening, Jr.*

Alfred Court.

Alfred Court.

Promotion of the slightly built, mannerly, middle-aged Frenchman was a problem for the Ringling advertising men. There was no difficulty in promoting a Clyde Beatty, whose fifteen-minute battles in the big cage gave youngsters summer long dreams of running away to join the circus and made every dog and cat in the neighborhood the subject of souvenir whip and cap pistol training sessions. But Court's appeal had to be based on a more sophisticated approach. However, for the public relations staff that made "Ubangis" and "Gargantua" household words, the solution was easy, and the mystique of the European trainer was born. Earlier in the century, Americans had been convinced that German trainers were superior. Now the Ringling promoters extended this to include all foreign animal trainers. The image was of suave, cool people in total command of themselves and their animals. Because of their remarkable patience and ability to dominate wild beasts, they were never injured and did not have to fight the cats with whips, chairs, or blank pistols. Journalists and authors readily accepted the publicity stories and the approach proved so successful that the Ringling stories have rarely deviated from it. The Ringling ad in the *New York Times* gloated:

First Time in America Dangerous Man-Killing Wild Animals That Are Really Educated! Direct From Europe – Three Great Mixed Groups of the Most Bloodthirsty Savage Beasts Ever Assembled – All Perfectly Schooled and Inculcated with Inconceivable Intelligence, Presented Under The Personal Direction of the Incomparable ALFRED COURT Master Trainer of the Ages.
Polar Bears, Tigers, Lions, Himalayan Bears, Siberian Snow Leopards, Black Jaguars and Panthers, Pumas, Cougars, Ocelots, Black and Spotted Leopards and Great Dane Dogs – Natural Enemies Since the Dawn of Creation, Taught with Understanding, Kindness and Patience, combined with Gray Matter – Performing Together in the Most Hazardous and Exciting Exhibitions in History – WITHOUT USE OF GUN-FIRE, CROWBARS, ELECTRIC PERSUADERS, PYROTECHNICS, OR DRAMATIC PRETENSE on the part of Court or his Retinue of Experts. A SIGHT THAT MAKES ALL OTHER WILD ANIMAL TRAINERS FEEL LIKE NINCOMPOOPS![6]

Court believed his 1940 appearance in Madison Square Garden was the high point of his career. The "Old Master," as he was known, and two assistants presented three acts of eighteen mixed animals working simultaneously in the three rings. Synchronization was of greatest importance in this unique presentation. All the props had horizontal surfaces of unbreakable glass illuminated from within by searchlights. Each act consisted of five tricks that ended in an ensemble pose. As a grand finale, the circus was plunged into total darkness and the searchlights suddenly flooded the groups of animals from below.

Court (seated) and his assistant trainers: Fritz Schultz, Damoo Dhotre, and Joe Walch (1942). – *Robert Good*

The rehearsals became almost too exciting for the reporters. An Indian leopard killed the only performing snow leopard, another cat escaped, and Court's face was slashed by a black panther. The wound was bloody but superficial and the trainer did not wipe his face for fear of blood poisoning. John Ringling North, pleased at the unexpected publicity, asked the Frenchman if he had staged the accident on purpose. "Sure!" Court replied. "Good boy, Alfred," said North, and turned to photographers who were standing near to announce grandly: "To see another trainer like my friend Alfred Court, you'll have to wait a century!"[7] *Time*, which reported the incident, declared naively that Court trained "beasts by wrapping hunks of meat around his chest and waist so that if they get hungry they won't nibble off him."[8]

Court himself was a talented trainer and quite candid in his autobiography and later memoirs about his injuries and training methods. He worked with a great number of different species, developed beautiful and unique acts, and passed his knowledge on to his many assistants. A *Collier's* feature story in 1940 said that rather than use a pistol or chair, Court and his assistants relied on "superb handling of the body" as protection. "He and his trainers move their bodies like matadors and their footwork resembles that of prize fighters, as they elude the swift, savage charges of the beasts." The writer called Court's method of subduing the most humane known in the business of

Court and his assistant prepare to treat a lion with the help of a squeeze cage. – *Tom Henricks*

Alfred Court.

wild animal education. Still, Court had been injured many times. Unlike others in his profession
he did not look upon his scars as medals. Instead
he considered them a reflection upon his ability
and good sense. His worst injury had occurred
when blood poisoning set in after a lion attack. He
had had to sell his animals and retire for two years
to a hotel he built in Nice. Finally fighting his way
back to health, he confessed he would have "committed suicide, but for the fact I am a religious
man."[9]

Court's autobiography reveals his love of working with the big cats, but it also describes the
intense danger and often brutal battles of the
training arena. He believed that rewards and
punishments were the basis of all training and that
both had to be administered swiftly to be effective.
The initial encounter with a new animal was the
most important one. If the beast did not attack,
gentleness and patience could be used, but if he
did attack, then "the trainer must defend himself
in every way and with all the strength at his command. The animal must at once be given severe
enough correction for him to realize at first encounter that he is not the stronger. There are
times when it is a struggle to the death."[10] Court
claimed he loved animals as much as any man and
often wept over their death, but during these first
encounters he killed two animals in self-defense.
Neither of these was a big cat: one was a polar
bear, and one was a Great Dane.

One of the most unusual animal acts was broken by
Court and his nephew, Willy Storey. It featured
twelve leopards trained to work with six Ringling
showgirls. Damoo Dhotre presented the act. — *Fred D.
Pfening, Jr.*

Damoo Dhotre and the leopard act with Ringling showgirls. — *Fred D. Pfening, Jr.*

"To understand animals and to love them, to possess infinite patience, to be calm and capable of great physical endurance and to have a little courage" were, Court wrote, the qualities necessary to a good wild animal man. Courage was least important, caution was more valuable.[11]

The gentle methods stressed by so many authors in describing European trainers certainly were not always evident behind the scenes. In discussing these training sessions, Court relates this: "Held by his lasso, he could not reach the smaller tiger. Immediately he received four or five lashes and was sent back to his place."[12] Concerning training lions: "Dropping my chair, I grasped the stool in front of me with both hands, shouting, 'Caesar, back to your place!' and flung it at his head,"[13] and in another instance, "I rushed after him, lashing him with the whip as hard as I could, all the time repeating 'Menelik! To your place!' "[14] One episode, far from "Peace in the Jungle"—the name of

Cageboy cleans tigers at RBB&B winterquarters in Sarasota. — *Dyer M. Reynolds*

Court's act—found him seizing "a heavy training stool made of wood and steel weighing a good eighty pounds. Raising it above my head, I flung it at Artis, catching him on the hindquarters. The animal gave a terrible roar, a cry of pain rather than attack, and turned in an attempt to spring at me. But the poor beast did not get far. The iron stool had hit him harder than I had intended and had snapped his leg."[15]

These occurrences were, of course, desperate situations but they demonstrate that wild animals are never tame. The quiet beauty of the European style acts is often deceptive and does not reveal the underlying hostility and struggles involved in breaking the beasts. Not only did Court suffer two years from blood poisoning, but in another attack, Brahma, a tiger, inflicted fifteen wounds, which included a four-inch gash on the trainer's stomach. The big cat furrowed his cheeks and shoulders, slashed his forearms, and sunk his four fangs completely through Court's thigh.[16] Another tiger, Bengali, killed two of Court's assistants, before the "Old Master" gained control over the beast in a savage do-or-die battle before an excited Spanish audience.

Some authors have forgotten his accidents and occasional brutality in the arena. For them he personifies the "good," humane method of training as opposed to "bad," cruel American practices. A 1949 work, *We Fell in Love With the Circus*, agreed

When Court's acts first appeared in Madison Square Garden in 1941, the three rings contained a total of sixty animals (including lions, tigers, spotted and black jaguars, snow leopards, black panthers, pumas, Great Dane dogs, polar bears, Himalayan bears, leopards, and ocelots). In ring one was Court's only female trainer, May Kovar. During the season she alternated working the act with her husband, Harry. In 1949, she was killed by a lion.—*Fred D. Pfening, Jr.*

May Kovar.—*Fred D. Pfening, Jr.*

May Kovar.—*Fred D. Pfening, Jr.*

Michael Konzelmann (Konzelmann's polar bears),
Roman Proske (tigers), and Damoo Dhotre (leopards,
jaguars, and pumas) starred with RBB&B in 1947.

that "Alfred Court . . . believes in studying the
character of the animals individually and training
without brutality, making noisy guns and cruelty
of earlier trainers unnecessary." The author,
Claire Fawcett, writes: "Now and then a flick of
the whip is all the guidance that is needed. Even
when the animal is sulky, the trainer's voice must
be the guide."[17] Fred Bradna, longtime Ringling
equestrian director, paid the greatest compliments
to Court in his autobiography. According to him,
the "Old Master" "belies the popular conception of
the bold demigod, cruel and stern who bends
jungle kings to their duty by an overpowering personality and bitter goad." He had no patience with

PROGRAM of DISPLAYS

DISPLAY NO. I   ALFRED COURT, MASTER TRAINER OF THE AGES

IMPLACABLE ENEMIES OF JUNGLE WILDS EDUCATED BEYOND BELIEF

Great New Mixed Groups of the Most Ferocious Wild Animals Ever Assembled

Lions, Polar Bears, Black Bears, Black Jaguars and Great Dane Dogs	Performing Lions, Tigers and leopards	Tigers, Polar Bears, Kodiac and Brown Bears and Lions
	Alternately Presented by	
Presented by	**ALFRED COURT** and	Presented by
JOSEPH WALSH	**PRINCE DAMOO**	**FREDERICK OLSEN**

Caricature of Alfred Court in the 1940 RBB&B Circus Magazine.

trainers of the so-called fighting school, who "fire blank cartridges into their animals' faces, snap vicious whips, and poke chair legs into their eyes." He proved that kindness, a soft voice, and patience "soothe the savage beast much faster than cruelty. In all his years of exhibiting—he has never once used whip or gun. And he alone of the first-rate exhibitors has never been seriously hurt." He never frustrated his charges, but diverted the lethal power of their claws by calmly holding out a piece of wood, or even a newspaper, allowing them to satisfy themselves by scratching it to shreds. Bradna concluded that Court was, without question, the greatest modern cat trainer.[18] John and Alice Durant, writing in their history of the circus,

came to the same conclusion. "Court never used a gun or chair, never raised his voice even when mixing species which were natural foes of each other. . . . A trainer's trainer, Court is one of the very few who has never been badly hurt."[19] Even after Court's autobiography was published, Henry Ringling North wrote: "To my mind Alfred Court is the greatest wild animal trainer the world has ever seen . . . he is none of your whip-and-pistol bully boys . . . cowing the cats by sheer brutality. . . . Instead he makes it all seem easy and polite as an Arthur Murray class in ballroom dancing." It was, North thought, "through his patience and system of reward for effort, [that he] got his animals to respect him without fear. Of course when it came to teaching the more involved tricks he had to use a whip." If an animal got out of control, he would flick it on a sensitive area, so that it would immediately know it had done wrong.[20]

But there was a minority report too. An article about Pat Anthony in Bill Ballentine's *Wild Tigers and Tame Fleas* calls attention to contradictions in Court's memoirs. Anthony, an American fighting act trainer, who patterned his style after Beatty and Jacobs said, "If you'll read Court's own book, you'll find out he was bad hurt more'n a couple of times. He didn't use blanks, he did use a whip and a stick sometimes. In training he used a blunt-pointed fork with tin cans tied to it to make noise."[21] The legend of perfect control and veri-

table invincibility on the part of Court seems to be the dream of circus press agents. Statements that the Frenchman greatly disliked American "bully boys" are also belied in Court's recent memoirs. "Pat Valdo [Ringling performance director] invited us to his home and showed me, I remember, a picture show of Clyde Beatty's act, a wonderful showman, who later became my friend."[22] In fact, Joe Walch, one of Court's assistants, later broke animals for Beatty, and Willie Storey, the French master's nephew and a former trainer himself, managed the Sells and Gray Circus, which was a subsidiary of Clyde Beatty–Cole Bros.

In 1944, the worst fears of John Ringling concerning caged wild animal acts came true. Eight

The disastrous Hartford fire strikes the Greatest Show on Earth. — *Herbert Duvall III*

After the fire, Court's cage wagons are starkly framed by the charred remainders of the circus. —*Herbert Duvall III*

thousand people were attending the matinee performance of the Ringling show in Hartford, Connecticut. The second act, which featured wild animal turns, had just ended, and three rings of cats were headed toward the steel mesh runways that fanned out from the arenas, when the music suddenly changed to "The Stars and Stripes Forever," the circus disaster warning. The big top was on fire and the cats had to be cleared out. The trainers fought desperately to drive the cats quickly through the runways. Mae Kovar turned a hose on four of her balking leopards to hurry their progress. The beasts headed back to their cages, but by then the whole canvas was in flames and people in the front rows had no way to escape but through the hippodrome track itself. The panicked audience found the runways an almost impassable barrier. First the fleeing patrons hurdled them, but

those who failed and fell built a human pyre that trapped the ones behind. Chunks of burning canvas hurtled to the ground and finally the six center poles fell one by one.[23]

Ringling officials took blame for the catastrophe that had left 168 dead and 487 others seriously injured. They had applied for fireproof canvas but because of wartime restrictions it was unavailable. They paid fines and damages and served jail sentences. The disaster did not cause another ban on wild animal acts, though it might well have done, but instead, under the Norths, who knew their popularity, the acts continued for many years in three rings, simultaneously, as before. Alfred Court retired in 1945, living well into his nineties (he died in 1977). His Indian assistant, Damoo Dhotre, remained with Ringling until 1949. In the early 1950s the Norths featured in the steel arena

Damoo Dhotre, Alfred Court's understudy.—*Harry Chipman*

Damoo Dhotre.

Oscar Konyot (1952) and Damoo Dhotre (1949) work at Sarasota. —*Dyer M. Reynolds*

the unique mixed bear act of Albert Rix and the comedy lion routine of Oscar Konyot. Between 1953 and 1964 Trevor Bale starred in the center ring. Bale, a member of an old circus dynasty, is Danish by birth, British by upbringing, and an American by choice. It is his belief that tigers are as trustworthy as homicidal maniacs. Once, when he was asked what he thought about when other trainers were injured, he replied: "You feel sick. You think, 'It could of [sic] been me.' But unless you're going to chuck the game for keeps, you go in—you go in somehow. And you put your faith in God."[24] Bale looked the part of a children's book animal trainer with his haughty air, waxed mustachios, and colorful turn-of-the-century military

uniform. Still an active performer, he has managed to instill in his son, Elvin, a daredevil instinct. The younger Bale is now a star aerial performer with Ringling.

An almost twenty-year domination of Ringling by foreign trainers was interrupted in 1959 when the Big One featured a most unusual big cat handler. George Jacob Keller fulfilled a lifelong ambition at sixty-two when he appeared with his act in the center ring of Madison Square Garden. A retired college professor, Keller taught from 1921 to 1950 at the State Teachers College in Bloomsburg, Pennsylvania, where he headed the fine arts department. The professor used a whip and blank gun when the cats entered and exited

In the early '50s, RBB&B featured the large mixed bear act of Albert Rix. Here he rehearses the bears at Sarasota.—*Dyer M. Reynolds*

The bears' cage wagon.—*Dyer M. Reynolds*

but for the main routine he donned a pair of white gloves and cued the cats by hand signals only. He called it his method of "progressive education" and claimed, "It's the same thing as with humans, you let the animal express itself in a natural way, but you teach him the right time and place for the expression." He found the beasts, "more cooperative than 90 per cent of the kids." The cats also had more respect for their instructor. Keller thought it deplorable that for providing a few minutes entertainment, he received five times more than he got for teaching.[25] While performing with a Shrine Circus in Texas during the autumn of 1960, the

sixty-three-year-old Keller fell dead of a heart attack. He had appeared with the Big One for three years, but a long term reign of German trainers was at hand.

In 1965, McCormick Steele, a 1916 graduate of Yale and administrative engineer for Ringling Bros., invented a collapsible, lightweight, meshed steel screen big cage. The new forty-foot-diameter arena made up of ten thousand feet of woven aircraft cable weighed 180 pounds and could be raised in two minutes and dropped in thirty seconds.[26] It also gave the audience far greater visibility of the acts than obstructive steel bars.

In 1953, Trevor Bale debuted with RBB&B with his six tigers. He appeared from 1953 to 1957, then returned to the big show in 1961 through 1964. — *Ken Whipple*

Trevor Bale.

George Keller appeared with the Big One in its 1959, '60, and '61 Garden dates. — *Tom Henricks and Fred D. Pfening, Jr.*

The man to star in this arena and, in fact, to appear longer with Ringling Bros. than any other trainer, has been Charly Baumann. His tiger routine, geared for symmetry and beauty in presentation, rather than breathtaking thrills, is one of the most emulated in the circus world. In circus hyperbole he is introduced as:

Monarch of Ferocious Felines, Devastatingly Dashing and Daring Dynamo of Jungle Demons Classically Flirting with a Fierce Cluster of Treacherous Tigers, Trained but Untamed, Exhibiting Unmatched Bravery and Brilliance in the Big Cage, Calmly Capturing the Attention of His Striped Cast of Cats, Who Provide a Peerless Performance Unexcelled in Wild Animal Training.[27]

Cool, debonair, and suave in the arena, he has assumed a "James Bond" of the center ring image both in his appearance and life-style. Presenting an

unruffled, casual manner, he sends his striped cats through their paces while managing to look slightly bored. Edward Hoagland, one of America's leading essayists, has written of Baumann that he is a "cool, good hearted, hulking fellow, neither brilliant nor inspired; but he likes the work. He's relaxed and rather dawdling and friendly with the cats, makes the hard look easy and doesn't travesty or humiliate them, just exhibits their elegance, their lovely coats. With little fuss and clatter, no snarls, just a few pleasantly resonant drum-like roars—he keeps them reaching upwards for the point of his whip or doing gentle stunts."[28]

Baumann spent a pleasant early childhood in Germany where his father owned his own trick horses, worked as a movie stuntman, and gave riding lessons. From 1935 to 1940, young Charly played juvenile roles in a dozen films. But all this ended when his father was found aiding a Jewish riding patron to escape Germany. The elder Baumann died in a Belsen gas chamber; Charly's mother, also interned, became the subject of medical experiments. Charly was placed first in a Nazi orphanage and then on a work farm, but he fled and managed to rejoin his mother, who had been released after serving nineteen months at Ravensbruck and was living in Berlin. But he was seized there and drafted into the Navy where he served until he was captured by the Americans and held

In 1966, Charly Baumann first starred with the Greatest Show on Earth. Extremely stylish and demonstrating an amazing rapport and innovativeness with his tigers, he has been the most imitated trainer in recent years—but no one has matched his sophisticated, excellent act.—*Tom Henricks*

Charly Baumann.—
*Fred D. Pfening, Jr.
and Tom Henricks*

at a large airdrome near Hamburg. He was seventeen years old. Escaping again, he scavenged in garbage cans to provide for himself and his mother. It was his mother's friendship with circus owner Paula Busch that got him a job shoveling horse manure. From Circus Busch, he joined Circus Williams as a horsetrainer. It was while he was there that he saved a trainer from an attack during a rehearsal. In recognition of this bravery the circus offered him an animal act of his own. Baumann refused, believing as he did that these acts were completely brutish. When Circus Williams closed following the owner's death, Baumann, out of a job, relented and took a position as a lion trainer.

Charly Baumann. — *RBB&B*

Baumann's 1975 autobiography is far more romantically oriented than Hoagland's characterization of the man. The fact that Playboy Press published it may have something to do with this. A major theme of the book is "that something in human psychology drives females to pursue males who train wild animals."[29] His escapades, according to this account, have included sticking his head in a lion's mouth simply because a girl dared him and attempting to kill himself when he was rejected by the same girl. In this instance, he got drunk and climbed into a cagewagon full of lions. Once another girl friend blew up his Mercedes, and one's irate brother tried to have him arrested on kidnapping charges. (He was exonerated when he explained he had put her on a train home after she followed him from Rome to Vienna.) When he was invited to perform with the Russian State Circus in 1960, the first western European wild animal act to appear in the Soviet Union in thirty-five years, the Russians set up a "love trap" to lure him into staying as a teacher. (Baumann grew suspicious of the Russian girl, and her confession of her role confirmed his fears, so he eluded the ruse.)

One affair, with Circus Roland owner Eva Aureden, proved to be profitable. Baumann originally worked lions, which he thoroughly disliked, and when he came near a nervous breakdown in

Baumann's tigers.

Baumann hoses down his tigers shifting cages.

1967, Aureden insisted on buying him his first tiger act. Baumann felt that the techniques necessary to handle lions as compared to tigers were as different as playing the drums or a violin. He controlled his fighting lions with a sledgehammer handle, wooden forks, and stout poles wielded by his assistants. He considers the male lion a beautiful animal, but dull and lazy. It is hard to make training stick with him and the tawny cat turns into an extremely vicious beast during the breeding season. "Today," he said in 1975, "I would have to be in extremely bad straits to return to training lions."[30] Lions, who live in prides, become involved in power struggles, but the tiger is a solitary animal with less aggressive drive for status. Baumann felt at ease with the great striped cats. He transmitted his love and understanding for tigers to the audience through the excellence of his performance and the response of the big cats. It was then that John Ringling North "discovered" him and that he began a phase of his career that would

see him both star in the center ring and eventually become performance director of Ringling's Blue Unit.

Baumann seems exceptionally proud that he learned his profession from Willi Hagenbeck of the noted family of wild animal men. This training has left him highly critical of American audiences, which he believes enjoy an act most when it falls apart and the trainer's life is in peril. But the performances, he argues, should be the animals', not the trainer's. "The poorest acts focussed on the trainers—and not really as a trainer, at that, but as some Hairbreadth Harry facing imminent death and bodily damage." Performers, he thinks, cater to this "thirst for blood. Instead of concentration on tricks that demonstrate the animals' remarkable capabilities, they often appear with acts presenting their animals' most beastly manners, perpetuating the idea of a death-defying business that draws blood if you watch long enough."[31] But while Baumann doubts that American audiences appreciate what they have seen, he observes that in Europe, and especially in Russia, animal training is considered an art. There, success is measured by the animals' achievements rather than the hazards faced by the trainer.

For Baumann, Clyde Beatty with his pistols and whips typifies the worst image of the animal trainer. Still, he shares with the American a resentment of the term "tamer" which implies forced submission. But Beatty, according to Baumann, was not even what is known as a "primary" trainer, one who breaks his own acts; though for a large part of his own career the German did not break his acts either. His lion act, plus any replacement animals he needed, were already trained. The tiger routine that gained him his starting spot with Ringling Bros., was also purchased "from a private zoo in Hanover." Already trained, it was com-

Charly Baumann, 1966.

GREAT NEWS!

Turnaway business greeted Ringling Bros Barnum & Bailey Circus throughout its entire current season. **STUPENDOUS!**— There is no other word for

THE GREATEST SHOW ON EARTH ®

Ringling Bros AND Barnum & Bailey Circus

— PRODUCED BY —
JOHN RINGLING NORTH

HAROLD GENDERS
General Manager

MAE LYONS
Publicity Director

NOW BOOKING FOR 1965-66

Address Communications to: **Rudy Bundy,** Vice-President and Treasurer
c/o Circus office, Madison Square Garden, New York, N. Y. 10019 • CIrcle 5-0084

Wild animal trainers were good subjects for ads, as
this RBB&B Circus Magazine example shows.

Opposite: Amusement Business ad for the Greatest
Show on Earth introducing their new star, tiger
trainer Charly Baumann.

posed of five cats who cost twenty thousand dollars, and the trainer came along for the season, Baumann acknowledged, "to introduce me to the act and pinch hit."[32] Nowadays Baumann breeds his own tigers because of importation laws of endangered species. He contends that his successful breeding program has resulted in thirty-one new tigers. The complex routines he has taught these homebred cats result from painstaking, patient work. The tricks he has perfected—the multiple rollover, the hind-leg walk, the revolving mirror globe, and double hoop-jump—are widely imitated by both European and American trainers. None has achieved Baumann's finesse and style.

While Baumann was appearing as a horsetrainer with Circus Williams, the owner was tutoring circus skills to a boy with a war-scarred background similar to Charly's. This was Gunther Gebel-Williams, from the Silesian village of Schweidnitz, where he was born in 1934. The son of a theatrical

Gunther Gebel-Williams, 1978.

The most heralded trainer of the decade, Gunther Gebel-Williams, rehearses his mixed cat act. —*Fred D. Pfening, Jr.*

set designer, Gunther, his mother, and sister fled to Western Germany when his father was drafted into the German Army and sent to the Siberian front. They were utterly impoverished, living on Care packages and Hershey bars until his mother found work as a seamstress with Circus Williams. Gunther, at the age of twelve, quit school and began his circus education. When his mother left the show, the boy remained and was taken into the Williams family as a son. "Gunther, keen as the orphan Dick Whitington, learned how to juggle and dance on a wire, flip like a tumbler, ride [*sic*] liberty horses and swing from a trapeze."[33] He had a way with animals, so Williams steered him in that direction since he considered it a rare gift. When the elder Williams and his son both lost their lives in circus accidents, the show was left in the hands of Mrs. Williams, herself a member of a European circus dynasty, the Althoffs.

In 1960, Gunther married her daughter—hence his hyphenated name—and although he divorced his wife in 1967 (he married a model in 1968), he has kept the name ever since. To insure that the circus remain in the family, Mrs. Williams chose her nephew, Henry Schroer, to be tutored by Gunther as his successor. Gebel-Williams stayed on with Circus Williams until 1969 when Irvin Feld, producer of Ringling Bros., brought this now accomplished performer to America with enormous fanfare. Feld reportedly spent $2 million to buy out the 150-year-old Circus Williams, making Gunther's foster mother a wealthy woman.[34] Along with the animal training star, an entourage of nineteen elephants, nine tigers, thirty-eight horses with thirty grooms, trainers, and keepers disembarked in New York. The new trainer proved his worth by working forty-three minutes of the two hour-fifty-minute circus performance, two and three shows a day for forty-eight weeks.

Gebel-Williams became the object of Irvin Feld's promotional talent. A very successful rock music impresario before he took over the Greatest Show on Earth, Feld created the image he wished his new star to project, that of a dazzling-costumed, bleached blond sex symbol. *Time* thought he looked like a "manic, peroxided Tarzan" when at the climax of the act his Bengal tiger leapt on the back of an elephant, he straddled the tiger, and then saluted the audience.[35] Most popular articles have placed great emphasis on the fact that "his skill with tigers extends to his handling of women, both the ex- and current wife work in his act, one in the center ring, the other in a side one."[36] (This is no longer true since his first wife married aerialist Elvin Bale, but they, too, have since divorced.) Although television interviews and a "special" have

Gunther Gebel-Williams unloads his elephants from RBB&B train
(1978).

Gebel-Williams leads elephants from the train to the arena (1980).

concentrated on his gaudy image, he has also been the subject of some of the most penetrating pieces written about the circus and animal training.

Prize winning essayist William Hoagland described Gebel-Williams as

> probably the best all-around animal man to come to America in twenty years. First he works alone with his cats, as lithe and on top of things as Clyde Beatty once was, but with a gentle, fertile, inventive delight, a sinful, delicious intimacy, and frank joy—he works like a genius, in other words. He has a Fighter, a Stealthy One, a Hatstand, eight altogether. He gives them the "How" salute of an animal man to a tiger, hand raised and palm flat, and bats them with the butt end of his whip to keep them slinking and roaring, nonplussed. He could go on playing with them forever, blending and understanding his feats, but all pleasures must end, the 14 elephants come on and he gives them a run for their money as well, with a Peter Pan grin, a crucifix bouncing on his bare chest. In his slippers, he roller skates on their backs. . . . This fellow treats them like mothers or sisters, however, or maybe overgrown tigers. He leaves leeway for their bashful grace, does practically all the directing with his voice alone, and runs and runs and runs like the wind in order to be everywhere at once.[37]

McCandlish Phillips, the *New York Times* theatre critic, thought Gebel-Williams "looks strapping and roughly 6 feet tall when he works in a cageful of tigers at the circus. It is therefore surprising to find out there is actually little of him . . . a mere hors d'oeuvre for a tiger. He stands 5 feet 6 and weighs 137 pounds. What shape he takes in the eyes of tigers is wholly imponderable. Perhaps he looks 10 feet tall to them. In any case he enjoys mastery over beasts that has nothing to do with his stature." Phillips's impression that Gebel-Williams "entering the center ring in purple tights, gold boots and a fire-flashing jacket of imitation diamonds . . . looks like a prince of some impossible kingdom," coincided with that of *Times* writer, John Culhane.[38] "When I was a boy, I read a teriffic book called *Tarzan and the Golden Lion*. Now this guy in the giant cage loked like a combination of Tarzan and the Golden Lion. His long golden hair looked like a lion's mane. His hard muscled physique looked like Tarzan's and his bright red boots and tights, his jacket that glitters like gold and the big golden cross on his chest, all added up to my idea of how a Lord of the Jungle should dress." Culhane believed Gebel-Williams revived the original magic of the circus involving real men and women who overcame humanity's age-old fears of wild animals and falls from high places, instead of *ersatz* circus where performers play it safe in brilliant costumes and rely on "mechanics"—safety devices normally used in learning an act, now used during the performance principally by eastern Europeans.[39]

Like Baumann, Gebel-Williams favors tigers over lions. He feels that lions are noisy bluffers who would change the pace of his act, which he wants to appear natural and easy. Lions have been likened to infantry men—loyal to their friends, they roar and charge straight ahead at their foes. But tigers are delicate and solitary. They will not defend each other even against the attack of a lion, satisfied to remain noncombatant observers. They are creatures of emotion and mood, like "the proverbial hundred flowers. There are no leaders for the trainer to watch; any one of them will stick out a paw and the earth may become his sky."[40] When tigers become excited or angry they move faster and faster, and if they begin to fight "very, very quick is one tiger dead."[41] A cage crowded with tigers is totally unreliable. They are solitary, uncooperative, self-absorbed, willful and foolish. Gebel-Williams calls the tiger "very much animal."[42]

Gebel-Williams often contemplates the nature of his performance. "For me," he says, "the pistol and chair and the noise just aren't right. Audiences know that the animals can kill the trainer. I know

Wolfgang Holzmair worked a lion act on RBB&B that was called reminiscent of Van Amburgh (1971).—*Tom Henricks*

Chutes between Terrell Jacobs's cage wagons on the 1939 RBB&B show.—*George Hubler*

Training area at the former Sarasota winterquarters.

Tunnel leading to training area at RBB&B's former Sarasota winterquarters.—*Dyer M. Reynolds*

Tunnel car used by RBB&B to transport shifting dens of trained wild animals. — *Fred D. Pfening, Jr.*

Cage comes down ramp (1960). — *Fred D. Pfening, Jr.*

it, too, but my job is to make everything a smooth performance." Although less caustic than Baumann, Gebel-Williams also believes the audience lacks understanding: "It is possible to do something very good and very different and very difficult and the people don't understand. It has to look good also."[43] Because he avoids violence in the arena, many in the audience believe no danger exists, although circus people know an unexpected movement in a cageful of wild animals can mean serious injury or death. Gebel-Williams has received wounds requiring over two hundred stitches

on his arms alone and if he "didn't abhor doctors and hospitals, if his macho style did not make him pretend he was perfectly O.K. when he could barely move without excruciating pain, he would lead the league in emergency room appearances."[44]

Cleveland Amory, however, has called his big cats so domesticated that they are little more than unhappy house pets.[45] Another critic, in a letter to the *New York Times*, complained that "circus animals are caged, poked, dressed in ridiculous costumes, hauled across the continent, forced to do unnatural things and as a result are extremely ner-

Gebel-Williams performs with his stepdaughter.

vous, unhappy animals that die a premature death. It is people like Gunther and his circus who have taken these magnificent creatures from their own environment and for the almighty dollar prostituted them in a most degrading way in front of thousands of children and adults."[46]

Gunther Williams has denied these charges, insisting that most animals are born in some kind of cage, either physical or mental. Working and training gives animals excitement and an escape from boredom. "Training is a beautiful thing, I think. When an animal's brain power is enhanced, life becomes more natural, easier, more pleasant. To get inside the head of an animal and communicate, that is wonderful. That is what I live for. Absolute."[47] He claims that animals are like children, they demand patience, praise, and reprimands.

They must "learn to respect you and learn it is to their advantage to do what you tell them."[48] Only a foolish trainer would completely trust a wild animal, he says, but the animal must have absolute trust in the trainer.

Although Gunther Williams utilizes a long stick and two crackling whips, his voice is also important—he issues his commands in German. But his ultimate control is personality, or what Curry Kirkpatrick called in Sports Illustrated, his "incredible will."[49] He has been described as having a satanic grin, a cloven-hoofed, urchinish, and inspired look. In reality, he is neither mystical nor driven by a death wish. Versatile, charismatic, and inexhaustible, he is not overly ambitious or compulsive. His performance differs from others in that it is not a wrestling match or the precise,

Gebel-Williams seems best suited to his tigers.

Although his leopard act has real crowd appeal with its humorous touches.

sophisticated routine of a Court or Baumann. It is more closely related to the fighting act because of its interpretive nature.

The great fighting showmen, Beatty and Jacobs, were not less knowledgeable than Gebel-Williams, but they cast their cats as killers and emphasized their own courage and agility. These trainers catered to the image of tigerish tigers and ferocious lions. The lions especially enjoyed the tumult of "created confusion" and quick mood changes. Although no animal could really be as continually ferocious as they pretended, mock adversaries easily turned into serious ones. The trainer's chief role was to be alert and stave off impending battle royals. But the big cats are not mythical dragons, their charges can be fought off, and their paws are really no faster than the hands of a man, especially if he is equipped with a whip.[50]

Gebel-Williams's interpretation emphasizes the correlation between the jungle cat and the house cat. He attempts to draw his tigers out in a casual manner, with blended routines. He works them with great concentration and no visible sweat which earns him comparisons with Rudolf Nuryev in ballet, El Cordobes, the matador, and Jean-Claude Killy on skis. *Harpers* calls these performers all very human "precisely at the moment when they are at their most superhuman," having styles that "push unconsciously against the boundaries of tradition."[51]

He is a man of this era, *Harpers* continues, because he "does not impose his courage or skill heavily upon us." He understands that his talent is rather foolish and unimportant, although no more absurd than most human endeavors. What is important is how he does it. "He tosses off the act at great speed—cool, insouciant, and very self-possessed. Thus the cats, seemingly so like him in temperament, have a peculiar rightness for him." Because of the circus's present relatively low estate, it is uncertain Gebel-Williams will achieve great fame. It is an area for aficionados, buffs, and parents who take their children out of a sense of obligation to their past or in a search for nostalgia. It is called an innocent, unworldly, quiet backwater, a living anachronism. Its stars develop in a certain purity away from distorting pressures of the celebrity system.[52] Although Gunther Gebel-Williams has been discovered by the press and television, one author concludes he will remain as fundamentally untouchable as a cat. His image is too complicated to stamp his identity on the public. He can also foresee a time when he concentrates on training only horses, since his versatility precludes an overwhelming drive to remain in the big cage. Pushed as a sex symbol with a "presence wired for sensuality—flowing yellow locks, revealing tights, bare chest, smile, charisma," it is doubtful he can become a child's hero.[53] In fact, one woman columnist gushed that he was "the embodi-

Beatty works his act at his zoo.—*Fred D. Pfening, Jr.*

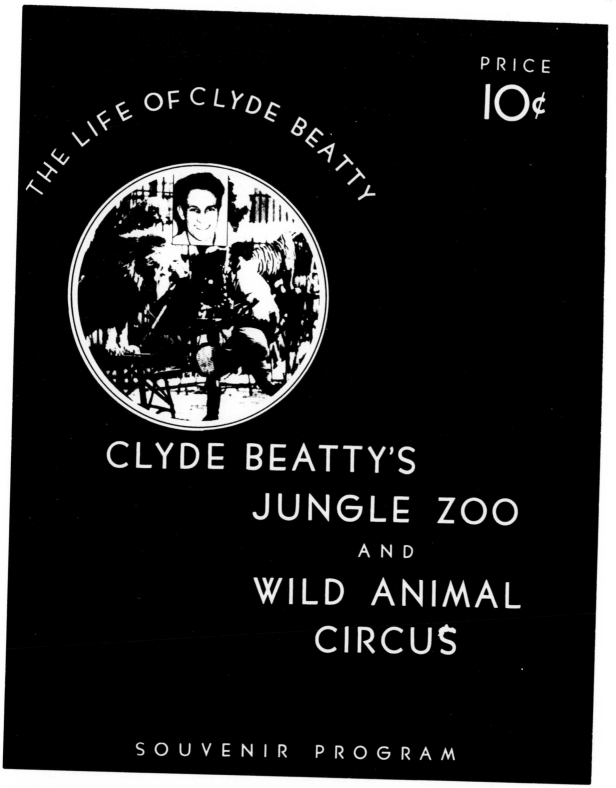

THE LIFE OF CLYDE BEATTY

PRICE
10¢

**CLYDE BEATTY'S
JUNGLE ZOO**
AND
**WILD ANIMAL
CIRCUS**

SOUVENIR PROGRAM

Soon after Beatty left Cole Bros., he built his own zoo in Ft. Lauderdale.

Beatty works a lion at his zoo.—*Harry Chipman*

ment of everybody's idea of what the Creator had in mind for the human race. . . . He's almost too good. It's difficult to believe he was born of woman."[54] The Siesta Key writer concluded that, "Wild animal acts aren't for nail biting anymore. Gunther has dropped whip, chair and gun, replacing it with a boyish grin and affection.[55] His act is not violent enough to gain him a villainous role, although to some it seems he degrades his cats by treating them with an air of casual indifference. Gebel-Williams does not play the daredevil either, since his routines do not appear wildly reckless or include an incredible number of animals.

In the mind of the public, Clyde Beatty will probably remain the stereotype of the wild animal trainer. Once he gained fame, he worked to attain and then maintain legendary status. Beatty achieved his goal and today even years after his

death, his name is synonymous with "lion trainer." It is also part of the most widely known circus title besides Ringling Bros.–Barnum & Bailey in America.

When Beatty left the Cole show in 1938, his career could easily have been over. He had possession of his act, three elephants, and little else but his reputation. Luckily, during his rapid rise to stardom Beatty had ingratiated himself with many wealthy and influential circus fans. A railroad executive and his wife had gone on record as calling him "one of the finest young men of our acquaintance."[56] Another was Frank J. Walter, a Houston, Texas, millionaire and amateur animal trainer who owned 150 animals and presented an annual circus for underprivileged children. He aided Beatty in locating and purchasing property north of Fort Lauderdale, on which the trainer

CLYDE BEATTY'S JUNGLE ZOO

A number of years ago when scouting the entire country in search of lions and tigers, to make up the largest mixed group of jungle beasts ever assembled in the steel arena, Clyde Beatty, for the first time, conceived the idea of a jungle zoo.

Realizing then that these animals were becoming extinct, his plans were to find a place where he could establish breeding grounds.

Taking all parts of the country into consideration where he had traveled, Florida was the most ideal spot, both for the different varieties of animals and a home for himself and family.

Fort Lauderdale, Florida, was the town he had chosen as the place for his dream to come true.

ENTRANCE JUNGLE ZOO

The Clyde Beatty Jungle Zoo is the wonder and thrill spot of all the Southland. It is one of the most picturesque zoological institutions in the world.

Nature plays a big part in this institution, for Clyde Beatty helps her preserve its beauty and the weirdness of the jungle. Natural surroundings for one of the largest collections of wild animal life in a privately-owned zoo, consisting of lions and lionesses, Royal Bengal, Siberian and Sumatran tigers, elephants, elks, brown Russian bears, water buffaloes, chimpanzees and many other animals too numerous to mention. Beside all these Clyde Beatty has a very rare collection of birds from all parts of the world.

Here among the lagoons, wild brush and trees, Clyde Beatty has established his jungle zoo. Caves for the jungle beasts and waterfalls for its charm.

In this jungle zoo, Clyde Beatty breeds and trains his ferocious man-eating friends. Clyde Beatty started these breeding grounds in the fall of 1939 and today it is one of the largest privately-owned zoological gardens in the world.

Performances of the Clyde Beatty Wild Animal Circus are given daily.

Tours of the Clyde Beatty Jungle Zoo, which is open the year around to the public, can be taken by riding in the howdahs on the elephants' backs.

WATERFALL

LAKE, SHOWING MOAT

MRS. HARRIET BEATTY

Mrs. Harriet Beatty, wife of the renowned wild animal trainer, is a typical American girl who displays the nerve and daringness of the modern lady of today.

Mrs. Beatty, a very attractive blonde, stands about 5 feet in height, weighs approximately 104 pounds, and was formerly an aerialist. She first handled wild animals in 1935 with a circus of which her husband was part owner. Mrs. Beatty, being a determined person, braved the dangers that faced her in the steel arena.

Jungle Enemies Perform In Harmony

For the first time in American circus history and at the present, Mrs. Beatty offers the public a distinct novelty act. A Royal Bengal tiger rides on the back of a huge Siamese elephant. This presentation combines thrills with danger as the two natural enemies are in the steel area. Not being satisfied with only having the tiger ride on the elephant's back, she has also trained the tiger to leap through a flaming hoop of fire. The fact that all beasts are afraid of fire makes this act seemingly impossible. The act is much more difficult to handle than the average person would imagine.

Several years ago Clyde Beatty ordered such an act. He insists that one of the worst battles he has ever witnessed in the arena took place between a tiger and an elephant. The tiger was perfectly willing to work but the elephant refused to allow the tiger to mount on his back. A scene of desperate battle between a tiger an an elephant took place. The pachyderm literally knocked the tiger all over the arena.

But none of these dangers seem to faze the petite and charming Mrs. Harriet Beatty, for she herself must have nerves of steel.

Harriet Beatty

Clyde Beatty in Big Cage

Harriett Beatty loved the Ft. Lauderdale Zoo. Even though the zoo was lost to city rezoning and development, Beatty's wife, who died in 1950, had requested to be buried in Ft. Lauderdale.

built a tropical zoo that offered open grotto displays and featured cat acts presented by himself, his wife, and his assistants, an elephant routine handled by his sister-in-law, and a chimp turn. The unique zoo opened on December 2, 1939, and gained Beatty more favorable publicity.

In 1940, George Hamid, who owned the Million Dollar Pier in Atlantic City, where he had featured Beatty in 1939, established a new, under-canvas Hamid-Morton show featuring the cat man. The venture proved successful, but the early war years forced Beatty to link his unit to the Johnny J. Jones Exposition, then the largest carnival on the road. This seemed an unholy alliance since circuses and carnivals traditionally have had little love for one another. But it was obviously profitable enough for *Billboard's* New York columnist to say: "To be vulgar about it, he [Beatty] seems to have a great deal more folding money, a fairly important commodity and an unusual state of affairs for an animal trainer to be in." He called Beatty a "nice guy" with a "Grade A" reputation. "In the cage he works like three men and when he's thru he's maybe lost five or six pounds and come out dripping with sweat. For our money, he makes his the hard way, and when he has his own show next season we hope he gathers in plenty of coin."[57] Beatty worked first in cooperation with Ray Rogers and Wallace Bros. In 1945, he fielded his own show for the first time. Obtaining the Wallace Bros. truck show equipment, he profitably toured the eastern half of America, although the circus met every conceivable disaster: wrecks, floods, blowdowns, stock killed, and even the theft of the "red wagon."

Back at his Macon, Georgia, winterquarters, Beatty dreamed of owning a railroad show. Arthur Concello, the great circus aerialist, also known as a brilliant showman, inventor, businessman, and

During the early war years, Beatty toured the unit he had salvaged from Cole Bros. on the huge Johnny J. Jones Carnival.

Beatty's cats were transported in these trucks when he traveled with the Johnny J. Jones Carnival. — *William Koford*

Lineup of Beatty's cages in 1945. – *R. E. Conover*

strategist, had purchased Russell Bros. when he left Ringling in 1942. Beatty had turned down a deal to purchase Arthur Bros. Railroad Circus but could not refuse Concello's offer. For a flat salary and percentage, he joined him and sold his truck show to Floyd King, who then began the King Bros. Circus. Concello's routing of the Clyde Beatty Circus, as the show was titled, was considered a stroke of genius. He headed the railer into western Canada, where no circus had visited for eight years. On Vancouver Island huge crowds, many of which had never seen a lion, tiger, or elephant, arrived by horseback and

wagon. The railroad cars had to be brought in singly and parked in the middle of town in Trail, British Columbia, a village located at the bottom of a two-thousand-foot gorge along the Columbia River. When the show reached winterquarters in Nacogdoches, Texas, it had traveled 14,315 miles, played 122 cities and given 384 performances.[58] It had enjoyed one of the most phenomenal seasons in circus history, with profits in the seven-figure category. But Beatty and Concello had grown more and more at odds as the season had progressed. Concello announced he was planning to close the show and he offered to sell it to Beatty for

Cage wagons are unloaded from Beatty's 1953 rail show. – *Ken Whipple*

Beatty's arena is unloaded
(1953). – *Ken Whipple*

Beatty faces down Prince, killer of his two prize tigers during 1951 Detroit Shrine Circus run.

cash. Beatty accepted, buying the entire circus except for Concello's private sleeper. The ex-flier returned to Ringling where his relationship with John Ringling North was just as stormy as it had been with Beatty. But since North knew he needed Concello's genius (Concello was introducing several important innovations), he often left the country rather than fire the little manager.

Beatty now owned the railer he had long wanted, as he continued to amaze audiences with his arena daring: "The one and only Clyde Beatty outstanding personification of intestinal fortitude, presented his assembly of thirty lions and tigers of both sexes in an act that has not now nor never will be duplicated. His control of the denizens of the jungle was extraordinary and unbelievable. The audience thrilled beyond expectation, remained motionless with amazement, mouths agape, as he humbled the royal beasts with masterful skill and unlimited courage."[59] *Colliers* called Beatty after almost thirty years in the center ring "still the foremost wild beast subjugator in the world." "While it is not a pleasant thought, the prospect of seeing a man eaten alive is irresistable to a great portion of the population and so this summer, assuming it is a normal season, something over a million persons will again crowd under the big top to see 'Clyde Beatty in person in the most dangerous, suicidal, blood-curdling wild animal display ever conceived and performed by man.' "[60] Up to six thousand eager customers had to be turned away at each performance of the Detroit Shrine Circus in March of 1951, when Beatty had five all-out battles with Prince, a lion. the fights culminated in the deaths of his two most valuable tigers. The gruesome melees drew nation-

Beatty in the arena (1944, Clyde Beatty–Russell Bros.).—*Tom Henricks*

wide publicity, and as with "Detroit," fifteen years earlier, Beatty at first refused to remove the lion from the act. But as the disruptions continued, he quietly replaced the killer with another lion, also named Prince.

By that summer only two railroad shows were left in the entire country: Ringling's and Beatty's.

The Beatty circus, now valued at $300,000, traveled on fifteen blue and orange cars and employed almost five hundred people. Beatty himself traveled in a private car "furnished with rattan furniture from Manila and entirely suitable for a jungle planter. There is a painting over a desk of a tiger defending her cub, a number of tropical

Clyde Beatty and his wife, Harriet at their Ft. Lauderdale, Fla. Zoo.

Be sure to hear
the adventures of Clyde Beatty
brought to you 3 times each week in

"THE CLYDE BEATTY SHOW"

on

THE MUTUAL NETWORK

Monday · Wednesday · Friday
5:30 p.m. by

Kellogg's RICE KRISPIES

The cereal that goes 'Snap! Crackle! Pop' to tell you how fresh and crisp it is

Announcement for Radio Program – 1951.

CLYDE BEATTY

"Mr. Circus" himself! He travels the sawdust path of the circus grounds into the tangled web of Africa's darkest jungles . . . for adventure . . . danger . . . and suspense!

Advertisement for Comic Book – 1953.

"SOMETHING TO BOAST"
By EDGAR A. GUEST

At dinner time I chanced to say:
"I met Clyde Beatty yesterday"
At which the children shouted:
    "Wow!"
And promptly asked me where and how.

At me the questions fairly flew:
"Did you meet all his tigers, too?
Did he invite you in the cage?
At you did all his lions rage,"

There's little children have to boast
About their grampas at the most,
They're old and tired and like to rest;
They're merely common folk at best.

Today their eyes much brighter seem,
Since I have grown in their esteem.
And boastfully to all they tell:
"Our grampa knows Clyde Beatty well."

plants and a miniature lion for a doorstep, to say nothing of two bedrooms, a galley and a real bathtub."[61]

To keep his name before the public, Beatty began a weekly radio show for children and in 1954 made another movie. Warner Brothers's *Ring of Fear* costarred detective book author Mickey Spillane, who wrote about Beatty:

> now there's a man. He's a guy you don't describe. You have to see him. You have to watch a cageful of jungle wild animals hating each other and all hoping for the same thing . . . that the guy in there with them comes a little too close or makes one little mistake. Yeah, this you have to see. This you have to sweat out for yourself . . . because for those minutes that Clyde stands inches away from ripping, tearing death he becomes you . . . and those shaggy manes and starkly white teeth are looking into your face . . . and all you can think of is that you have to be good. You have to be real good! He is great![62]

No one guessed then that a spectre hovered on the horizon, that the horrible nightmare that was the season of 1938 was returning and would become real in 1956. Circuses experienced their usual difficulties. But problems that shows tried to shrug off would not go away and finally they became really insurmountable in that pivotal year. Rising costs, a scarcity of good management personnel, growing competition from television, and a need to make changes that went against the grain of tradition were all involved. The buildup of suburbs was another thing, for that made good sites rare and difficult to find. And if this was not enough, unions again attacked the circuses. The American Guild of Variety Artists (AGVA) and Teamsters picketed and sponsored competition shows. Jackie Bright, a former nightclub comic, led the union against the Greatest Show on Earth and glibly cracked: "I'll lay you 100 to one the Ringling show doesn't make it to August. Long before then, they'll have to fold up their tent and go back to Sarasota."[63] He was right. On July 16, the Ringling circus put away its canvas for the last time and went back to winterquarters, John Ringling North vowing the show would return the following spring. (He was right too, but the Big One was now an indoor extravaganza and the *Wall Street Journal* nostalgically editorialized, "So now the sawdust will always be hard and perhaps there will be no tatooed lady at all. They are still going to call it Ringling Bros. and Barnum & Bailey but next summer it will be under dull, everyday roofs. . . . The new children will doubtless have new wonders to tell about when they are old. But it makes us feel already wintry to watch old wonders pass into permanent winter quarters.")[64]

Similar difficulties forced King Bros., the largest truck show on the road to close the week before Ringling and at about the same time Beatty on the West Coast also met disaster. His circus had left

Beatty in the '50s.

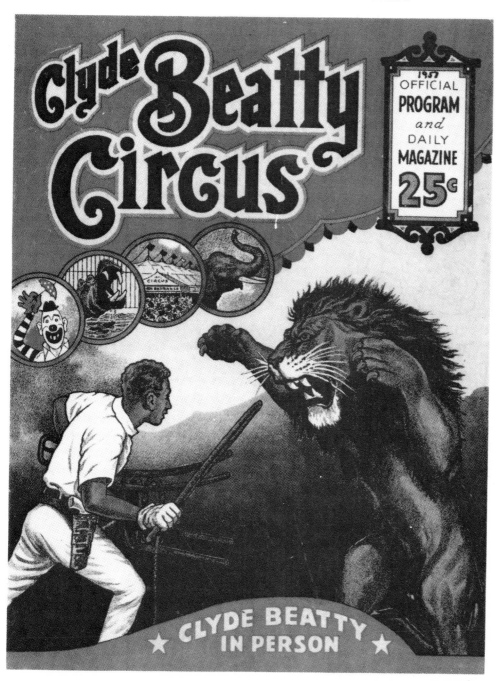

Like all circuses, Clyde Beatty's faced desperate times in 1956. Following bankruptcy, it was reorganized and became the last tented railroad circus in America. In 1957, it went out on trucks, but the program depicted Beatty in the usual manner.

Deming, New Mexico, winterquarters in March only to face bad weather and worse crowds. The normally prosperous show could only meet its $5,000 per day nut six out of forty-three days! Then the AGVA struck, pulled fifty-five performers off the show and insisted Beatty pay $15,000 in back pay. Loyal employees agreed to stick out the lean times, but Beatty's National Circus Corporation declared bankruptcy. It claimed $281,758 in debts with assets of $260.[65]

As in 1938, Beatty was in deep trouble, but again misfortune turned into success. Some former Ringling officials who believed a circus without a tent was no circus at all approached Beatty with a proposition. Ex-Ringling managers, Frank McCloskey and Walter Kernan—along with attorney, Randolph Calhoun, and dog and horse track owner, Jerry Collins— offered to buy out Beatty entirely, including the title and the trainer, retaining him as the star attraction. But Beatty had

Typical Beatty publicity shot in the '50s.

cleverly kept his animals and equipment separately incorporated (the Monarch Corporation), and now he agreed to sell all his physical equipment and other necessities, but insisted on keeping his act and his name. Knowing the success of the show depended on his name and act and that without either the circus would be undistinguished, he agreed only to lease the use of his name. That done, he then bargained for an "unbelievable salary." Among the perquisites and emoluments granted him were payment of the cats' meat bill, transportation, a cageboy crew, and generally anything else he needed in relation to the animals. He also received a new white Cadillac annually and an Airstream trailer every other year.[66] During the ten year "consolidation of the show," Beatty was guaranteed insurance against loss of life, sickness, or permanent injury; his wife was beneficiary.[67]

The reorganized Clyde Beatty Circus reopened on August 24, 1956, to become the last undercanvas railroad circus in America. Previously West Coast-oriented, it now routed in the eastern half of the United States, wintered in Florida, and switched to more economical trucks in 1957. The new Acme Circus Corporation purchased the DeLand, Florida, fairgrounds for $47,000 to serve as winterquarters. In 1959, the show was retitled Clyde Beatty–Cole Bros. (The Cole title had become inactive and was purchased from the Wirtz family in Chicago.) The new name was appropriate for it linked the scrappy, traditional Beatty circus to the original Indiana tenters where Beatty had achieved fame. Beatty's own shows, although always second in size, have always appealed to circus buffs who often find the larger Ringling organization rich, haughty, and untouchable. Like its predecessors, the new Beatty-Cole circus never backed off from direct competition with the Big One.

In 1959, it played a month's run at New Jersey's Palisades Park, simultaneously with Ringling's Madison Square Garden appearance, and as usual Beatty drew accolades. Robert Coleman wrote in the *Mirror*, "His is the most exciting, the most dramatic wild animal act I've ever seen, and I caught the best of them in Europe and the U.S. I have come to this conclusion: Clyde Beatty is in a class by himself; there is no wild animal trainer that can be compared to him. He leaps into that steel barred arena like Mars, himself, and the impact on the wild beasts and the audience is terrific.

. . . Clyde knows his jungle pupils as he knows himself."[68] The show itself, said *Billboard*, "is all circus. That's been said about many shows, but seldom has it applied and better than in this case. Take the performance, the management, the rolling stock and equipment, the look of the lot—it's all real circus."[69]

The three-ring circus was the feature of the 1962 thirty-four-day Christmas Festival at the New York Coliseum. It became the first show to play in New York during the holiday season since Barnum in 1872.[70] Beatty-Cole settled into its role as preeminent in the tented world. It featured established stars like the Wallendas on the high wire, the human cannonball Zacchinis, the Hannefords and Cristianis (bareback-riding families), clown Emmett Kelly, along with new talent such as the Gaonas (flying trapeze) and the aerialist Elvin

—Circus City Festival, Inc. Museum

Press releases from the '50s. — *Harry Chipman*

A TRAINED JUNGLE KILLER -- Clyde Beatty, the world's most famous wild animal trainer and star of screen, radio, television and his own huge 3-Ring Railroad Circus, makes one of his jungle-bred **iiឆឆx** man-eating lions stand on it's hind legs as he presents his death-defying battle against a mixed group of lions and tigers in the big steel arena, one of the thrill-packed features of the all-new**x** big-top show coming to _____ on_____ for _____ under the sponsorship of the _____. The Circus tents will be set up on the grounds at _____ _____ with performances scheduled for ____ & ____ P.M. Doors open one hour earlier so that folks can visit the FREE menagerie containing strange and unusual animals from all parts of the world.

MAN VERSUS SNARLING KILLER -- Facing sudden death daily,
Clyde Beatty, the world's foremost wild animal trainer, shown
with one of his huge jungle-bred Bengal tigers, will present his
sensational single-handed battle against a mixed group of
man-eating Lions and Tigers in the big steel arena as one of the
thrilling features of the huge Clyde Beatty 3-Ring Railroad Circus
coming to _____ on _____.
This year's all-new Big-Top show will be set up at the _____
_____ Circus grounds, with performances
at ___ & ___ P.M. Doors open one hour earlier to allow folks to
visit the FREE menagerie, containing strange and unusual animals
from all parts of the world.

The Beatty winterquarters moved to DeLand, Florida, following reorganization. —*Roy Zinser*

Bale. Years after the reorganization, *Amusement Business* reported "it was shouldering everything conceivable on a day-by-day basis, that helped drive a tented Ringling-Barnum to its knees . . . years ago. This is plenty big enough. So if this be circus—the old traditions are upheld quite nicely."[71] The Acme Circus Corporation became a true holding company with the addition of Sells and Gray and King Bros. in the 1960s. It provided complete coverage of the eastern United States. Even today Beatty-Cole is a thorn in Ringling's side with its popular suburban mall promotions.

Thus Beatty's association with McCloskey and Collins did nothing but enhance his legendary status. The program introduced him as:

The Greatest Thrill of All Time
Presenting in the Huge Steel Arena The World Acclaimed Mixed Group of Veldt and Jungle Mankillers—Over 20 Black Maned Numidian Lions and Royal Bengal Tigers, Trained but Untamed, Obeying in Snarling Fury The Commands of the One—The Only—The Universally Acknowledged Master Wild Animal Trainer— Claw and Fang Torn, But Utterly Fearless, The Debonnaire, The Gallant, The One—The Only —The Incomparable—Mr. Circus Himself—Clyde Beatty[72]

But to become a legend, Beatty needed more than arena triumphs and florid circus announcements. He needed to keep his name before the public by creating a good working relationship with the press. In fact, Edward Anthony said Beatty's most endearing qualities to writers were his candor and distaste for hokum.[73] But coverage alone was not enough. His image as the king of trainers and an all-American boy also had to continue unblemished and, as far as the general public is concerned, he succeeded in this too, remaining a hero to the end.

Writers found his courage fascinating. Author Dale Carnegie wrote of Beatty: "If he's got to die, he'd rather be gored to death than bored to death."[74] Mark Hellinger concluded: "He's the only living trainer who has succeeded in teaching a tiger to roll over at his command. How long he will remain the only living trainer is problematical."[75] Even his appearance drew comment. Drew Pearson was surprised at Beatty's size: "[He] looks as if a lion cub could knock him over." Pearson was just as shocked that Beatty's voice was low and pleasant and "his eyes—well there seemed to be nothing unusual about them."[76] Another columnist reported: "Clyde is a smiling chap with surprisingly mild eyes—none of the 'gimlet eyes' that writers tell about." He was astonished to find nothing different about Beatty and his wife, except their occupations.[77] But more reminiscent of the early *New York Times* articles about the Hagenbeck trainers was Bill Ballentine's book in which

Beatty circus in its heyday. — *Roy Zinser*

he reported that there is a "deep, almost Neanderthal thrill in close communion with wild beasts. You sense this in Beatty. Full face, he has a strong resemblance to his handsome tigers. His large nose hooks and flattens a bit, the nostrils flare high. His cold blue eyes are penetrating; they seem like a cat's eyes to look through you, rather than at you." Ballentine concluded that Beatty's greatest asset was his style and first class showmanship. While traveling with the trainer, the author continually heard the comment, "After ya seen Beatty the rest of them stinks."[78]

He not only impressed strangers, he impressed his wife too. In 1965, Jane Beatty had a children's book published, *Davey's Adventures with the Clyde Beatty Circus*, in which she added to her husband's heroic image. The story is that of a boy spending a few weeks of his summer vacation traveling with the circus. When Davey first meets Beatty, the story goes, "Davey felt his heart swell until it seemed too big for his chest. For once a sense of awe paralyzed him. Yet Mr. Beatty looked like any ordinary person—he was so friendly and informal."[79] Later, a cageboy discloses that [Beatty] " 'really enjoys his work. Guess he must enjoy puttin' his strength and will against those wild beasts. But that's what life is. Any way you look at it—big or small—it's always a challenge.' Challenge—it meant you had to stand up against forces as big as yourself—maybe bigger. And it meant you had to give life everything you had."[80] Davey decides, "Clyde was a real live legend. Just as the knights of old, he combined courage and bravery whenever he was in the arena with the big cats."[81] Eight pages later, Davey's thoughts get even more profound. "Perfection was more than

Interior of Beatty show in the '60s.—*Roy Zinser*

Beatty signals a tiger to begin his rollover.

mere muscle control" he is made to think. "It had to do with timing and love of your work. Heart and muscle were the winning combination. You had to follow through, that, he knew was why Clyde was tops."[82] So wrote Mrs. Beatty.

Beatty himself was never reticent about the injuries he had received in the arena. He claimed he was proud of his "formidable collection" of scars. A story in the Cleveland *Plain Dealer* in 1935 supports this. The writer visited the trainer at his home in Indiana and remembered: "While Mrs. Beatty and Miss Evans [Beatty's sister-in-law] were getting supper, Beatty took off his shirt and pants and showed me his many wounds. His legs and arms bear many huge teeth and claw marks. He has been sent to the hospital numerous times. Only a few weeks ago a lion socked him with a paw and broke several ribs. No insurance company will sell him a policy."[83]

But the acid test of Beatty's popularity had to be

his performance. When it came to a wild animal act, no trainer has ever understood better what would excite an audience. For example, Beatty developed a routine that probably was the ultimate in "hypnotic eye" tricks—the Spinning Tiger. The big cat crouched on her pedestal and Beatty slowly brought her down to the arena floor as if by sheer will power.

She follows as though I might be drawing her by hypnotism or an invisible rope. . . . I back out to the center, holding out two fingers, level with her eyes. She starts following and in the hush I hear people say, "Look, he's got the eye on her." Dropping flat on the floor, she lies there as if under a spell. Now I make a sudden circular motion with my right hand, her cue to come to life and begin her whirl. Her eyes twisted on my hand, her face screwed into a snarl, her teeth bare and her lips curling, she rises slowly to her feet and suddenly starts whirling around and around on her hindquarters. . . . Faster and faster she goes until the

gold and black of her coat merged in circular
stripes and she seems a dizzy disc of motion. . . .
"Ladies and gentlemen," says the announcer, "the
one and only spinning tiger in the world!"[84]

The act was extremely dangerous to both the
trainer and the tiger, since the other cats remained
in the arena and Beatty's total concentration was
riveted on the Spinner. Although he felt he owed
it to his audience to add some new features to his
act occasionally, the clean classic pattern excited
writers even three decades after its introduction:

> The show is almost classic in its unfolding. Beatty
> is about the same as thirty years ago. Curly hair—
> one errant curl dancing on his forehead. The
> ringmaster makes pretty much the same old
> standard spiel, warning the audience to remain
> seated. . . . Beatty materializes in a spot of light
> and the arena swells with a rolling fanfare. . . . He
> looks bigger than life—12 feet tall, not 5' 6", age-
> less with the vigor of youth, not 58, pound for
> pound a match for any superbly muscled lion.
>
> The band comes to life. It plays the storm scene
> from Rossini's *William Tell Overture*. Pulses
> quicken . . . in the big cage lions already prowl.
> There's Buddy, the topmounter, Pharo, the
> Brothers Sultan and Brutus. Leo enters. Simba
> enters. Then King and Caesar and Congo. Last is
> Henry. . . . Now the Bengal tigers. Ravel's *Bolero*
> accompanies them. Saber leads, with Rajah,
> Prince, Princess and Frisco following. Beatty puts
> his talent and ability against the wily tigers and
> lions, always mindful of the audience—not in
> numbers but in what he feels it wants.[85]

Edward Anthony summed up four main factors in
Beatty's rise to preeminence in his field: a love of
wild animals; a warm, friendly approach to them;
an intuitive knowledge of their mental processes;
and utter fearlessness.[86] This was written at the
time of Beatty's death and shows a positive change
from the drive and ambition at earlier stages of his
career that overshadowed his good sense and love
for animals. In *Jungle Performers*, Beatty's second
book, published in 1941, the trainer gave great emphasis to gory battles involving "Sammy" and "Detroit," the killer lions. Indeed, the publicity received from these bloody arena feuds and subsequent confrontations between wild beast and man
was invaluable. In describing Big Ross, a tiger, he
declared, "I saw not only a killer, but an animal
bent on escaping. . . . I resolved now that he must
be put into my act. This meant I must face him in
the arena and train him. His seemingly indomitable will must be made to yield to mine."[87] About
Sammy, he said, "It was a thrilling, though appal-

ling moment for me. I was seeing the primitive passion of the king of the jungle at its height and I
stood transfixed. Here was all you ever imagined a
lion to be. Bone crunching, skin tearing, tail-
switching, roaring like a rumble of thunder. . . .
He looked standing there, a criminal among animals, the ruthless murdering cat that the lion is
supposed to be."[88]

He claimed he could never kill a cat, even
though it hated him, or if a mercy killing was in
order. Anger and fear were the reasons for most
attacks on a trainer, and he believed he did nothing to arouse either emotion. Animals were
usually vicious because of faulty training and they
became "obsessed with a lust for injuries inflicted.
By failing to supply that cause for violence, I manage to escape much of the trouble that might
otherwise come my way." "These cats are funny,"
he told one reporter, "they don't exactly carry

Beatty (early '50s).

Beatty (1945).—*R. E. Conover*

Beatty (1953).—*Ken Whipple*   Beatty in the '60s.—*Tom Henricks*

Illustration from 1965 Clyde Beatty-Cole Bros. Circus program of Clyde Beatty, his wife Jane, and their son, Clyde, Jr.

grudges or feel resentment, but they can always tell when anyone—a human being or another cat —is afraid of them. And whenever they find such a person, or animal, they'll attack."[89] Beatty candidly admitted that, "Lions hate tagers [sic], that extra hazard is what has kept my act on top all these years."[90]

The trainer's last book, published by Doubleday in 1965, may have been influenced by various wildlife conservation movements and the best seller, Adamson's *Born Free*, or perhaps by the end of his career Beatty had no need to further his daredevil image. He again collaborated with Edward Anthony, author of *The Big Cage*. It was far less bloody than the earlier volumes, since it concentrated more on the psychology of the big cats. In it Beatty showed much greater sympathetic understanding for his beasts and also gave his definition of wild animal training.

> It is because of the basic savagery that causes them to revert to type when you least expect it that I have to play this game of keeping them off balance. For as fond as I am of these rough, tough, wonderfully endowed playmates of mine, I simply cannot afford to trust them fully.
>
> Some people never cease to be puzzled by my position that, although I do not place complete reliance in my cats I love them. Nature has endowed them with certain Jekyll-Hyde qualities,

and that is something the animal trainer must accept. It is not unusual for a lion or tiger that tries to wreck me one day to show affection for me the next. There are those who believe that an animal that behaves this way is "two-faced" and should be removed from the act. To me it merely reaffirms the to be expected mercurial characteristics of basically savage creatures.[91]

Some lions were naturaly nonkillers, while others suffered from what could best be called mental aberrations.

More than once I have confused people by referring to a lion or tiger as a friend. Without any illusions about their trouble making potential, a trainer develops an affection for his animals. It is possible to love them without fully trusting them. There are little ways in which these big ferocious beasts convey that they have confidence in you and trust you—to a point. [They] are friends that have to be carefully watched. It doesn't alter your affection for them—to some extent, it must be admitted, because they help you earn a living. But there is more to it than that. A bond that is hard to describe without seeming to be somewhat maudlin . . . The big cats, even the wildest and potentially most dangerous of them—have a way of subtly getting under your skin.

In both the wilds and in captivity they are creatures of moods. The unpredictability of these moods is what gives them their never-ending fascination. Not even the greatest animal psychologist in the world can say with absolute certainty if the big cats are motivated more by the kind or the cruel side of their nature.[92]

Beatty with Clyde, Jr. (1954).—*Tom Henricks*

Beatty and his son, Clyde, Jr. (1953).—*Tom Henricks*

Page from "Clyde Beatty Comics" (1953).

He also admitted that he finally took the advice of fellow animal men and removed lionesses from his act. Females in heat excited the males to such an extent that disruption was inevitable. He kept working tigresses, however, since their inhibited nature created no unnecessary hazards.[93]

Beatty said an animal trainer starts with a love of animals.[94]

The crack of a whip and the bark of a blank cartridge pistol are so synonymous with my work in the arena that I am regarded by some as a tough guy who likes to push animals around. It comes as a surprise to some that I love these animals and that the big cats and I have had a lot of fun together over the years.[95]

To some of the cats I am another animal, a formidable one they don't seem able to figure out. True, I am one against many, but one that puzzles and awes them because I am a creature equipped with advantages no other animal has; that something I use as a shield (the chair), that long snake-like device (the whip) which makes that cracking sound, and that other noisemaker (the blank revolver).[96]

1962 Detroit *News* feature.

Don't Be Afraid to Live

January 25, 1962

By Clyde Beatty

"Man is born to live and not to prepare to live."
— BORIS PASTERNAK

THERE IS one question people often ask me: "Why do you do it?" They wonder why I risk my life daily entering an arena to face a pack of snarling lions and tigers.

In reply I like to ask, "Who today lives in complete safety?"

Crossing a busy street can be a hazardous adventure. So can a plane ride. So far we have no protection from atomic fallout. Strife between nations hasn't exactly ceased, and most of us have lived through the greatest war in history.

Then there are the calamities of nature — hurricanes, earthquakes, floods. . . . I don't mean this to be a catalogue of horrors; I am merely saying that life today has its risks for everyone. Probably that has always been true.

Yet we go right on getting born, growing up, marrying, earning a living and bringing into the world new generations. We do it without too much fuss or grumbling. And we have our full share of enjoyments despite all the doom. "We're used to it," you say.

Well, I'm used to my lions and tigers. I admit they've given me some bad times. Still, I know them and know how to handle them — usually.

Animals have fascinated me since boyhood, when I had my own backyard circus. I've worked with them all my life. You can bet I enjoy my job or I wouldn't have it. In fact, any other kind of work would be dull to me. So dull I would lose my interest in life, which is the worst kind of death.

Danger? No job, no life in the world is without it. I think the important thing is to do the thing we like best and gamble on the risks. By doing that we master the uncertainties of life. We reach self-realization.

Life becomes a full-time, worthwhile adventure.

OUT OF MY LIFE—No. 3:
Clyde Beatty has been risking his life in wild-animal cages for more than 30 years. His article is the latest in a new series in which THIS WEEK readers share their experience. Next week: Dr. John A. Gius: "Is There Anything I Can Do For You?"

Bluffing is as important in animal training as in poker. A lion or tiger fully aware of the relative might of the big cats and mere man would make short work of any trainer. Thus animal training might be described as the art or science of keeping wild animals from learning the facts.[97]

In a wild animal act, the trainer can demonstrate that the wildest of wild animals can be taught to concentrate, pick up cues and affirm they are thinking creatures. And when these stunts and formations are brought off effectively, they also give people who are fond of animals an ever-changing view of them in action that they could not get any other way.[98]

Edward Anthony, in a final tribute to the trainer following his death said: "A little known fact about Clyde Beatty is that he was a brilliant naturalist, without benefit of schooling. He had more first-hand information about wild animal behavior and psychology than any of the scientists in the field, to whom he deferred because of his respect for their scholarship and erudition and their dedication to his favorite subjects, zoology and natural history." Even Dr. Raymond L. Ditmars, curator of the Bronx Zoo, called Beatty an "intuitive naturalist."[99]

Little is known about Beatty's personal life. Perhaps a feeling of inadequacy because of lack of formal education, a childhood spent in an isolated hill community in southwestern Ohio's Paint Valley, plus traditional circus close-mouthedness about that side of one's life explains Beatty's vague background. His arena battles are well-documented, but he never wanted his legendary image clouded by events not related to his performance. He refers to childhood circus games, numerous pets, and excitement over traveling shows, but none of these are unusual in small town life. His boyhood friends recall him keeping and training rabbits, guinea pigs, a raccoon, and a chicken. Described as a neat, clean, lively, well-liked youngster, "Buster" was also the town show-off who would stand on his head at the general store for the attention and pennies of amused customers. Researcher Dave Price found no county or state birth records on file. Beatty himself recorded different places and dates of birth on various official documents. The two hometowns listed, however, Bainbridge and Chillicothe, Ohio, are adjacent to each other.[100]

The first feature story on the young trainer ran in the *Detroit News*. According to it, when his

Screen Thrills magazine of the early '60s featured illustration of Beatty in *Darkest Africa*, re-released as *King of Jungleland*.

father took him to the Cincinnati Zoo, he recalled, "I saw all the wild animals and was so fascinated I never got over it. I dreamed wild animals, lived wild animals and could not get them off my mind." After finishing high school, he got a job as a cageboy in the circus rather than become a partner in his father's bakery.[101]

In 1928, a major article about Beatty appeared in the Kansas City *Star*. According to this story, the boy first became interested in circuses when his parents took him to a little show in Chillicothe. He was thrilled by the German trainer and his six lions and vowed to be an animal trainer himself. His father put a stop to his son's small menagerie of dogs, rabbits, and guinea pigs after some skunks were delivered. While in high school Beatty ran away and joined a circus, but on the second day out his father met the train and ordered him back

This picture of Beatty with two tiger cubs was used for ad for Rolex watches in the '60s.

Beatty co-starred with Mickey Spillane in Warner Bros. 1954 *Ring of Fear*.

home. His parents agreed to a circus career for their son if he completed high school, which he did.[102] In 1929, he was honored with a special homecoming day in Chillicothe when Hagenbeck-Wallace played the town. The two-page article in the *Scioto Gazette* on the "Bainbridge Boy" said nothing about his family life or boyhood except that the "outstanding trait of the big animal trainer is mother love."[103] (This same theme was followed in a 1968 "Childhood of Famous Americans" book about Beatty's poor but devoted mother, Clara.)

Two years later, when Beatty starred in Toledo's Shrine Circus, the *Blade* called him "Hagenbeck's greatest European importation."[104] In 1931, *The Literary Digest* stated he was "an American stripling not long out of college."[105] The *American Magazine* the next year reported that he ran away from college his junior year to join a circus, but his father prevailed upon him to go back and graduate. "Diploma in hand, he returned to the same circus to become a menagerie boy and demonstrated so clearly his unbelievable ability to handle animals that he progressed by rapid steps to his present position of unchallenged preeminence."[106] Just a month later, Beatty wrote in a *Colliers* story that he began his circus career after going "AWOL" from Chillicothe High School.[107] Another article

Beatty and his wife Jane accept ¼-scale train and model of his circus from Jerry Booker (left). Beatty planned to use the display at a combination zoo-winterquarters and museum in Phoenix (1955). — *Jerry Booker*

repeated the Cincinnati Zoo story, but claimed the boy ran away and joined the circus at fourteen.

A 1935 Cleveland *Plain Dealer* article called Beatty a Bainbridge farm boy who ran away at seventeen.[108] This story became the most consistent, only his age at the time he joined the circus varied. The same year, Floyd King, press agent for the new Cole show, wrote Beatty ran away at eighteen with the first circus he ever saw. He had worked as a newsboy, "baker's boy," and farmer to help support his widowed mother. But after he visited the show, he left the family mule hitched in front of the court house and began his circus career.[109] Stories issued at the time of his death also said he lost his father at six and worked at odd jobs to help his mother until he went with Howe's Great London Circus at sixteen.[110] His hometown paper, the *Chillicothe Gazette*, presented another variation about Beatty's widowed mother, Margaret.[111] Beatty did nothing to clear up these discrepancies. As he became more legendary, the lack of information about his personal life added to his mystique. Even his three marriages had a vagueness about them. He had a daughter, Joyce, who lives in Peru by his first wife, and a son, Clyde, Jr., a professional surfboard designer in California, by his third wife, Jane.

Virtually nothing was written about Beatty's short-lived first marriage to a Peru girl, Ernestine Pegg, except that the couple had a daughter prior to the divorce. But in 1933, his new wife Harriet, also a circus performer, joined in the confusion when she stated on her marriage license that she was the daughter of Chick Evans, the first amateur golfer to win the U.S. Open. Evans had no children, but the story, recorded as fact even in the *New York Times*, became part of circus legend. Beatty developed a special act for Harriet and their seventeen-year marriage was highly publicized. (The second Mrs. Beatty died of heart disease in 1950.)[112]

Throughout his career, Beatty spoke far more freely about his feelings concerning the dangers of his profession. The addictive and compulsive nature of wild animal training often led to highly contradictory quotes about life, death, and retirement. At the end of his career, Beatty demonstrated the same overriding obsession to stay in the big cage that had marked Mabel Stark. This drive was not as clear-cut as Karl Wallenda's intention to remain on the high wire. Wallenda said simply that he had an edge over most men in that he always knew how he was going to die. (Wallenda was killed in a fall from the wire in 1978.) In fairness to Beatty, he was much younger at the time of his death than either Stark or Wallenda.

From the beginning, when he started as a twenty-two-year-old trainer, he had admitted that

Beatty on the circus lot in the '60s. — *Tom Henricks*

a cat could get him anytime, but the fascination of the arena was irresistible. "It is the most thrilling work in the world and I would not give it up for anything. When will I quit? I'll stick it out until they get me. Of course, they will chew me up some day. It may be today or tomorrow. They always get you sooner or later, but I am ready and quite willing to take the chance."[113] Seven years later, in 1933, after his first book and movie, *The Literary Digest* reported, "he is at the peak of his career—and realizes he can't stay up long. He hopes to make an extensive tour of Europe in 1934 and then retire."[114] In 1938, he discussed his reason for casting his lot with Adkin and Terrell's Cole Bros. "I was twenty-nine years old. This meant I had perhaps nine or ten years to make enough money to support myself and family for the rest of my life. The arrangement suggested by my business associates involving a percentage of the gross 'take' for the season, would make this possible. . . . [by 1937] I felt myself getting closer and closer to my goal of independence and retirement by 1942 or 1943."[115]

The publication of *Jungle Performers* in 1941 marked Beatty's twentieth year in the circus business. Far more optimistic than when he was twenty-two he boldly concluded: "I have no intention of letting one of my cats kill me. It's my firm belief that I'll continue working the arena as long as I can get around, and then eventually die of old age,

inertia or overeating. While I'm badly scared every time I go into the ring, I almost never feel that this is going to be the time." Beatty claimed that in spite of apparently settling down in his new zoo he had no retirement plans and instead would travel with his own railroad show—which he did.[116]

Ohio Bell produced a radio program on Beatty in 1955. It began—"Clyde Beatty . . . forty-nine years old and still very much alive despite all reports to the contrary," and went on to describe some of his adventures and accidents. This program concluded, "Well you'd think that after an experience like that Clyde Beatty would have quit while he was still ahead. But he keeps going on, year after year, providing the thrills that have made him the world's greatest showman. All told Clyde's playmates have sent him to the hospital some thirty times . . . six times in serious condition. Every now and then you hear that Clyde is considering retirement. Sometimes you even hear that he has already died. But the lure of the big cage with its spine-tingling thrills and death rattling danger, will probably always hold its grip on him."[117]

Beatty speculated in an article a few years later that he would still like to take his act to Europe or perhaps play Las Vegas. Then he repeated his earliest feelings that "I expect one day I'll get chopped down." Beatty told Bill Ballentine, "To go quick, that wouldn't be too bad. But I'd shore [sic]

Detail from 1957 Clyde Beatty circus program.

In the '60s, the Clyde Beatty–Cole Bros. Circus featured this illustration on program covers.

Clyde and Harriett Beatty in the '40s.

hate to linger on with what we call arena shock, a mysterious breakdown that sometimes ends a trainer's career."[118]

In 1962, *Newsweek* wrote the "star performers were real lions, real tigers and a battered, scarcrossed man of 58 who faces more danger each working day than a white hunter would meet in a year of safaris. His name, of course, is Clyde Beatty." The act, it explained, is one of the rare illusions of show business because it is more convincing the closer it is examined. It also showed clearly that performing with the big cats had, indeed, become addictive and that all earlier retirement plans had been pushed out of his mind.

> Nerve and courage are plainly essential. For all his skills, Beatty has been clawed or bitten a hundred times and severely mauled on a half-dozen occasions. Both his forearms are laced by long claw scars and spotted with tooth marks. A deep scar runs the length of his right thigh, crisscrossed by smaller ones. He was in a coma twelve days after a lion seized him in its jaws and carried him around the ring. His right eye is developing cataracts after repeated backlashings from his own whip. . . . Why does Beatty go on . . . it is more than money. As the star of a dozen jungle movies, sometimes zoo operator and partner in the profitable over-the-road Clyde Beatty–Cole Bros. Circus, Beatty is well enough fixed to keep himself in pretzels and tigers. "Every year, I keep telling my wife this is gonna be the last. But it's like getting

1953 comic book cover featured Beatty and Saber.

something by the tail. I can't let go. It never gets monotonous. Like today. When Brutus came in today, maybe you noticed he circled out front. He was looking for Buddy, up on the perch. Brutus was looking around for him to say 'c'mon, let's get this guy.' "[119]

Beatty explained his feelings best in another story. Remarking that nobody lives without some danger, he stressed that the most important thing was to do what we like best and gamble on the risks. It was the only way to reach self-realization. "In fact," Beatty said, "any other kind of work would be dull to me. So dull I would lose my interest in life, which is the worst kind of death."[120] Although his bold defiance of death was too exhilarating to give up, the Wallendas' 1962 fall in Detroit, where Beatty was also performing, seemed to alter his thinking. Always very mindful of the audience, he observed: "I think they come to see death. I don't think they wish it. That's too horrible. But after the Wallendas fell . . . we didn't have any standing room in that arena which seats fifteen thousand people. Bernard Gavzer's AP story continued:

> "I want them to see me close. I want them to see the cats right up to me; to be close enough to smell the cats. I don't think about the people when I'm in there. I don't know if there are a hundred or a thousand in the audience. I really don't. It doesn't matter how many. I'll give them anything. I'll give them everything."

"But not that one thing."

And then Clyde Beatty laughs.

He is a man of action, not of philosophic contemplation. He doesn't really like to talk about death. Danger, yes. Death, no.

And yet death is like some monster cat—neither lion nor tiger alone but something of both—that sits unseen at every performance, licking its chops, waiting its turn.

There have been dozens of times it seemed the frightful cat marked death had claimed its victim. But each time, Beatty had risen, a new scar on his body but the old strength and will right where it had always been.

He claims you can get killed crossing a street or in an airplane, and the answer satisfies most. But there is a vast difference between perishing in an accident and deliberately and intentionally doing something that has danger as one of its basic characteristics. As Beatty says, "If there wasn't danger, who'd come see the show?"

He had grown into a feeling that he did not want to die in the ring, and give the cats and a bloodthirsty audience their final victory. "I go in there because I like it. It's my job. It's bread and butter. But most of all, it's been my life since I was a boy. I don't know anything but this. I want to give the audience excitement. I want them to see me close. But I won't give them that last thing. I won't give my life."[121]

The cats never killed Beatty. It was a stealthier, more treacherous thing than tigers that killed him.

Illustration from comic book.

fatal enemy with a courage he showed throughout his life."[122] On July 19, thirteen days after he entered the hospital, he seemed to rally. But right after his wife left his room, at about the time the matinee would have started, cancer finally clawed to earth the man *Time* called the "King of the Beasts."

For forty years Clyde Beatty had pushed his luck to the limit and "carried on a dramatic intense and chilling flirtation with death—a flirtation that left him scarred, clawed and spotted with fang marks. It was a flirtation, too, that made him a symbol of the eerie, bizarre world of the circus, a world of hokum and high drama, of show biz and sudden death."[123] If the true test of the strength of any legend is how long it persists in people's minds then the legendary status of Beatty seems secure. As the little Chillicothe *Gazette* editorialized on the first anniversary of the trainer's death, his end "was believed by many to be an end of an era in circus history. It was a belief that will not come true, at least not in our time—circus men say . . . ."

Beatty programs always emphasized the ferocity of his cats.

It was in the summer of 1964 that he underwent surgery for stomach cancer at the University of Chicago's Billings Hospital. He recovered sufficiently to return to the circus for its opening on Long Island the following spring and even went with it on the road when the show began its long season of one-night stands. Although weak, he worked his full act, occasionally even three shows a day. His third wife, Jane, who in fourteen years of marriage had only watched him perform less than a dozen times, continually urged him to retire. "I'll never quit!" he vowed. But, finally, at his doctor's insistence, he made a final appearance in the ring in Salisbury, Maryland, and reluctantly returned to his Ventura, California, seacoast home for a rest. On July 6, he hemmorrhaged severely and was rushed to Community Memorial Hospital. His wife issued the announcement that he was suffering from terminal cancer of the esophagus, and she added: "He is fighting against a nor will the name or the image of the valiant Ross Countian be dimmed in memory."[124] This was more than mere pride in the local boy who had made good, for Beatty created such an indelible image in America that his name is virtually synonymous with "wild animal trainer" here.[125] His singleminded drive made him epitomize the three-part characterization of the trainer. To those who disliked wild animal acts, he was the ultimate villain, who exploited the dominance of man over beast. His tools—the whip, chair, and blank gun—were the cruel symbols of a proud, unfair, relentless bully. Others saw him as a fool, or daredevil, whose overoptimism and courage carried him to reckless extremes in a basically frivolous occupation. Of course, he was also a hero, in all three senses of the word: an invincible conqueror with almost magical power, the self-made small town boy and, finally, the audience-oriented splendid performer. If it is true he aroused the basest instincts of the crowds he sought to please, he also represented what has been considered the most American of qualities: a defiance of nature and insurmountable odds. But in the world of the circus, his legend is strongest. His name proved to be one of his show's strongest assets. It still opened its performance with a fighting act, which was introduced this way:

In the giant steel Encircled Arena. A Triumphant Tribute to Tradition—Capt. Dave Hoover Personally Challenging the Fearsome Ferocity of the Clyde Beatty–Cole Bros. Jungle Bred Wild Animals. Handpicked Protege of the Master Battles Bravely In Adding Plaudits and Praise to Death Defying Demonstrations.

The 1966 program continued, "No person in the world today shares the legendary prominence in the wild animal field with the late great Beatty. Unmatched in all of history, in every section of the universe, were the risks and narrow escapes the circus man undertook day after day, week after week and year after year."[126]

Today the Clyde Beatty–Cole Bros. Circus still crisscrosses the country under canvas. Dave Hoover's cat act (Beatty himself selected him as his successor) is introduced as "an exceptionally exciting exhibition of the Clyde Beatty ferocious wild animals" and the lead story in the program is about Beatty.

No one has ever entered the large steel arena and paralleled the showmanship and veracity of . . . Clyde Beatty, still considered the world's most extraordinary wild animal trainer. . . . As a mere animal groom, the least applauded and most obscure circus chore, [he] was all eyes and enthusiasm. He would see the world and later the world would clamor to see him. . . . Always ready to the rescue, full of self-confidence and unabashed theatrics, [he] swiftly catapulted to circus fame. Within a mere decade, [his name] was synonymous with wild animal training. The best and most exciting ever seen under the Big Top!

The circus today continues to carry the name of the most astonishing sawdust sensation ever . . . the master of sneering, sinister jungle beasts—the one and only Clyde Beatty."[127]

Chapter IV

THE WILD ANIMAL TRAINER IN AMERICA
HERO OR VILLAIN?

The wild animal trainer is unique in the circus world. Appearing out of shadows, neither the child of a trainer or any other member of the circus hierarchy, nor the product of a circus school, he somehow discovers an ability to handle big carnivores and embarks on his singular career. His performing days often end with tragic physical mutilation or death, but amazingly, another young runaway or dreamy romantic appears, ready to take his place.

All this has excited the curiosity and worked on the imagination of writers of fact and fiction alike. Probing the methods and motives of animal trainers, they have tried to explain their domination over the big cats in terms ranging from the biological and psychological to the supernatural. Dime novelists used to think there was something in the hypnotic power of the human eye, and Jim Tully, in his 1927 work *Circus Parade*, continued to stress the same idea. Much more recently, Daryll Ponicsan has suggested that successful domination of the big cats depends less on eye contact than on the total involvement of the animal trainer's personality and his detachment from everything else as especially important for understanding the act of wild animal training. Thomas Duncan's *Gus the Great*, for example, published in 1947, explored in detail the personalities of two animal men: the egotistical, imaginative Captain Latcher; and the boorish, brutal cageboy, Willie. Edward Hoagland's prizewinning *Cat Man* (1958),

which also examined the personality of a cageboy, sympathetically portrayed a young social outcast who discovers strength and love in his association with the big cats.

Trainers who have written or talked about their unusual profession have much to say about the way they control—or imagine they control—the wild animals they handle. But again it is their personality which engages interest. The autobiographies and interviews of a host of trainers reveal an almost compulsive drive to remain in the arena and convey the impression that the excitement of handling wild animals is something almost addictive.

Some commentators, ignoring these kinds of questions, have simply denounced trainers as villains and declared their acts debasing to performer and audience alike. These kinds of outright condemnations, however, have evolved into serious discussions among professional animal experts about the value of training to the beasts themselves. A significant influence in these discussions is the heightened interest in ecology and wildlife conservation, which has been responsible for legislation severely limiting the importation, transportation, and breeding of animals usually featured in circus acts, notably polar bears, elephants, tigers, and leopards. And while these laws probably will not eliminate wild animal performances entirely, they may well serve to relegate them to the position they held seventy-five years ago, when they

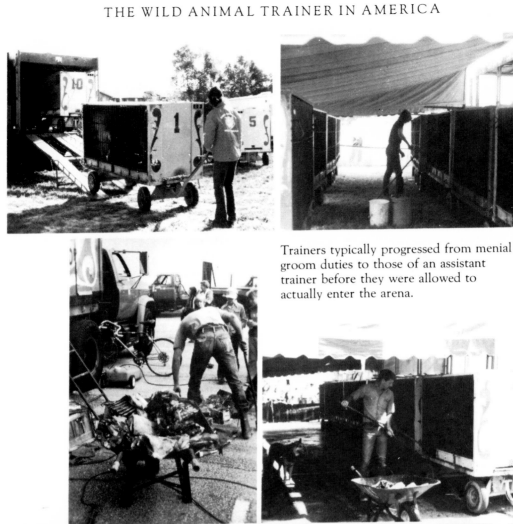

Trainers typically progressed from menial groom duties to those of an assistant trainer before they were allowed to actually enter the arena.

were exhibitions in permanent parks. Questions turning on the personalities of wild animal trainers or the methods they employ would then become largely academic, for the circus would once again be mainly a presentation of equestrian and canine skills, and demonstrations of acrobatic agility.

Miraculously over-night the shabby wall had blossomed into thralling splendor. What was

Daniel in the lions' den compared with Herr Alexander in the same? Not as the prophet is pictured in the farthest corner from the lions, and manifestly saying to himself: If I was only out of this! But with his head right smack dab **in** the lion's mouth. Right **in** it. Yes sir! "S'posin'!" we gasped, all goggle-eyed, "jist s'posin' that there lion was to shut his mouth! . . . Ga-ash!!"[1]

If a fellow only **could** run off with a circus!

Wouldn't it be great? No more splitting kindling and carrying in coal; no more: "Hurry up, now, or you'll be late for school; no more poking along in a humdrum existence never going anyplace or seeing anything but the glad free, untrammeled life, the life of a circus boy. . . . And then . . . and then . . . Travel all around, and be in a new town every day! And see things! . . . And when the show came back to your own hometown next year, people would wonder whose was that slim and gracile figure. . . . They'd screw up their eyes to look hard, and they'd say: "Yes, sir. It is. It's him. It's Willie Bigelow. Well, of all things!" And they'd clap their hands, and be so proud of you. And they'd wonder how it was that they could have been so blind to your many merits when they had you with them.[2]

Under the witchcraft of the dreaming blue, each boy had a firm and stubborn purpose. Over and over again he rehearsed how he would go up to the man that runs the show, and say: "Please mister, can I go with you?" And the man would say, "Yes." (As easy as that) . . . You don't know. Things not half so strange as that have happened. And if you were right there at the time.[3]

This 1905 reminiscence of circus day was the dream of most small town youths then. The glitter of show life, attracting boys willing to join the circus in almost any capacity, held out the promise of excitement, freedom and, as so many dime novels assured them, a chance for wealth and fame as circus owner or star animal trainer. It was a special American fantasy, akin to the imagined lot of the western cowboy. But for those who did join the circus when it passed through their town, the rude awakening to the hardships and arduous work they had taken on usually put a quick end to their dreams. Ellen Velvin, a close observer of circus life at the beginning of this century, estimated that as many as ninety percent of the boys who entered the circus this way very quickly left it.[4] Clyde Beatty disclosed most cageboys talk their way into their jobs by insisting their big goal in life was to be near wild animals and look after them. There was no limit to what they would do to demonstrate their dedication and willingness to learn. But the majority of cageboys only sought adventure and travel and had no desire to actually enter the steel arena.[5]

Yet it was just this way that the American wild animal trainer typically did enter the circus. Joining it at some spot on its seasonal tour, he started out as a cageboy, tending to the needs of the cats and hoping for more important tasks, such as those falling to the gun boy or the assistant trainer. If it meant becoming a trainer himself, an eager cageboy regarded no job as too difficult. "How can I describe my delight," Clyde Beatty wrote when recalling his own days as a cageboy, "in finding myself an assistant, even in a humble role, to honest-to-goodness animal trainers. It was an honor to clean the cages, to fetch water for the animals, to do anything that was asked of me."[6] Because of what Ellen Velvin called a "wonderful equality" among the employees in the trained wild animal exhibitions she visited at the turn of the century (she noted that little social distinction was made between the star performer and the small boy who sold peanuts), it was a real possibility for able and energetic boys to rise in the circus ranks from laborer to star. Given the simple necessity of having to replace trainers as injury or age incapacitated them for their work, it paid experienced performers to keep close watch on everyone joining the show with hopes of becoming a trainer. After all, the youngster who sold peanuts now might become the featured star of the future. Trainers and semiretired trainers alike took note of the newcomers, looking for signs of courage and aplomb. They noticed if youngsters studied the traits and idiosyncracies of the animals, and whether they showed a willingness to talk to the beasts—always considered a good indication of future success. The ambitious cageboy kept his eyes open too, watching the trainer and his assistants and, if he was like Beatty, secretly knowing that he could make the animals perform as well as they.[7]

Because trainers have so frequently come out of the ranks of circus cageboys, the popular idea of the cageboy has all along had a bearing on the idea of the trainer. For as long as the cageboy was represented as a free-spirited lad who, as incipient trainer, promised to fulfill themes of independence and success through laborious effort, the trainer might plausibly be seen as the virtuous culmination of a life dedicated to these American ideals. But with the publication in 1947 of Thomas Duncan's seven-hundred-page novel, *Gus the Great*, this idea was struck a devastating blow. Instead of rural innocence (using phrases like "honest-to-goodness"), the cageboy in this epic work embodies all that is cruel in the misshapen life of a vicious delinquent.

Willie Parr, a son of a three-times married North Woods trapper and guide, is one of numerous brothers and sisters. Alternately beaten or ignored, he commits various misdeeds, one of

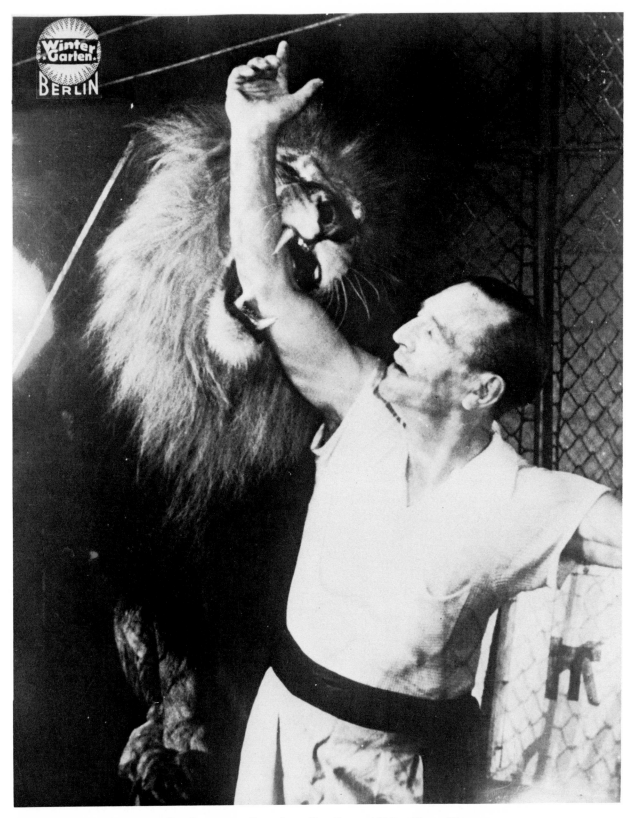

Bob Mathews with King Tuffy, the wire-walking lion (Kay Bros., 1936). — *Harry Chipman*

which is cutting up neighbors' cats and dogs. After learning he is to be sent to an industrial school, he takes to the road and changes his name to Krummer. Willie spends two years on the bum—stealing, rolling drunks, kidnapping pet dogs, and living off the land. In 1918, he is discovered in a boxcar, but escapes aboard a circus train. Thanks to a labor shortage, Willie is hired as a canvasman. The hard work and plentiful food toughen the seventeen-year-old, but he retains his sneaky road kid mannerisms. He fights often like an animal with other boys in the circus, and on those occasions when he is beaten, like an animal he crawls off, ever after to lick the winner's boots.

The wild animal trainer with the circus is Phillip Latcher. The name is a pseudonym he has taken to disguise the identity of his family, wealthy Canadians he fears he will embarrass if his association with a circus is discovered. He has been to military school and has medals for rifle shooting, boxing, and fencing. Handsome, courtly, precise, and charming, he has satisfied his longing for an adventurous life in a wild animal act he himself owns. The first time Willie sees Latcher's performance, the effect is immediate. "Deep in his soul something stirred—an awakening half painful, half pleasurable. A tide of craving passed over him, craving to wear a smart uniform like Captain Latcher, to stride into an arena looking hard and masculine and to subdue wild beasts. It was the only thing he ever wanted to do, and he felt bewildered and almost stunned that he had not thought of such a career before. He had always had a way with animals. The stray dogs he had

Jules Jacot ex–H-W trainer, presented the featured act at the St. Louis Zoo for many years. — *Fred D. Pfening, Jr.*

Royal Bengal Feats—A royal command performance by a stunning troupe of trained tigers, under the masterful direction of Karoly Donnert, is one of many thrilling highlights featured in "The International Circus Festival of Monte Carlo," a unique, one-ring, European-style, multi-media extravaganza presented under the high patronage of His Serene Highness Prince Rainier III.

taught tricks, the crow he had taught to speak after catching it and slitting its tongue. . . . A way with animals!"[8] Latcher who thinks of himself as an English nobleman, is rapidly drawn to Willie, too, for as the boy begins to pay deference to him —almost to worship him—he exalts himself into something of a knight. "Willie" he thought, "was medieval, he had the soul of a loyal aide-de-camp. . . . it appealed to Captain Latcher's imagination to toy with the possibility of acquiring such a faithful follower, valet, bodyguard, servant, all in one."[9] Willie Krummer, obedient to the Captain's suggestion, frightens away the cageboy and takes the job for himself.

Thus begins a strange relationship in which Latcher treats Willie nearly as an animal himself, to be both tamed and civilized, while Willie responds with a cringing subservience that is matched only by a growing inner brutality. When the boy's inclination to be insubordinate surfaces, Latcher simply beats him until he induces abject surrender. He attempts to teach him grammar and some of the social graces, and occasionally he allows him to enter the arena with some of the older cats. But Willie, whose idea of courage in the ring is to dominate beasts by beating them into submission, arouses only resentment in the animals. His respect for Latcher fades when he notices

(Above) Striped Champions—Karoly Donnert and his handsome array of trained Royal Bengal and Siberian tigers make their North American debut in the elegant, European-style, multi-media "Festival International Du Cirque De Monte Carlo Spectacular." Donnert, whose family has long been associated with circuses throughout the world, was honored at the 1978 International Circus Festival of Monte Carlo as one of the outstanding artists in the world's most prestigious championship of circus talent.

Magazines have typically dramatized the goriest arena incidents. – *Tom Henricks*

THE TOP HALF OF REINER WAS STILL HANGING FROM THE BARS WHEN THE LIGHTS CAME BACK ON. THE LIONS WERE EATING THE REST.

fear in the trainer, a dread even to enter the ring, especially with unbroken animals. The Captain suffers from arena shock, and he claims that this comes to all animal trainers eventually: It "sometimes creeps up on you gradually, like a damned tiger stalking you for days through the jungle, and sometimes it hits without warning and you go to pieces in the safety cage and are never any good after that. Maybe, old man, it's a way the beasts have of evening up the score, eh? We cage them up and put them through their paces so that a lot of

dullards can sit with their hearts in their throats. But it's all a damned unnatural business, eh? So Old Dame Nature takes it out on us."[10] When Latcher marries, his fear of the arena increases; soon his act is unacceptable in any circus. His only hope is to introduce young and vigorous cats, who frighten him pathetically. Willie, already contemptuous of his former hero and prepared to take over the act anyway, murders Latcher by knocking him on the head and tossing him to the unbroken cats. In the process, the cageboy himself is attacked but manages to escape. In the hospital, he learns the newspapers have made him a hero for his brave attempt to rescue the Captain. He has even been nominated for a Carnegie Medal.

Having dreamed for years of being a star and already having picked out a professional name for himself—Baron Karl Otto von Krummer—Willie now develops a fine act, complete with studied German phrases and mannerisms. A nationally acclaimed hero with many circus contract offers, Willie is regularly quoted as saying that patience and kindness are the only way to train wild animals. But in his winterquarters, the cats emit terrifying sounds: "roars, shrieks of wild beasts in horrible agony as if from hot irons and ammonia."[11] His brutality, however, cannot disguise his own special fear of being found out a murderer. He is afraid to drink, lest he reveal his crime, he is afraid of being injured in the arena, lest he talk while anesthetized. So, brutal as he is, "when the Baron entered the arena—the only person frightened and thrilled was the Baron himself."[12]

The act succeeds when the Baron forces his wife —the Captain's widow—to present the lions and tigers. Her "valor in the arena was inspired by the animal whip in the Baron's hand." In the arena her "footwork was graceful and precise like a dancer's. And the whole act took on a flowing ballet quality. Lions undulated and the tigers were sinuous . . . cracking her whip [she] was suddenly not so much Venus as Diana. . . . because her fear was so primitive the act became primitive."[13]

Duncan researched his book carefully. He included many circus legends and stories surrounding animal acts, such as: arena shock, the gullibility of the press in accepting a "foreign trainer," and the popularity of female trainers in the twenties. The title character was patterned after controversial circus owner Fred Buchanan. The wild animal scenes are accurate because many of the descriptions are virtually lifted from Beatty's *The Big Cage* and *Jungle Performers*. Because of this appearance of authenticity, the characterization of the cageboy turned trainer, though softened in more recent years, has become the commonly accepted view to this day.

Roman Proske, a noted European trainer, did little to enhance the cageboys' image in his 1956 autobiography. Writing that he always tried to have at least one helper who was familiar with animals and clearheaded enough to cope with an emergency, he declared that such a one was hard

Roman Proske's risky tiger act led to many severe injuries.

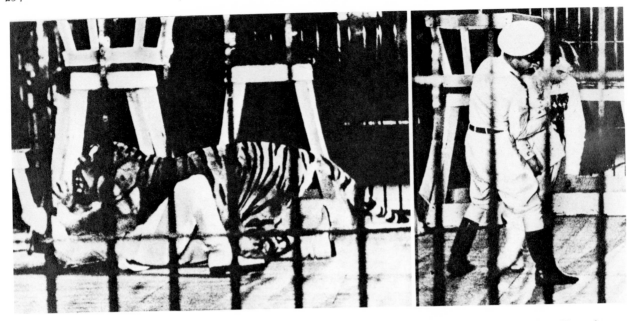

Proske is attacked by one of his tigers—one of the sequences available of an actual attack.—*Tom Henricks*

to find. Two distinct types, he wrote, seem particularly attracted to wild animal acts: alcoholics and exhibitionists. The drunk believes the danger of his work excuses his drinking and the show-off basks in the exotic setting of wild animals and the circus. Neither can be depended on in time of crises. Proske claimed that occasionally one of these weak personalities becomes a trainer, but the career of any performer "who goes in for strong drink or for showing off is not long for this world."[14]

Two years later in 1958, the prize-winning *Cat Man* was published. Edward Hoagland, the author, was a Harvard student who traveled for a year with the notorious Dailey Bros. Circus as a cageboy. He fictionalized his adventures, changing the setting to the Ringling menagerie department. His book depicts a violent, brutal world of "winos" and misfits. The young cagehand, Fiddler, escapes the depravity by forming a tenuous and ultimately fatal alliance with the big cats he tends. Hoagland's recent acclaimed essays are strongly influenced by his initial experiences as a cageboy. His favorite topic is the intricate bond between the world of animals and the world of men. Like Fiddler he is drawn especially to the predators since Hoagland believes that these adventurous carnivores, "just as they *eat* all other animals, somehow *contain* all animals." Thus Hoagland's and Fiddler's emotions are inextricably inter-

Cavalier depicted the attack on Proske in sensationalistic style.—*Tom Henricks*

Proske appeared in 1947 with RBB&B.—*Fred D. Pfening, Jr.*

twined when the author writes: "But just touching those walls and feeling them shake, he pictured the cats. Giant, one-muscled, shattering, foreign. That could turn this town upside down. Leopards lithe as smoke in the wind. Tigers glittering like cymbals . . . The cages were his."[15] Fiddler takes more and more liberties with the big cats as he learns their individual personalities and idiosyncracies;

the dazzling fast leopards, the great, massive regal tigers and, of course, the lions.

The boy found the lions the most awe-inspiring of the big cats. "They weren't half so active as the tigers, half so shifting—moody and yet opening the tiger cage didn't carry half the shock. . . . Just lying there and not trying they packed the power to make you never in your life forget what lions

Frank Phillips (1942–43). — *Fred D. Pfening, Jr.*

were."[16] "Joe was the gruffest, biggest, best lion Fiddler had ever seen. . . . The dots which constantly swirled in his eyes might have been shaped like arrowheads without making his gaze any wilder. When he looked at you you couldn't keep from hopping, you'd swallowed hornets, you wanted to bite on a knife and run hog-wild."[17] Then there was the tiger: "Unless you stopped to imagine what Ajax with his strength could do, he wasn't awesome. . . . He was above squabbling, this great regal cat who never growled or wrinkled up his face . . . [But] once a week or once a month, if somebody's arm was laid across his paws Ajax would tear it off. He'd happen not to want to be touched. Nobody could save the man, nothing could be done. Off would come the arm like a twig."[18]

"Daring" Dick Clemens. — *Fred D. Pfening, Jr.*

Just being around the cats was enough for Fiddler. The world of the performer was totally alien to him. When he saw the wiry, well-groomed trainer, surrounded by a bevy of beautiful girls, "he quickly didn't want to watch — it made him feel as dead and seedy as a flop house janitor."[19] In fact, Hoagland's *Cat Man* stresses the totally separate worlds of the performer and worker. No trainer, however, could be more dedicated to his animals than Fiddler when he rushes to protect his beloved lions from teasing black roustabouts only to fall against the cage bars and be ripped apart by the big cats.

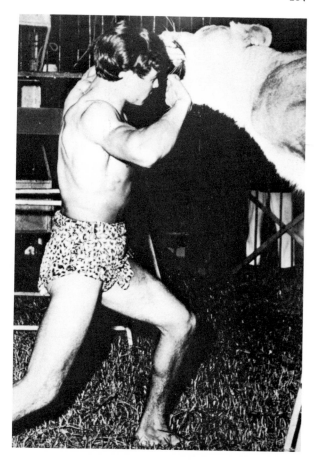

One of the most dynamic trainers in recent years is Jon "Tarzan" Zerbini.

After traveling with the Ringling show for a year, showgirl Connie Clausen wrote down her experiences, including her opinions of the cageboys. They are very similar to Hoagland's. Both see the boys as weaklings or misfits who enjoy vicarious power in associating with carnivorous felines. She noticed that the "men who took care of the big cats mooned around the cages like stage door Johnnies."[20] The cageboys, she felt, were of another breed than the men who worked with other animals. "There was a kind of tension, a concealed explosiveness about them so strongly reminiscent of the cats themselves, that seeing them around the lot one knew instantly they were cat men."[21] They idolized their charges and bragged about the beasts' deadly fierceness, stealthy cunning, and sinister swiftness. "They even kept score of the man-killers, the maimers, the eye-gougers . . . as though the animals were underworld heroes, temporarily imprisoned, but still full of fight, ready to strike out at their jailers with every weapon nature gave them."[22] The boys' unreasoning admiration for their charges led them to take senseless chances with them.

Even though the boys themselves were often the cats' targets, they still stuck their thin arms into the cages and felt rewarded if the animals condescended to be petted and did not bite off their arm. While Clausen was with the show one of the boys was suddenly, without warning, pulled close against the bars of the tigress's cage. He screamed horribly but before anyone could reach him, he lay dead in front of the cage, as the tiger cleaned her fur, her eyes cool, almost bored. Clausen was unnerved by the experience and asked an old circus hand why it occurred. He explained: "There are men who know they're men and who animals are animals. They like animals, respect them, but they don't let the animal forget who's boss. They don't take chances either. Now the other kind aren't men yet—like that cageboy. He's not sure what he is or who's boss, him or the tiger. A poor skinny boy thinks he can prove he's a man if he can control something as big and deadly as a tiger. The more danger, the more important he feels." Although Clausen thought she had seen great devotion between the men and their animals, the old hand quickly contradicted her romantic notion. "You suppose that poor bastard cageboy would look to a tiger for love if he had a woman to love him. You think a man, a real man, would spend his time talking to animals, if he wasn't

scared to death of people? . . . We don't hate the towners as we say. We're afraid of them, that we aren't good enough. That's why we're here, talking to animals that can't talk back."[23] Hoagland and Clausen could sympathize with the cageboys, but years later Daryll Ponicsan created a character as despicable as Duncan's Willie Krummer.

"Po Chang" is the psychotic cageboy in Ponicsan's 1978 circus novel, *The Ringmaster*. Newly hired, he becomes enraptured with his first close-up view of the wild animal act. "His blue-flecked eyes—there was tumult inside of them—took in every gesture, every nuance of Rico's performance and of course every twitch of the cats. With each crack of the whip he found his right hand jerking involuntarily, simulating the snap. Before the show he had put that hand into the cage of the one called Hondo and for the first time in his life had actually felt the fur of a live lion."[24] Unlike Fiddler or Clausen's cageboys, Po Chang is an exhibitionist, who loves to have people watch him feed and clean the cats, and his fantasy of one day working the beasts grows until his seething jealousy for the trainer finally drives him to murder.

Thus, in the last thirty years, the characterization of the cagehand has shifted from the innocent small town boy seeking adventure to an emotional cripple running from reality. If cageboys have provoked authors' imaginations and become the victims of sensationalism, then the actual trainers themselves have provided more mystifying questions to be probed. Why can certain people dominate the big cats, how do they control these animals, and why do some quit from fear, while others overcome their fright and become addicted to the arena?

When an assistant acquires his first act, it is usually one trained by another person. Technically, then, he is a "handler." Dr. J. Y. Henderson, the veterinarian of Ringling Bros., claims that there is a world of difference between the two animal men, although the public is unaware of the distinction. Real trainers, he insists, take raw animals, break them, teach them tricks, and then perform with them. Handlers perform with animals already broken and trained, simply repeating a given set of signals.[25] Hoagland writes that as long as discipline is maintained in a pretrained group, the animals will keep on doing the chores they have been taught, and if casualties occur, a yearling or two can be inserted, "which mingling in,

Three ex-Clyde Beatty assistants: Joe Arcaris, who worked with Beatty at his zoo and won a Carnegie medal for rescuing a man from the lions' pit; Joe Walch, who assisted both Beatty and Court; and Manuel "Junior" Ruffin, a former Beatty assistant and one of the very few black trainers.—*Fred D. Pfening, Jr.*

The European Circus Knie features this unusual combination. — *Fred D. Pfening, Jr.*

will pick up the cues and gradually reach some understanding of what is expected; their quirks, if exploited can even enhance the act. Generally it deteriorates to a patchwork, but there is a market for it," with royalties sometimes being paid to the first trainer or the impressario who employed him, and who may still own the animals he performed with.[26]

So, an act may be worked by a succession of trainers, some quitting for less dangerous or tiring work, others because they are overcome by a feeling that they too are somehow penned in with the animals, a sense akin to what jailers often feel.[27]

If the handler is well acquainted and expert with animals, there is little reason to disparage him. Thoroughbred horsetrainers do not usually break the animals they work with, and neither do professional show riders or dog handlers.[28] They may add to the animal's training, but their value is in getting the beast to perform to its maximum potential. This is often true of the wild animal handler. If he is carefully chosen and trained, his gifts of showmanship and rapport with the big cats inject color and life into a performance that might be technically good but dull.

Thus the criticism frequently leveled against Clyde Beatty, that he was primarily an actor-showman-handler rather than a primary trainer, even though untrue, seems unwarranted. The risks, danger, and arduous work were still his. When he acquired Pete Taylor's act, Danny Odom — Hagenbeck-Wallace's general manager — made it clear to him that the circus had thirty thousand dollars tied up in the cats, not counting equipment, training, or the trainer's salary. Since it probably was the show's largest single investment, it was considered just as important that Beatty keep the big cats alive as himself. They expected him to separate battling animals and then nurse the injured beasts back to health. He was his only protection, for there were no loaded guns to help him and not a man on the lot who would enter the arena to save him from the cats. At the Kansas State Fair, during one of his first seasons as a featured performer, Beatty had to fight the cats during a thunderstorm. When the boy (he was only in his early twenties at the time) came out of the arena that night "he was panting for breath and wet with perspiration. Great seams of fatigue creasing his face made him look ten years older. He had put on a great show, the rest of the circus family said."[29] This episode illustrates an important point. Whether the performer is a primary trainer or a handler, he must be able to control his animals.

Control is paramount to the success of any wild animal act. The two earliest theories maintained that the trainer either was endowed with supernatural powers or that he brutally beat his creatures into complete submission. These beliefs persist. Those condemning these performances will always believe cruelty is an essential ingredient, just as circus publicists will continue to utilize the idea of a magical force. For example, the Friends of Animals, Inc. officially contends that the training of wild animals is generally accomplished through great cruelty and deprivation, while a recent Ringling publicity piece describes Gunther Gebel-Williams as a dynamic German-born performer with "almost mystical communion with all creatures."[30]

Circus Parade, Jim Tully's sordid novel of a small circus traveling in Mississippi and Arkansas at the turn of the century, is considered a classic. It describes the show's lion tamer as a lithe two-hundred-pound Negro, who was the "king of our small world." Twice a day he went into a cage with six lions, three of them proven killers. He kept his courage up with liquor, although he claimed never to worry about dying. "Curious as to how he managed to control them, I asked him the secret. 'It's nothing,' he said, 'You must always look an animal in the eye. They can tell by that how game you are. You never can fool them.'" When the trainer is killed by a brown bear, the narrator muses: "How can you catch a blind bear's eye?"[31]

Trainers deny both the supernatural and cruelty theories. There is no way they possibly could keep their eye on all the animals in an act at once. The big cats have to be watched since they naturally attack moving objects, and training cannot change inherent traits. But, the only power the human eye has is that, when watched, the animals generally behave. Nor is discipline ever a venting of the trainer's temper or anger; only fools would attempt to handle animals by force or brutality. Hagenbeck-trained performer Franz Woska insisted: "It is no more than a perpetual invitation to death to do so. Like human beings animals resent brutality,

The last of the fighting act showmen, Dave Hoover, center ring star, with Clyde Beatty–Cole Bros. since 1966. This photo illustrates one of Hoover's first acts in 1952.—*Fred D. Pfening, Jr.*

Dave Hoover.

and will put that resentment into sudden action at the first offered opportunity. . . . The first law of animal training is to know your animals. The rest is easy. Just a matter of mutual trust and patience."[32] Dave Hoover claims that animals obey because they do not know how weak the trainer is. If the cats are pushed or bullied, they will soon "realize you're hitting them as hard as you can. Then there's no stopping them." Years ago, he says, trainers knew all this but did not know it was based on animal psychology.[33]

A circus historian contends that almost nothing is known about how a "comparatively puny man can bend a great and treacherous beast to his will." According to Murray, the trainer must move assuredly in the cage, speak firmly, and never show fear. He has to possess indomitable courage, patience, respect for the animals, and intuitive understanding of their individuality and group psychology. Most important of all, he must have a "deep and inborn conviction that he will be able to control his animals. A person who can make a beast of prey obey does certainly have some unusual force, an inexplicable authority, which the mighty predator immediately recognizes and accepts. Such power is given to only a few human beings." Murray insists no one knows its origin or can explain why one trainer wants to control only lions while others are obsessed with tigers. But given the power and the obsession, the trainer is eternally dedicated. "He may be torn almost to bits and still insist on going back into the cage. His urge is incurable." Among lions, Murray writes, there is always an animal in the act that attempts to dominate the arena. The trainer must be alert to insubordination, for to the lion he is another

Dave Hoover.

Dave Hoover.

Dave Hoover.

Dave Hoover.

cat, perhaps a "lion god," whose demands are law. But the animal will turn on his master if given the chance, so the trainer must maintain eternal vigilance and "heaven-given assurance" that he is all powerful and cannot be hurt. Murray concludes that although it might not be immediately recognized, the ability to dominate wild animals must be inborn.[34]

British animal man Jimmy Chipperfield also discusses control in his autobiography. He believes wild animals' perceptions are extremely keen. They can sense a person's frame of mind from his physical movements alone. That is why it is important for the trainer to enter the arena firmly and slam the door in a determined way. Then the cats

know they have met their match. If a man shows nervousness, hesitation, or even has a cold, it is risky for him to work. Chipperfield writes that "to go into the cage, after a couple of drinks is the act of a madman."[35] The trainer may think his voice and movements are perfectly normal, but the animals know better. Their sense of smell is acute and they detect the difference at once—often with lethal results.

Domination is one thing, training another. "Few people outside the circus realize how dreadfully boring training can be." Patience must be inexhaustible because no one can beat a cat into doing what you want. Hit hard, he may go berserk, and his future relationship with the trainer is ruined.

Dave Hoover. —*courtesy Dave Hoover*

Dave Hoover. —*courtesy Dave Hoover*

Robert Baudy, noted ani-
mal breeder, with his
Siberian tigers. — *Fred D.
Pfening, Jr.*

beasts with fewer individuals to tyrannize are more brutal.[38]

Animals often treat man as a member of their own species. When a man enters into the social organization, he must play the part thrust upon him in accordance with the rituals peculiar to that species. Among the large carnivores man must assume at all cost the alpha position and keep it. If man were socially inferior in a group, he would be in severe danger, for the animals would take any liberties. Much of the unpredictability trainers speak of is really a manifestation of social crises induced by biological impulse. Animals must know if they are socially inferior to their partners and vice versa, and if the trainer misinterprets an animal's moves or puts off decisive action, he gives initiative to the beast. At the least expected time, the animal will test him.

Luckily for the trainer, most quarrels over social rank can be settled by calm, unruffled behavior. One that is able to intimidate its opponent is recognized as superior, so that a fight is not necessary. In the case of the big cats, where the animals are clearly superior to man physically, the trainer must behave at critical moments like an unquestioned master. Importantly, man can assist himself by meeting the beasts in surroundings unfamiliar to the animals, for strange environments tend to inhibit animals' aggression.

In the circus, the trainer first openly takes possession of the ring before allowing the animals to enter.[39] He must ostentatiously stake his claim to

the cage as his territory.[40] This puts the animal in an inferior position, especially when the man stands in the center. (The lack of corners removes all chance of the animal taking cover and man can give his superiority full play.) When the trainer becomes accepted as the alpha animal, he enjoys all the privileges of that rank, especially complete freedom of movement. All inferior animals must obey his orders without reservation. He can then interfere within their ranks, subdue quarrels, and protect those who are bullied.[41] But animalization has its risks. The task of recognizing fights between his animals as early as possible and then suppressing them before even the most stringent measures will not work is often difficult for the trainer, and in entering into the animal society he establishes himself as a rival in fights over superiority and prospective mates.[42]

The dangerousness of the big cats is almost entirely caused by "critical reaction," that is, a defense reaction that automatically occurs at a critical distance, the demands of social rank, or even by pure accident, as in play.[43] Mishaps with wild animals cannot be totally prevented because man often fails to understand the beast's position or because it is impossible to keep constant watch. The experienced trainer comes very close to the ideal of foreseeing the reaction of any situation. But despite everything, he too will probably meet with injuries since human watchfulness can only be kept at its maximum for a few seconds at a time. There will be times when his attention flags and it

"Tarzan" Zerbini. — *Fred D. Pfening, Jr.*

is probable the animal can recognize this. The number of accidents a trainer suffers is in direct proportion to his attentiveness.[44]

Even with theories as scientific as Hediger's a bit of the mystic appears. In the best interests of man and animal, he writes, the relationship should be "positive." He argues also that not everybody has the same emotional attitude toward every group of animals but that beasts prefer certain people to others. He concludes, in fact, that no amount of teaching will help some people since there are "born animal men."[45] As early as 1904, a trainer wrote in *McClure's Magazine* that "no man living knows all about animals, or more than a very little about them. Some who are dead thought they knew."[46] Rather than exciting, he found the career of animal trainer marked by long periods of

monotony, which is broken by some terrible and tragic circumstance. The reason, he concluded, was that a caged animal, just like an imprisoned man is unbalanced. He is not necessarily insane, but some of his faculties are dulled while others are unduly sharpened. Even worse for the animal, is that he must deal not with his own kind, but the domination of an alien. "He must measure his altered faculties against the unfathomable mind of a superior being. So is generated the deep-seated terror, the smoldering rage, the treacherous uncertainty and changefullness that flash out in such deadly guise. Is it any wonder that the wisest and most experienced trainers must confess to knowledge so slight, an ignorance so vast of those untamed and sullen minds which for a time they perilously control?"[47]

Caged polar bear acts have always been a rare but exciting type of wild animal act. Ursala Botcher displays her large polar bear act on RBB&B.

Jeannette Rix works a mixed bear act assisted by her father, veteran trainer Albert Rix. — *Tom Henricks*

Control of wild animals is consequently tenuous at best, and the fear of loss of control is always present in every animal trainer. In the early wild animal shows, it was recognized that no matter how courageous a man might believe himself to be, he could never be absolutely sure and that "courage [would] not ooze out at his fingertips when he finds himself shut in alone with wild beasts and face to face with creatures who can as easily tear him limb from limb as a cat tears an unfortunate mouse."[48] When courage was self-conscious, it usually betrayed great fear. A lion trainer in *Circus Parade* is described as very nervous before each performance, although he declares he never let the cats know he is afraid. "I've always thought he was the bravest kind of guy," his successor says, "he knew he was takin' chances but he kep' right on. A boob never knows when he's takin' a chance. A brave man's a coward lots of times, jist like a lion."[49] J. Y. Henderson agrees. The chief reason for injuries, he argues, is overconfidence. The trainer who is always aware of the danger and the capabilities of his animals is much less likely to get hurt or killed.[50] Fred Powledge, who traveled with Hoxie Bros. Circus for a season and wrote his observation in *Mud Show*, tells of a trainer who was attacked at a five-thirty performance, worked the next show, and then could not go on again for eight whole days. "But I knew if I didn't get back in there right away, I might not **ever** go back in

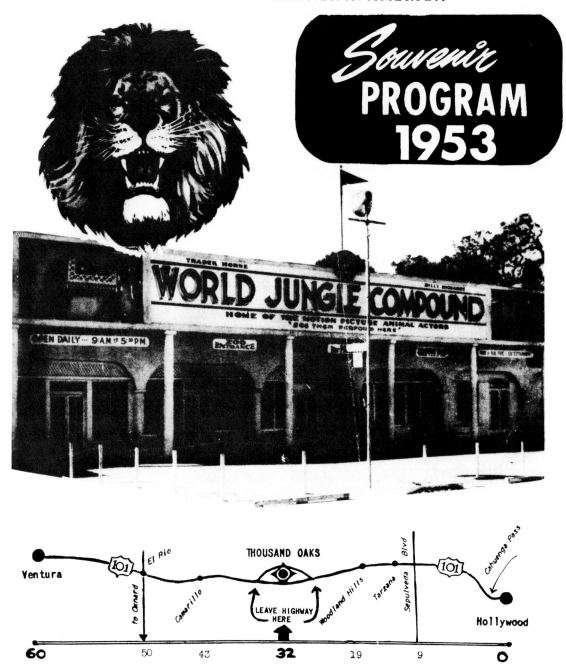

Birds, Beasts and Reptiles from the Jungles of the World

On Ventura Boulevard • Thousand Oaks, California

PHONE THOUSAND OAKS 2515

THOUSAND OAKS   32 Miles North of Hollywood on Ventura Boulevard

The World Jungle Compound, later renamed Jungleland, in Thousand Oaks, California, not only provided trained animals for the movies but was an excellent training center for young potential American trainers.

The bankruptcy of the center eliminated a good school for American trainers.

there. . . . If you lose your nerve you'll never do it." When the trainer returned to the arena, he was attacked again. Later, Powledge writes, he "blew the show." Another trainer commented that even for a twenty-year veteran like himself, getting hurt is a terrifying experience. "It seems like you get the butterflies just as much after twenty years as you did the first time you went in. I sympathize with him, and I know how he felt. He was hung by a claw. They took him to the hospital and they stitched him up, which they never should have done. And he got an infection and his whole arm swole up. A lot of times you can't get that across to a doctor. . . . It's pretty painful."[51] But when a trainer developed self-confidence in his own mastery, his fear was minimized. As Richard Sawade, one of Hagenbeck's first and most successful pupils declared: "I am never afraid when I am in the cage. If I were, I should have to pay for it. I must believe in my own willpower against that of my animals;

never give in to their moods and always demand they do their duties."[52]

Accidents could never be avoided, however, and when they occurred they were usually serious. When Bostock's trainers showed Velvin the injuries they considered routine—deep lines like furrows, red and drawn patches, muscles drawn up until the limb was out of shape, and deep dents from teeth meeting right through the arm—she did not find it surprising that after suffering for several weeks with such a wound, many decided to give up animal training as a career.

But established trainers did not believe these accidents seriously harmed anyone, unless they were permanently crippled. On the contrary, they felt such wounds did a man good. They made him alert, courageous, and compelled him to practice self-control.[53] When he was twenty-one, Clyde Beatty suffered his first injury from a lion attack. "It sure was a test," he said, "and almost got my nerve. But there I was well on my way to be what I wanted to be, and no big cat, linked with my own carelessness, was going to stop me."[54]

Involved in the belief that if a trainer enters the arena feeling nervous, or if he loses his nerve during a performance, he can be certain the animals will know it and attack, is the implication that animals can sense fear. It is sometimes argued that animals smell fear in human perspiration, and some scientists report that animals can smell it in man when cutaneous pH or acidity is radically changed.[55] But the veterinarian J. Y. Henderson insists that animals see fear rather than smell it. "You got to bluff all the time. Even if your knees are shaky, never back up. The sweat can be running down your face, but as long as you don't show an outward motion of fear, chances are you're okay."[56] If animals sense fear, he writes, it is

The first man to study animal training under the G.I. Bill was Ohio's Pat Anthony at the World Jungle Compound. — *Picture Perfect*

through the tone of a person's voice or from his actions. He has talked with cageboys and trainers who have admitted being really afraid yet were able to keep their animals from knowing it simply by maintaining an attitude of dominance and a firm, strong, commanding tone of voice.[57] There is no getting around it, says Dave Hoover. The slightest mistake, a momentary lapse can cut short a career. But it all boils down to one thing. The trainer must repeatedly convince the caged beasts that he is invincible. Once he loses that edge, his cats will not obey him. Although Hoover has been injured seriously thirteen times, he has always stayed in with the cats until the act was over. If the big cats realize they have hurt the trainer—especially if he is forced to leave before the act is completed, he believes, "he might as well forget working those again."[58]

Young Dick McGraw proudly presents a small group at the Compound.—*Picture Perfect*

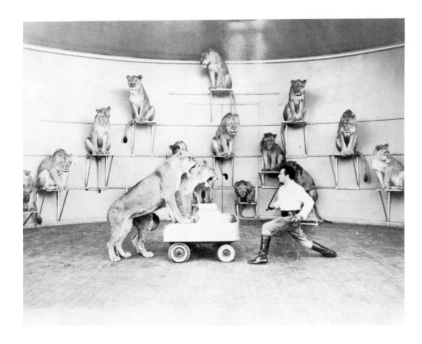

Pat Anthony first appeared with this lion act.—*Picture Perfect*

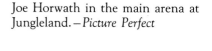
Joe Horwath in the main arena at Jungleland. — *Picture Perfect*

The strain of maintaining this arena supremacy causes some trainers to suffer the incongruity of striding out of a cage full of lions where he has been braving death and exercising his formidable will, to lay down the whips, the dominance, the belligerence, and defer to the performance director, step around the children in the entry way, sidestep the ballet girls and their husbands, avoid offending police and arena officials, and speak civilly in the dressing room. According to Hoagland, not all trainers can manage this. Instead, they go off in a corner, shout at the walls, and whale with their whips for half an hour, as if in a decompression chamber.[59]

Of all the students of the relationship between men and animals one of the most perceptive by far was Ernest Hemingway. His observations of bullfighting taught him to understand fear and what it

Dick McGraw with large lion
groups. — *Picture Perfect*

meant to lose control. Much of what he wrote about bullfighting is apropos to animal training. For example, he considered it to the bullfighter's credit if he did something highly dangerous but carefully thought out, and to his discredit if he courted danger through ignorance, physical or mental slowness, or through a blind folly that disregarded fundamental rules. Tallying precisely with that of the trainer in Tully's southern circus of 1905: "A boob never knows when he's takin' a chance."[60] Hemingway's matador, like the animal trainer, must dominate his animals with knowledge and science. If this domination was accomplished with grace, it was beautiful as well. And, as with the animal trainer, Hemingway found that courage was always precarious: "Courage comes such a short distance; from the heart to the head; when it goes no one knows how far away it goes.

Jungleland trainer cues his lions.—
Picture Perfect

... Sometimes you get it back from another wound, the first may bring fear of death and the second may take it away. . . . [Many cowards) stay in the business relying on their knowledge and their ability to limit the danger and hope the courage will come back and sometimes it does and most times it does not."[61]

Hemingway wrote of the inner satisfaction of being in a ring in which an animal was attacking with the conscious intent to kill. Such an experience provides enough of a sensation that there will always be men wanting to have it. It requires bravery, but he found that, like animal trainers, matadors may be frightened before the fight begins, but almost all of them are brave. Bravery as the ability to temporarily ignore possible consequences was the most common kind, but there was also the bravery that comes from exhilaration: it was the ability not to give a damn for possible consequences.[62] It is easier to be stupid and naturally brave, according to Hemingway, than to be exceedingly intelligent and still completely brave.[63] It was Hemingway's idea that if an animal man becomes afraid, his actions will become cowardly, dull, and defensive and it is better that he retire than rob the public with poor performances. The public, in Hemingway's mind, is vitally important, because the bullfight, like the animal act, engages spectators in a shared sense of immortality. "In

Most famous trainer of animals for motion pictures, Mel Koontz.—*Picture Perfect*

playing with death bringing it closer, closer, closer, to himself . . . he gives the feeling of immortality, and as you watch it, it becomes yours."[64]

But there are differences between the two activities also. The bullfighter never fights the same bull twice. Once a bull has been exposed to a man and a fight, he is considered too dangerous to match against a man again. In outlying districts where bulls were refought, matadors were usually injured or killed. But the animal trainer has to face his cats daily, including animals that might have previously injured him or tested his domination, so there is an added danger in animal training that is not often present in bullfighting.

Despite the danger or maybe because of it, many trainers have an obsession to remain in the arena. When discussing this drive, authors typically refer to Clyde Beatty and Mabel Stark. They loved the circus with its adventure, excitement, and hardship, but they also were captivated by the thrill and excitement of stepping into a cage with magnificent felines facing the danger every day of being mauled to pieces, and never really knowing what would happen. The challenge was the affirmation of their superiority over brute force. Perhaps this was childish, or perhaps it satisfied their egos, or some more elemental need.[65] Roman Proske, expressing gratitude for having the opportunity and privilege of working with "truly majestic wild creatures," has stressed the allure of danger. All the time a big cat is kept in its cage, prevented from exercising its natural bent, desire

keeps mounting up in it. "It keeps building up and building up, until the moment comes when he can express all this pent up explosive force in one murderous onslaught."[66] An enraged wild beast has tremendous power, is insensible to pain, and appears unimpressed with barriers.[67] But, quipping that "God protects fools and drunkards and sometimes wild animal trainers," Proske has written eloquently of his profession:

> Yes, I am sure there must be better ways to make a living. But this does not answer the question! How does a man come to be a wild animal trainer? Maybe he suffers from a lack of plain ordinary common sense. Or maybe it is vanity or exhibitionism, certainly a man does not put his face in a tiger's maw just to get a better view of the animal's tonsils. Then, too, there may be an actual chemical need, in some people, for the drug we call danger, the sensation of fear. I know in my own case that after moments of the greatest danger—when moments seemed hours and fear possessed me utterly—I have always felt delightfully refreshed. On the other hand when I retired from the steel arena after 40 years . . . and the shock of fear and danger was removed, I suffered as cruelly physically and mentally as any confirmed drug addict deprived of his narcotic.[68]

For Edward Hoagland it is all quite simple. Watching a trainer bring water to his biggest tiger and then, finishing, touch noses with him, appeals directly to his own memory. When he worked as a cageboy, he also finished his chores this way. "I still love crowds," he writes, "just as I still love

Jungleland Christmas party: Albert Fleet, Frank Phillips, Mel Koontz, Pat Anthony, Dick McGraw, Arky Scott. (Front) Henry Tyndall, Steffanno Repetto.—*Picture Perfect*

Anthony walks a tiger.—*Picture Perfect*

Anthony would have one of the last major fighting acts featuring lions and tigers.—*Tom Henricks*

Pat Anthony.—*Tom Henricks*

tigers, and keep going back at convenient occasions to feel the breath of each: neither taste withers away with age."[69]

During the one hundred and fifty years in which the wild animal trainer has developed in America, scientists, psychologists, sociologists, and trainers themselves have attempted to explain why certain men can master the big cats while others cannot. Much is now understood about this but an element of mystery remains to pervade even the most recent literature on the subject. In the 1978 novel, *The Ringmaster*, a compound of science and folklore exists. Here an animal trainer, Rex Starback by name, loses control of a lion in his act and attempts to crawl out at the top of the arena. But "Old Dan," the lion grabs Starback, severely biting and clawing him. "Starback himself knew only that he had to have complete control or he had nothing but luck, and nobody's luck lasts forever. . . . It hurt beyond all imaginable pain. The scream twisted in his throat."[70]

Starback had been drawn to train lions in his teens and the big tawny cats had been his work and life. Determined to go back to the arena after the attack, he finds himself almost suffocated in his own fear when he next approaches the lion. When he reenters the ring his hand shakes so badly he cannot crack a whip or breathe freely, and his injured leg turns rigid. "There followed that long dark night that always follows the end of

something dear, when death ceases to be the enemy."[71] He begins to drink. Every alley cat he sees seems to mock him. Nightmares of lions chasing him rack his sleep. He reflects that lions are "never really mastered, only held at bay by some mysterious force. To work them required an unknown factor [he] never really understood. He knew when he had it, he knew when it was gone, but he never knew what it was. . . . Every good trainer knew he had it. Whatever it was it was easy to lose."[72] Ten years after the attack he is still unable to face the cats.

When Starback returns to the circus as a ringmaster after the long hiatus, he has the choice to observe a newly hired trainer who quickly demonstrates his ability to control animals. Clean, sober, a vegetarian who abstains from tobacco, he is of a newer generation. He fasts periodically, practices yoga and karate, chants, meditates, hypnotizes himself, and works toward attaining "astral projection." But even as his first season progresses, Starback can see—and he alone can see it—that the young trainer is falling victim to fear, "the most malignant of human forces."[73]

In an emergency, Starback reenters the arena to face the killer lion Hondo, son of "Old Dan." "Starback grabbed a prod and went into the arena. When Hondo repels Bobo he will come after me thought Starback, and oddly he was not afraid. . . . Hondo stood alone. For a moment he moved

One of the few Europeans to utilize the fighting style was Guy Gossing. — *Tom Henricks*

WALLACE TABER'S

FISHING • SHOOTING • BOATING

Safari

AUTHENTIC
WORLD-WIDE
ADVENTURE

JANUARY SAFARI 50¢

Larry

aimlessly about the arena. Starback stood still. . . . He watched the cat, who seemed oblivious to his presence and he discovered the simple secret that had eluded him all these years. There are never a trainer and several trained animals in the steel arena, he realized. There is only a pack of animals, and one of them must be dominant, the alpha animal."[74] The novel illustrates the compound of science and folklore, raw realism and mystery (some intentionally created and some imagined) that surrounds the wild animal trainer. Perhaps this pervasive aura has led to misunderstanding, distrust, and criticism of the motives and methods of trainers.

In 1932 Ernest Hemingway wrote: "It would be pleasant of course for those who do like it if those who do not would not feel they had to go to war against it or give money to try to suppress it since it offends them or does not please them, but that is too much to expect and anything capable of arousing passion in its favor will surely raise as much passion against it."[75] He was writing about bullfighting, but the statement could equally apply to the wild animal act. The performances arose near the end of an era in which audiences amused themselves by watching the running, baiting, or fighting of lions, bulls, bears, badgers, dogs, and cocks. In 1835, the first act against these blood sports was passed in England. Attacks on wild animal acts soon followed. Condemnation of these acts employed various themes, but the ecological and conservation-oriented assaults of the last decade are the most powerfully organized and probably will have the most lasting impact.

The rising social conscience of the nineteenth century caused artists to condemn wild animal exhibitions because they tended to debase man. For example, when French painters like Renoir, Degas,

Opposite page: "Jungle Larry" (Dr. Lawrence Tetzlaff) is a wild animal catcher, zoo operator, scientist, and wild animal trainer. He has been called the successor to Frank Buck. Today, Jungle Larry operates his own park in Florida during the winter and in the summer has the "Circus Africa" display at the major Ohio amusement park, Cedar Point. Reminiscent of the turn-of-the-century displays at Coney Island, Tetzlaff and his fellow animal trainers present a diversity of wild animal acts throughout the day. The illustration is the cover of the January 1961 issue of *Safari Magazine.*

and Toulouse-Lautrec treated the circus theme it was to protest employing people without house or home and compelling them as a condition of employment to play with their lives night after night before unappreciative audiences. The performer is without identity and without defense against the materialistic forces that surround him. He represents the tragedy of separateness and of being cut off from society.[76] English writers also found the circus a promising theme for social reform. An 1877 article, "The History of an 'African Lion Tamer'" is an example of the sympathy-evoking literature often associated with the Victorian era. In it, readers learn of a certain John Carter, who was born in Dublin in 1845. (The story must be that of Macarthy who replaced the black trainer Macomo in 1870 and was killed at Bolton in 1872. He died almost immediately upon his removal to a local infirmary and did not linger on interminably.) His parents were wealthy and he received a good education. But his wild conduct led to banishment from his father's house. After wandering through Dublin, cold and wet, he acquired a job as a general worker with a traveling menagerie. His duties as a cageboy were menial but he enjoyed the excitement of travel and crowds. Eventually he rose to head keeper, married, and occasionally he ventured into the lions' den. The trainer was an African named Manto, described as courageous and strong, but also a drinker, who mistreated the animals when he was intoxicated.

When Manto became sick and died, Carter was offered the trainer's job at a salary of thirty pounds per week, far better than the two he was then receiving. The idea horrified his wife, but Carter darkened his skin and appeared as "Tonanti, the African Lion King." He dismissed the grisly thoughts that crossed his mind when "the proprietor took me by the hand, and conducted me to his private room; asked me how I felt, and told me not to be timid. . . . He laughed and joked as he handed me a loaded revolver, to place in my belt, a sword to fix by my side, and a whip to dangle in my hand."[77] As a last measure the owner gave him a glass of grog. Carter's debut was successful, "I made them jump through hoops, crouch at my feet; I slashed them with my whip, fired a blank shot among them, and retired perfectly safe, amid the acclamations of the beholders."[78]

Carter wanted to quit after the first performance, but the proprietor would not allow him. "What cared he whether I was killed or not, so that

David Teztlaff (*above and opposite*) at Circus Africa in Cedar Point, Ohio, carrying on in the footsteps of his father, "Jungle Larry".

he made money."[79] By the time of his sixth appearance, the new trainer had become hardened. Thereafter, for several years he worked the beasts and convinced himself he was born for the job. He laughed at fear, but he also drank heavily. Then the inevitable occurred and Carter was attacked. "Such confusion arose, that a stampede out of the house took place, while I vainly called for hot irons. After a while the keeper brought them, and they were applied to the teeth of the ferocious animal. Shots were fired, and just as I was sinking from loss of blood, she let go my arm, and I was pulled out."[80]

Six months later, "Tonanti" returned to his act, minus an arm. His wife, who was pregnant at the time of the attack, had miscarried and died. Carter hoped to save enough money to buy a cottage in the country and retire with his little daughter. But on the third night, as he put the cats through their paces, he slipped and fell. "Oh horror! my old foe, the lioness was on top of me." The audience shrieked, as the handicapped tamer, unable to fight off the beasts, was dragged from side to side by four ferocious cats. From the audience came the scream of his little daughter, Jenny: "Oh, save my poor father! save him!"[81]

He awoke in the hospital, with every limb bandaged, and for nine weeks suffered without rest or peace. He would have gone mad except for constant opiates. Although nurses encouraged him, he knew he could never recover, since half his body had been torn away. Finally he prayed for death, seeing himself a sacrifice to vain and frivolous curiosity. His father never knew that his "darling boy, in whom he placed all his hopes and joys" had become a lion tamer.[82] With his last gasp he lamented the "fate that drove him from his father's door and urged him to take up with the hazardous and cruel practices of 'lion taming' . . . he was born for better things, but chance, and perhaps an acquired love of popular applause, led him on through a perilous profession, which cost him his life."[83]

But this type of criticism in which the circus performer is seen as the tragic victim of a debased society was relatively short-lived. Instead circus people began to be seen as nonmaterialistic free spirits. Germans, first laughingly and then seriously, called these performers *Himmelreicher*—high fliers. It contains a triple pun: *Himmelreich* means the kingdom of heaven, *reicher* is one who reaches, but also one who is rich. Painters like Seurat, Bonard, Beckmann, Ernst, and Kirchner treat cir-

cus people "as if they were the last manifestations of the angelic spirit on earth since they are compelled to overcome the limitations of the world and its gravity by an almost religious asceticism and by their cheerful familiarity with death and what lies beyond." Picasso, too, found the circus motif as an expression of "a spiritual hope in something as yet unrealized." The treatment of the circus symbol by artists is an appreciation that performers have been able to overcome the destructive impact of the machine age.[84] This same feeling of superiority is reflected by the attitudes of the British performers in *Luke's Circus* (1940) who derisively call noncircus people "flatties":

Folk with a narrer look in their eyeballs, and narrer thoughts in their nuts; folks what dursen't live to-day for fear of what's coming tomorrer; folk what worrit themselves sick over the things their neighbors may say of 'em; folk what would

Star wild animal trainer at Circus World in Orlando, Florida, is David McMillan and his Flying Tiger act. His act features 16 Royal Bengal and Siberian tigers, an African lion and a black panther. The act derives its name from the cats' spectacular jumps. The animals also play leapfrog and drink milk from a baby bottle. The trainer rides on the back of the lion, has a black panther jump 20 feet into his arms, and sticks his head into a tiger's mouth.

Born in Liverpool, England, McMillan joined his first circus at the age of 14. Later he became an assistant to Gunther Gebel-Williams and accompanied him to America. The young Englishman reportedly left the circus when Gebel-Williams' son was born, believing he had little chance to be the trainer's successor. After a difficult period of searching for work as a trainer, he found a position at a California amusement park. From that time on his act rose quickly in demand and he travelled to New Jersey where he appeared at Great Adventure in Jackson and Resorts International in Atlantic City. His act features a great deal of close contact including the kissing and hugging of his cats. – *Circus World, Inc.*

sooner have their bodies clean than use 'em; folk what would sooner be ordinary than different, folk what prefer a feather bed for their old age above freedom for their youth, folk what walk with their pigeon toes in a rut, squinting at their troubles, folk what wish to live their lives over again and live 'em diferent, folk what envy those as ain't made like 'em, folk what has to be amused by circus workers such as because they're too darn silly to amuse themselves.[85]

But this did not mean that critical attention was withdrawn from the circus or wild animal acts. Instead it was simply redirected to cruelty to the wild animals themselves. Again England was in the forefront. The first protective legislation was passed in 1822 with the Ill-Treatment of Horses Act. In 1840, the Royal Society for the Prevention of Cruelty to Animals was officially founded with stress on education and propaganda.

An African adventurer wrote in a British magazine in 1867 that "be the lion what he may, he will not and does not treat man so barbarous as he is treated by man. They have all the affection and fidelity of the dog, if well treated but they will try before they trust." The lion, he wrote, will not injure man until he has been injured, or "known some of his race to be injured by man. . . . I have never found it difficult to render lions 'tame' . . . not only without injury to myself from them, but with a perfect confidence that they would suffer none to harm me," even when approached in their own habitat and at full strength. "I have no reverence for the dastardly arts of showmen, or 'lion kings' and I can conscientiously say, I found lions far less brutal than the men who hunt them."[86]

In 1873, Van Amburgh, although dead for eight years, came under attack in *Gentleman's Magazine.* Called very stupid, ignorant, and totally devoid of wit, the trainer, according to the author, had gained his success by declawing his animals. The writer, who had befriended the American in Paris, kept his word and did not disclose "the excruciating process, the refined agony, and despicable cowardice by which Van Amburgh made himself a Lion King!" until after the showman's death.[87]

Despite this type of criticism of wild animal performances, limited legal success was not achieved until 1900 with the Cruelty to Wild Animals in Captivity Law that imposed a ban on abusing, infuriating, or teasing an animal in close confinement or when pinioned or restrained. The Performing Animals Regulation Act that required the registration of trainers and allowed local authorities to send officials into training quarters was passed in 1925. It was preceded, however, by the Performing Animals Defence League (founded in 1914), which like the Jack London Societies later in America, encouraged the public to pledge themselves to walk out of places of entertainment showing animal acts.

The American humane movement began somewhat later with New York passing the first humane treatment of horses law in 1866.[88] The American Humane Association was founded eleven years later in 1877. The initial federal laws passed in 1873 and then amended in 1906 dealt with the feeding, watering, and resting of animals in transit by rail or ship. Fifty-two years elapsed before the next act—The Humane Slaughter Act. Not until the Animal Welfare Act of 1970 were circus, carnival, and zoo animals given any federal protection. This law plus the later Marine Mammal Protection Act and the Endangered Species Act are also supplemented by state standards for the maintenance of wild animals within their jurisdictions.[89] Since 1954 a number of powerful organizations that make up the "Kingdom of the Kind" have been founded: The Humane Society of the United States (1954), Friends of Animals (1957), the Fund for Animals (1967), and the recently organized radical Defenders of Wildlife.[90] International protection movements have met with limited success, although both the Marine Mammals and Endangered Species acts formally encourage worldwide cooperation. One of the first proposals was made at the Hague, Netherlands, in 1950 where the World Congress for Animal Protection proposed a Bill of Rights for Animals that would ban animal performances in circuses and severely limit zoos for scientific purposes only.[91]

The most recent position of the Humane Society of the United States is that animal abuse is "inherent in the nature of circus life. HSUS, therefore, opposes animal acts in circuses, not as a response to isolated incidents of blatant animal abuse but to those conditions, which of necessity exist in all circuses, that prevent even the simulation of a natural or comfortable environment for animals."[92] The problems are especially severe, they contend, with wild animals found in circuses, as opposed to the more adaptable performing domestic animals. Trainers, unless they presented acts featuring animals in unnatural behaviors (riding bicycles or motorcycles, wearing clothes, etc.) were not condemned as vicious brutes. The Society

This page and opposite: Clyde Beatty–Cole Bros. Circus cageboys and assistants at work.

even admits that many animals seem to enjoy training. But the HSUS insists that even if the USDA regulations enumerated in the Animal Welfare Act were rigidly enforced, the ethical question of "quality of life" for these circus animals would still exist. "It is this fact which cements our opposition to wild animal acts in circuses. Realizing that eliminating animal acts is a long term goal, we will continue to push for better enforcement of federal regulations and any other type of improvement that would bring immediate relief to these animals. But we will also work for the day when no wild animals perform under the big top."[93]

A typical modern proponent of animal protection is Phillipe Diole, the scientific and literary associate of Jacques Cousteau, who urges in *The Errant Ark* (1974) a genuine respect for the needs of animals and less haphazard protection. Diole maintains that confining animals for purposes of display is not the beginning of closeness between man and animal, but the start of their separation instead. Animals in captivity, he writes, are a constant prey to psychological imbalance, sexual disorders, and disequilibrium. They are psychologically demolished by being unable to flee from man. While some curators hope to alleviate the devastating effects of captivity by training, Diole dismisses this plan as just another form of servitude and degradation. It is his fear that eventually only those animals that have been domesticated or imprisoned will remain, and these he believes, will have been perverted, altered by controlled reproduction.[94] Men may "protect" animals, therefore, but only for their own sake. Diole argues that man needs animals to bear the brunt of his own hostilities and frustrations; he wants them as victims of the violence and rage which his inhibitions prevent him from unleashing at their proper targets.[95]

Following Diole, the public first became really infatuated with trained wild animals, especially the big cats, on a wide scale during the last thirty

Pat Anthony.

Cuneo's rare performing white tigers.

years of the nineteenth century. Trainers touched these great predators, stroked and caressed them in an exercise of an art which flourished two thousand years before and had been forgotten. The author questioned the purpose of the renewed contact and man's intuitive skill to handle animals. He said animal training was not a resumption of the natural relationship between man and animal but instead an affiliation that Edmond Jaloux believed "teetered on the brink of the absurd. . . . No animal is ridiculous except when man obliges it to be ridiculous."[96]

Even as vehement a critic as Diole admitted some value in animal acts since they served "to establish a certain familiarity—however violated it may be—between man and animal." He was impressed by the "utter confidence" early trainers showed in their animals, as these beasts were reportedly completely intractable. Wild animal training, he contends, is the result of a sympathy with the beast and two peculiarities of man: his upright stance and his voice. As long as man stands upright and confronts an animal, he has a chance of

mastering it. Their basic sympathy enabled them to demonstrate the intelligence of the lion and to show the beast's memory and reasoning ability could be used to teach the animal to perform.[97] The lion, in particular, has a special relationship to man, since it has always been an object of human terror and awe. Since the lion is assumed not to know the meaning of fear, it has been an undoubted act of bravery and courage to face a lion. Man, Diole believes, has always needed wild beasts to fortify his self-esteem, because it was not always certain that man would prevail in the conflict between man and beasts.[98]

A far less emotional appeal for conservation is offered by Bryce Rensberger, science writer for the *New York Times*. He discusses man's pervasive, though often unwitting, inclination to misunderstand animals in *The Cult of the Wild* (1978). It has become increasingly fashionable for people to argue that "it is man who is the savage beast, that the animals are quite humane," he writes.[99] Our misunderstandings have also led to disastrous consequences for some of the more persecuted wild

George Barrada and his lions.

species that fail to stack up to our pure and noble ideal of animal life, for example wolves and hyenas. Even conservationists have been unfortunately influenced by the moral classification of "good" and "bad" animals. Recently ecologists have become interested in the importance of all forms of wildlife, but even they still believe one "bad" animal exists—man.

Most of man's feelings about animals grew from his early experiences as a hunter. His study of animals' habits led to his observations of obvious similarities between himself and beasts. It became easy to project human qualities to animals (anthropomorphism). Taken a step further, human values were attributed to animals. The idea of animal values led to a belief that revenge became the driving motive of the hunted beasts' surviving kin. To atone for the sin of killing animals, man made the creatures objects of veneration and homage. This animal appeasement tradition has found its way into the present day conservation movement. The idea persists in those who fear that if we meddle

too much in the animal kingdom, some dire ecological catastrophe will befall mankind.

As man moved from a hunting to an agricultural and urban society, a process of alienation from wild animals began and pushed man's attitude toward the beasts further into the realm of fantasy and conjecture. Rensberger writes that the long process of alienation of Western industrialized man from wildlife has gone about as far as it can. It has resulted in the so-called "Bambi complex" which is often accompanied by a potentially dangerous loss of respect for wild animals. The author hopes that man can put away this impoverished view of nature and come to recognize that "man is also a part of nature and that there really never was any such thing as a constant or untouched wilderness."[100]

Since the rank and file of the conservation movement are largely urban, they actively preserve their idealized views of how people should relate to animals. Rensberger calls the new form of wildlife appreciation the "cult of the endangered

Eddie Schmidt's tigers.

species," in which these specific animals become the most valued. He writes that we must put away these childish attitudes if wildlife is to be conserved. Reasons for conservation today fall into three broad categories: ecological reasons, aesthetic grounds, and economic factors. Included in the aesthetic argument is the "desire to get back to nature." This reason is also the most intangible of the points since it is shaped by culture. Most American and European urban dwellers now want what remains of the wild animals and their wilderness to stay the way we like to think of them.[101]

The economic motive simply means that wild animals must pay for themselves—the conservation of animals must be more economically attractive than any alternate use of the animals or the natural land. One way they can pay is through tourism, the other is the harvesting and selling of animal products. The latter idea, Rensberger admits, is extremely repugnant to urban conservationists.

Even though zoo animals are not considered "whole" because they lack natural behavior, the zoo can still be a valuable gene bank. Those species that are able to breed in captivity, but are threatened or already extinct in the wild can be kept alive until there is some opportunity to reestablish a free-living population. Up to the time an economically feasible plan is devised to preserve ecosystems in the various biosphere zones, carefully supervised zoo and circus breeding programs can give valuable time to endangered species.[102]

So far, the views Diole expresses have found more emphatic support among various wildlife organizations since they allege cruelty in caging animals and accuse trainers of materialistic self-interest. Stressing a need for natural conservation, and having strong financial backing, they have influenced legislation dealing with wild animals. While many of the laws they have backed are excellent, some, for example those relating to the sales and trading of endangered species, may do more harm than good to the wildlife they seek to protect, by discouraging the breeding of rare animals.

Conservationists and reformers have not been alone in complaining about wild animal acts. Circus historians such as Chindahl have also questioned these performances though they have usually directed their criticisms at certain types of acts. Murray's 1956 circus history reported that Americans like the playing up of danger and the spectacular demonstrations of mock ferocity in the animal acts they watch. Beatty, he writes, drew "immense audiences" because of his "carefully exaggerated atmosphere of sound and fury." Like Van Amburgh, Beatty gave the crowd "ample opportunity to indulge its sadistic instincts."[103] But this criticism had been ably answered years before by a Cleveland drama critic, William F. McDermott, who pointed out that the circus is the primitive essence of the drama. It is make-believe in its purest form and quite unashamedly acknowledges that people like to be fooled. What Eugene O'Neill offered in a sophisticated way, the circus offers in simplicity; people rejoice in believing life is stranger and more wonderful than it really is. Of Clyde Beatty's act, he commented that it was genuinely exciting. The wicked scars left on his arms and chest by enraged lions and tigers proved that his performance in a cage of mixed wild animals was really dangerous. But, he added, it was not as dangerous as he made it seem. He had to coax the lions to roar and plead with the tigers to make passes at him. Some of the animals roared and leapt only out of a desire to please the trainer when they obviously prefer to lie down and take a nap. But the circus audience wanted to believe these roaring beasts were thirsting for blood and ready to spring, and Beatty succeeded in giving them what they wanted. "Beatty," McDermott wrote, "is the best of the showmen among the animal trainers. With the greatest grace and skill he tantalizes the spectators with the risks of his life amid beasts of the jungle and causes the circus leopard and the lion to seem more ferocious than the wild beasts of the Roman Coliseum." This make-believe, subconsciously understood as such by audiences, distinguished the circus and "explains the secret of its charm for children and the children that all men are."[104]

According to Jimmy Chipperfield, if the nature of a lion's personality was understood, then nothing cruel could be read into a fighting act. A lion is an extrovert, he argues, and he loves rough and tumble. "In making him swipe at you, you are teasing him, but in a way that he understands and en-

joys. Far from being cruel, you're having a game with him, and he is with you."[105] The big cats know they are part of an act and they enjoy it, as their willingness to breed and good appearance indicate. There is no way to disguise anxiety, for it would show up in the animal's physical condition.[106]

Recently, the American Museum of Natural History published a work that agrees that the seeming harshness of the "untamable act" is sheer histrionics, a carefully prepared performance based on a profound knowledge of animal psychology. Hermann Dembeck, the author, notes that the cats have been taught to snarl, strike out, and appear unmanageable, so that animal acts should be appreciated as dramatic demonstrations in animal psychology. They should, he suggests, increase our respect for animal intelligence.[107]

Critics of wild animal acts tend to be far more influential than advocates. Nationally known celebrities speak out on electronic media against wildlife abuse and in favor of conservation. Like the whaler, who was once a folk hero and symbol of New England hardiness, the wild animal trainer suffers a tarnished image. While he does not decimate beasts, he does cage and commercialize them. Since the proponents of wild animal acts are those who benefit the most from them, either financially or in personal enjoyment, their arguments, no matter how accurate and realistic, tend to lose credence.

One of the earliest defenses against the charge that caging animals was cruel to them was advanced by Dr. William T. Hornaday, first director of the New York Zoological Society, in 1906. "In the matter of disposition, wild animals and birds are no more angelic than human beings. In every family, in every herd and in every cage, from tigers to doves, the strong bully and oppress the weak and drive them to the wall." The director continued: "The virtues of the higher animals have been extolled unduly and their intelligence has been magnified about ten diameters. The meannesses and cruelties of wild animals toward one another form a long series of chapters which have not yet been written and which no lover of animals cares to write."[108] Ellen Velvin added that "evil passions"—anger, jealousy, greediness—exist in animals in great intensity. Lions, she claimed, could work themselves up into frenzies of rage through jealousy, especially of a newcomer, and tigers, leopards, and jaguars were characteristically

Left and below: Karoly Donnert's tigers on the
RBB&B Monte Carlo unit.

sly, cunning, and treacherous.[109]

More than sixty years later, a study of the cats of Africa revealed that food and sex interest lions most, and if the number one male is deterred in any way from the speedy attainment of either, there is an instant and occasionally fatal retaliation. In nature, lion society, like any communal animal society, is based directly on force or the threat of it. "The lion's share" is no idle phrase. It has a real and terrible meaning, deriving from the belief held by all lions that the shortest distance between desire and realization is a straight line. Edey, in the *Cats of Africa* (1968), writes that the basic philosophy of the lion is: "You want something—you go directly for it. The only thing that can stop you is something larger or more dangerous than you."[110] The leopard, Edey says, is the quintessential cat, secretive, quiet, agile, and the nearest thing to an animated steel spring that exists. Leopards usually kill with a lethal bite in the throat or neck. They like warm blood and they lap it up first, as long as it flows. They live strictly for themselves. If cruelty means to kill or injure for one's own amusement then only one cruel animal exists, and that is man. Yet the leopard is so remote, so cold, so implacable, observers find it difficult to label him. As a mankiller, he is efficiency incarnate.[111]

While this set of arguments derives from the nature of wild animals, a second attacks the hypocrisy of reformers. Clyde Beatty provides a good example of this in his first book where he wrote:

> My lions and tigers are better cared for, in captivity, than they could possibly be in their native jungle. They will live much longer than their average jungle brother. There is no roughness in the handling of them, except when it is necessary to use emergency measures to protect them or to protect the people around them.
>
> Some of the "humane" reformers don't realize this. Some of them are blind unreasoning fanatics who, in their zeal to tell their own story, are unwilling to listen to anybody else's. They are ignorant, and —worse still—ignorant of their own ignorance. They lack the saving grace of tolerance. Such "reformers" should develop a capacity for listening to the other fellow's story. Perhaps they might even start their editing of the human race by improving themselves.[112]

Other writers, who agree with Beatty, admit that when wild animal acts began, a lack of understanding did result in cruelty. When an animal inflicted a wound on a trainer, it was repaid a hun-

dredfold to show the wretched beast who was master. But since this course sometimes resulted in bringing animals to realize they possessed more strength than man, and since the result of that was always bad for both tamer and beast, that kind of activity was long since dropped by experienced professionals. Now an animal who wounds his trainer is never punished. In fact, the man makes every effort not to let the big cat see the extent of the damage. This is based on two principles: first, the injury might have been inflicted in play or by accident—though even in anger the animal can scarcely be judged by human standards, and second, the big cat should never be allowed to know its power.[113] The argument is also made that, although there may still be cruel trainers today, there are criminally negligent people in every profession. They may be found, for instance, as nurses, teachers, or clergymen. Child abuse exists, but all parents are not stigmatized as perverts. British circus historian Anthony Coxe concludes, "The 'antis' are a group of people too hysterical to be rational and too bigoted to learn, who state categorically that no animal can be trained to work under professional conditions by kindness." Any article complimentary to wild animal trainers, he declares, is immediately condemned as completely misguided.[114] Many other kinds of animal trainers outside the circus can be cruel, yet hunting and show dog trainers or horse breakers and trainers are never subject to the rabid criticism leveled against wild animal trainers. While people complain about the unnatural, commercial, and alien atmosphere of the circus, almost none find morally reprehensible the life of a race horse. In fact, it is extremely improbable that a race horse owner will ever be visited by an ASPCA inspector unless strong evidence of cruelty or suspected cruelty is given, but the circus trainer must always be open to inspection. Again it is argued that millions of sheep, pigs, and cattle raised in the most unnatural conditions are routinely slaughtered every day.

There is a third set of arguments for training too, one advanced usually by zoo directors and naturalists. It is probably the most scientific and rational. Zoo men differ of course, often violently, on the virtue of circuslike performances for some animal acts are incongruous where simulation of a natural setting is the goal. Others ask if it is better to have a listless, neurotic animal weaving back and forth than one that enters into a circus act

RBB&B Red Unit tigers unload (1980).

with unmistakable enjoyment. Again, Hediger's work is instructive.

Because of anthropomorphism, the idea of animals in captivity arouses sympathy. Famous prisoners are brought to mind, victimized men and women, pacing their cells, longing for a freedom they really deserve. (Recent field studies by Kruuk and Schaller indicate that the lion in the wilds spends between twenty and twenty-one hours a day sleeping or resting, virtually the same behavior seen in captivity.) The comparison is based on the belief that wild animals in nature are free and able to range at will over wide areas. In fact, nothing is further from the truth. Territories are restricted with psychological factors acting as powerful restraints, so that animals are spatially bound to conquered territory which they mark and defend. As early as 1909, Ernest Thompson Seton wrote: "No wild animal roams at random over the country," because as he knew, "territory is divided into definite beats."[115]

Confinement does mean the prevention of encounter with enemies and, of course, limitation of territory. The cage restricts the animal's attempts to get away **from something** (flight reaction). It does not prevent its getting away **to somewhere.** The newly captured animal attempts to escape because the cage has sinister significance reminiscent of its enemy, man.[116] Escapes occur because "overexcitement weakens all barriers."[117] The escaped animal is not a dangerous criminal, it is a beast exhibiting its natural flight reaction. It wants to put a safe distance between itself and man. The real danger of an escaped lion, for example, is not that it wants to devour the first man it meets. It is the release in the lion of its defense reaction and the critical reaction aroused by men closing in on it. There is a change from flight to defense.

Terror, caused by some unusual condition, motivates most escapes. This is why the big carnivores are caged for their performances: the behavior of

RBB&B lion act presented by Jewell New.

the public is usually far less predictable than that of animals.[118]

A good example of this occurred in 1950, when a leopard disappeared from a twenty-foot-deep pit in the Oklahoma City Zoo. Residents fled from the surrounding suburbs and sixty men with big game rifles stalked the beast. The cat was called "greased lightning," and it was said it would kill for the sheer sake of killing.[119] The following day planes brought in troops who burned the brush in the vicinity to flush the leopard from cover. Damoo Dhotre and Clyde Beatty were called and consulted, and both of them recommended tying a live goat in a portable cage. If the leopard was in the vicinity, they argued, it would find the goat to be an irresistible temptation.[120] Their advice went unheeded. When no one was able to find the leopard, Beatty told the authorities that it had probably never escaped at all but was simply hiding in a recess or niche. Drugged meat was thrown into the pit to test Beatty's theory and when the leopard appeared and consumed it, it died of a drug overdose. Officials contended the hungry cat had leaped back into the pit, but Beatty said: "He was right where I said he was all the time. Why would he make a terrific leap to get out of the cage and then turn around and jump back into it? If he had wanted meat he could have killed an animal on the outside. . . . I personally think the leopard was killed needlessly."[121]

By definition a wild animal has developed without the help or interference of man. Wildness means neither bloodthirstiness nor lust for killing, but flight tendency. The tamed wild animal has no flight tendency—unlike the newly captured animal it has become emotionally stable. When an animal becomes adapted to captivity, it means the original tension caused by the presence of man has been reduced, and the animal is willing to take sufficient food, undeterred by the presence of man. Training has been defined as "special treatment of an animal with continuous use of favorable mental factors so as to produce certain actions at a particular personal command. These actions are natural to it, at least their elements are, but would never be released in freedom by the same stimuli or performed under the same conditions."[122] The tamed wild animal does not suffer from restraint and it is not in a chronic state of tension that causes it to hide whenever possible. Tameness is attractive, healthy, and expedient.[123] It is true that the animal can still suffer from a lack of occupation since its two leading drives—the avoidance of enemies and the seeking of food—have been rendered irrelevant. But Hediger points out that biologically suitable training, which involves the importance of occupational therapy, can provide a new interest in life for the animal. He writes: "Societies for the protection of animals would do far better to insist, where possible, on good, i.e., biologically suitable training; they should foster understanding of this in the widest circles rather than oppose blindly any training of wild animals on the basis of arguments that have long been completely untenable. Through their opposition to training animals they do them real disservice." Training has been called unnatural, but Hediger insists that since what he calls "natural captivity" would mean forcing animals constantly to avoid enemies and struggle for food, training in fact should be seen as closely corresponding to the sports and athletic competitions of civilized man. It aids the muscles and overcomes the complex changes that arise from captivity and domestication. It enriches animals and releases them from extreme or morbid fixation of attention. Finally, training is aesthetically pleasing, since the good trainer creates something out of the inimitable movements of the wild animal just as the artist does with his colors or the composer with his notes.[124]

The final argument is that of the circus owners themselves. Both emotional and rational, it alleges that the trained animal is healthier than its counterpart in the wilds, more docile than it would be in a zoo, and contented in its relationship with humans. Patient and kind, the trainer of today makes sure his animals are fed an excellent diet, kept clean, and provided comfortable quarters. He understands beasts and realizes that no two animals have exactly the same personality or intelligence. He communicates with them before each performance to determine their mood in order to know what he will have to cope with when he faces them, and afterwards too, in order to praise or rebuke them, depending on how they performed. Between animal and man there is mutual understanding and respect.[125]

"Our animals," write Irvin and Kenneth Feld, "are the healthiest, and I would venture to say, they are the happiest in the world." But the argument is more than academic. Federal and state legislation (often conflicting and confusing) has already raised the possibility that circus animals may be confiscated if various requirements are not satisfied. What is more, according to the Felds, endangered species laws make it very difficult for endangered species to be anything but endangered. The Ringling show could easily breed eight to ten tigers annually, they point out, but there is no place they could sell them or even give them away, and since each tiger costs five thousand dollars per year to feed maintaining extra cats is unrealistic. If laws become even more stringent than they are already, it will not be feasible to transport or show animals in the circus. "How would you like to take your kids to the show," the Felds ask, "and try to tell them how it used to be in the great acts. You wouldn't have a tiger act. There wouldn't be a bear act. There wouldn't be a chimp act. For us, it's unthinkable."[126]

The circus has served as a medium of communications and an instrument for presenting wonders from all over the world. It has brought wild animals from the deserts, plains, mountains, and jungles and displayed them to hinterland America, at a time when large metropolitan zoos could be counted on the fingers of one hand. Most important of all, the circus has been and remains a visual joy and an enrichment to the human spirit. "Children and adults leave a performance feeling themselves better people. They have seen fellow human beings do incredible, wonderful things—and realize that it is within their own reach to accomplish the seemingly impossible, and with grace and beauty."[127] While these words were written by circus owners, who since the beginning of circus hyperbole have had their credibility often called into question, yet in many ways their case is the most valid one. It links the wild animal acts of today to the original performances of almost a hundred fifty years ago. Even in an age of scientific marvels, the sight of a man caging himself with a group of great carnivores and controlling their actions, still makes an emotional impact on the audience. If today's trainer is more often typecast as a villain than a hero, it is a role he has successfully reversed before. It is to be hoped this quote will remain just as fresh in the future as it was in 1902.

> One might go on indefinitely, describing the life of the members of different companies of trained wild animals captured in the remotest corners of the world and brought together in the arena around which the public has always been eager to sit as in the days of old.
>
> The popularity of the animal show is not likely to diminish. When those of the younger generation of to-day are the fathers and grandfathers of to-morrow they will be taking little boys and girls to verify the alluring lithographic signboard promises, hear the hoarse brass band, and inhale the peculiar circus-smell, made up of the odor of wild animals, pungent sawdust, crushed hay and grass.[128]

EPILOGUE

Reminiscences of a Cat Man
by Roger Smith

Anyone, particularly non-Americans, who has not been written into history has but two choices: honor the man who has, or succumb to common jealousy and let it make a fool of you. These non-Americans and their current servitors now rely on the passage of time to strengthen their own roles while trying to detract from Beatty, who not only worked the big cats, but also the largest polar bear act, at fifteen animals.

Most notably among those who never had a chance to equal Beatty's career, the show-business jealousy, unfathomably deep and simmering in resentment, surfaces in bitterness which easily becomes vicious.

But one man attained great heights of his own, and, for a time, equalled Beatty in the size of his act. Terrell Jacobs, working fifty-two animals, drew legions of admirers and attracted another faction among the organized circus fans—those who yearned to enjoy a feud between him and Beatty. Beatty's fans encouraged him to slight Jacobs. Both men laughed them off and remained friends. To put an end to it all, Jacobs said publicly, "Clyde has done more to advance the animal training profession than any other man." Scorning pettiness, Jacobs' example is failed by others.

The difficulty in listening to these latter-day critics lies in knowledge of their most shameful secret. Almost every one of them has found it convenient to have their animals surgically altered. The great trainers would never have considered this crime against nature. Their pride was in being exceptional men and women in an extraordinary profession; it was unthinkable to deal with other

than the full beast. Today, it seems impossible for presenters to face such animals. The cowardice which leads to butchery of fine stock has also stained their status now beyond recovery, and yet they wish to diminish those who were honorable toward their animals.

I worked once with a man whom I liked and respected. When I learned he had declawed his lions, I took it up with him. He had not long before been severely attacked and had endured a difficult recovery. He stated his injuries as the reason for declawing his lions. I thought of reminding him of the others of us who had gone through the same thing and had left our animals intact—after all, we asked for opportunities to assume these risks, and obviously the animal did exactly what he was known to be capable of doing. But I could see he had been shattered by the accident, and I could not bring myself to chide the man; nevertheless, I lost respect for him when, before I left, he grinned and said, "Look, if these elegant hulligans are getting away with it, why shouldn't I?"

This reflects the attitude prevailing with the advent of the star European trainers of today and the spread of information inside the field that many of their tigers (later nearly all the leopards) were altered, and most of the males (if not all) gelded. Nature comes back hard on those who defy her and ignore propriety for the service of vanity. I do not wish to share their fate.

But Mabel Stark put it another way. Her lesson reflects her character and remains indelible in my mind. She had seen the lesson taught severely: "The Mills of the Gods grind slowly . . . but he

Roger Smith. A low bounce from Congo as Benny
Bennett (the man in the hat who taught and safe-
guarded us all) and Dick McGraw look on. — *Roger
Smith Collection*

who does dirt with animals is grist for the Mills."

You asked for insights to Clyde Beatty. I had for-
tunate moments with him for one who wanted to
know the man as well as the legend. Within my
first week in his employ, I had graduated to the
tunnel door and, best of all, to driving his car and
trailer. From the door, with instructions to watch
him while he watched the cats, I had the best van-
tage point from which to study his style. It was
here I learned the fine points of managing mixed

animals in the arena. (But that's another story.) As
his chauffeur, typist, and cageman, I saw him
when others did not. Luckily for me, he was an
impatient driver and liked to be driven wherever
he went, although he sometimes surprised me and
took the wheel himself, humming cheerfully to
himself and driving at breakneck speeds. So it was
that I knew firsthand where he went and what he
did. And wherever or whatever it was, being the
kind of man he was, he always included me in his
plans as a startled and grateful companion.

Beatty had been to doctors in Philadelphia, as
he even noted in *Facing the Big Cats*, ironically.

Roger Smith's
Career Chronology

1960-1964*: Small zoos in Texas. Trainer: lions, tiger, leopards, pumas. Single animals, and pairs.

1964: Clyde Beatty-Cole Bros. Circus. Animal Attendant, Tunnel Doorman, Chauffeur to Clyde Beatty.

1965-1969: Jungleland Wild Animal Compound. Trainer: lion act, tiger act. Assistant to Mabel Stark and Dick McGraw. Assistant Caretaker and Meatcutter to Benny Bennett.

Toured Jungleland Fighting Lions on West Coast routes as follows:
1967 — James Bros. Circus
1967 — Kay Bros. Circus with Dick McGraw
1968 — James Bros. Circus
1969 — James Bros. Circus
1969 — Miller-Johnson Circus

1972-1973: Hubert Castle International Circus. Trainer: mixed lions and tigers.

1975: Clyde Bros. Circus. Trainer: tigers, elephants.

1976: Texas Lion Country Safari. Senior Ranger, Lion Section.

1980: Clyde Beatty-Cole Bros. Circus. Superintendent of Wild Animals. Assistant and Back-up Man to Dave Hoover. Winter Tour only.

1981: Clyde Beatty-Cole Bros. Circus. As
** above. Full canvas tour.

*People who let me in with the cats, while I was under age, still work in Texas zoos, none of which have training programs. To list them even now would jeopardize certain careers.
**Years not listed indicate those free-lancing, working only spot contracts. Includes those periods at liberty.

They had arrived at indeterminate diagnoses, and he seemed to me quite well. I remember then he was, to me, a man of vigorous health, a real man's man, with full and hearty appetites, who enjoyed vivid interests in life and had a great sense of fun. He disdained hunting but was an avid fisherman who never missed a chance to wet a lure. Deep-sea fishing was an obsession with him. He loved to wager, and he placed bets on every sporting event he knew of; he loved to go to the tracks and was very well-known in Vegas. That summer, he had read Ovid Demaris' *The Green Felt Jungle*, an exposé of the casino life, and wondered aloud how he, among the many written of, missed being included among the listed high-rollers.

In public, Beatty was quiet and gracious; he never drew attention to himself, waited in turn for service and was polite with his hosts. I have been with him in little diners along the road, barber shops, hotel dining rooms, and neighborhood bars where he liked to sip V.O. and soda and enjoy his Friday night fights. If he enjoyed his fame, he seemed more comfortable remaining unrecognized in public and never sought special treatment.

I used to enjoy watching him eat. It was a ritual in those small roadside diners: he invariably ordered a bowl of hot soup (almost any kind) and a hamburger—plain bun, not toasted, and a slice of raw onion—accompanied by coffee with a touch of cream. He felt lucky when he found a place with good Mississippi River catfish and ate generously of this favorite. The fun in sharing these pleasures with him was that each of them seemed to him a happy adventure. He was one of those special people who knew how to live and relished living.

Many today argue that Beatty was a poor businessman whose unfortunate decisions led his ownership of the show to a premature end, while others reason that if he faulted it was due to taking bad advice, at times by those bent on ruining the show, some of whom were around most conspicuously in 1956. However, Beatty was scarcely so inept as critics would like to believe. We see now that it was his circus corporation which fell into bankruptcy, and not Beatty himself. He had been sufficiently astute to salt away an important personal fortune, and wise enough not to put it into his circus during the fateful year of 1956. Circus insiders told me in 1970 that when Beatty died he left Jane and Clyde, Jr. two million dollars. I cannot substantiate the figure but find it well within possibility.

I know that Beatty liked a cold bottle of Michelob. In public, I never saw him order more than one drink. On a circus lot, if you drink, everyone knows it, talks it up, and you become another circus lush—specifically, another drunken cat trainer. When I knew him, Beatty handled his drink like a man.

Two stories come readily to mind in regard to his heirs. Beatty never encouraged Clyde, Jr. The lad, then twelve, showed little interest in the show other than joining the other kids in bouncing on the trampoline and playing baseball. In fact, it was he who taught me how to properly toss up a baseball and hit it to him in the field. Beatty liked me to spend time with the boy and told me he was glad to see us become friends. Clydie's desire then was to play professional baseball, and he shared a passion for the game with his Dad. But one night in the Cadillac on an overnight jump the boy asked Beatty how he told his lions apart and how he recognized the different tigers. Beatty replied, "Oh, gee, Clydie. They're as different as night and day." And with that, the subject was dropped. We know that Beatty also objected to his granddaughter's participation in the local circus activities in

Peru, arguing that "one Beatty in this business is enough."

The profession is too tough—too much about it cannot be taught. Enduring animal attacks and returning to work, living with the daily hardships of the profession, and making many difficult personal sacrifices with home and family while meeting the dictates of lives like ours are commitments you must be prepared to make at the beginning. To belabor an old phrase, we are either born that way, or we are not.

That Beatty could break and train is a matter of record. He took over a lot of stock in those early years, but, as he said, "We had to know how to train cats on those Corporation shows, or you didn't last long." There were too many willing to come on and take over an act—usually attractive to the owners because of a cheaper price on the payroll—but those who lasted were valuable because of one thing: animal training capacity. Beatty knew what to do to keep others disinterested in trying to supplant him. He created the most dangerous acts of his time. Hopeful usurpers let him be.

"Beatty never trained those cats" became a catch phrase when he assembled the Big Act of 1935. He honestly wrote of buying animals from zoos, circuses, and other acts for the act he agreed to have ready for Spring. Far more was demanded of Beatty here than if he had broken out all new, green cats for an act of such expansive ambition. The job he did then, which no one has ever touched, was to mix mature, veteran animals on a grand scale, maintain order, and open on time with a presentable act. I am well within certainty to state that his accomplishment will remain singular.

The fact was never hidden that many others were hired to train animals for Beatty's act. Here, we are required to look closely at who these people were, and then to examine who Beatty was. The hired trainers were technically capable men. If they could break and train, so could Beatty, but the difference is this: minus the trappings of fame and stardom, these fellows were free to train animals during their working day; Beatty, in an entirely different world than theirs, was much in demand in the off-season. Many winters found him busy with collaborators on his books, being constantly asked for interviews, making countless personal appearances, working in films, or running

Mabel Stark, with part of her six-tiger pyramid; behind Mabel is her ten-animal cage line. —*Kathy Wheeler; Roger Smith Collection*

the three different zoo operations he had at various times. Often, he went on long vacations weeks at a time (since he could well afford it) and took off deep-sea fishing. The repetitive chores of training were left to those who wanted the work (and took some pride in saying, "I broke those for Beatty") and who had no celebrity attached to their burden. But another fact that is not often mentioned is the knowledge that it was Beatty who returned to Winterquarters and mixed in the new stock with his older animals. This mixing, and the polish he then added to the revised routine, was the hardest part of the job. Others could not do the mixing as they did not know Beatty's veterans as well as he did.

Once, in 1964, he was breaking his last two cats, two young tigresses named Tiny and Judy. He turned in Sultan, a lion who sat high on the back pyramid wall, and then signalled for the tigresses. He seated them, checked the lion, moved the new additions about the arena to their second seats, and soon sent them out. As he exited the Big Top, he said, casually, "They're okay. We can put those two in tonight." They had not yet been fully exposed to the other animals, and I was fearful of their safety. But Beatty had read them right, and there was no incident.

[Regarding correspondence between Smith and Beatty] consider that here is a man famous to three generations, a living legend, taking time to sit down and write to a hopeful cageboy he didn't know—and twice in his own hand. What he wrote reveals very human qualities about the man.

Beatty told me of his deep regret that he did not have more formal education. He hated typing, calling his method the "hunt and peck system," and those chores fell to me. So we look beyond the diamond-in-the-rough aspects of his letters and involve our study with the thoughts he had as he wrote them.

In the letter of February 21st, he refers to the March 8th date we had set to talk.

> I recently returned home to find both your letters here, and am quite interested in your brochure which showed me you give considerable thought to what you do. . . . I'm leaving here next Sunday, March 1st, and will be at our circus winterquarters in DeLand, Florida (Fairgrounds) on Tuesday or Wednesday. I will call you on Sunday night, March 8th after 6:00 p.m. your time, and we can discuss this further. . . .

At 6:00 p.m. that night, I was in surgery after old

Duke had given me the once over at the zoo that afternoon. I had dispatched Dad home from the hospital to receive the call. Beatty sent his regrets over the incident. He told me to follow the doctors' orders and get well, and that he would hold the job for me until I could join. Jane had typed this letter.

His letter of April 24th he typed himself. He gave just a hint of his animal philosophy in the first paragraph.

> Your letter just received and glad you're feeling fine, and that the injuries are healed. Frankly, don't think you should have anything more to do with that lion, Duke, because I've found out thru experience that those ZOO animals are more dangerous than those born in the jungles. . . .

But his efforts to spot me in 22 Wagon, the old Silver Sleeper, surprised me.

> . . . Roger, am trying to work things out so you can join me when we show Philadelphia, Penn. the latter part of May. Enclosing route to that date. The sleeping accommodations are very scarce, and my problem is to find you a suitable place; which I'm trying to make arrangements for you in one of our Performer's Sleepers. I have berths for the animal caretakers in front of one of our cat cages but I've wanted something a little nicer for you. . . .

By this time, I was learning something about him I had not expected. Most circus men would let a new guy sleep anywhere, and would leave it up to them as a rule to find a bunk of their own. His offer was extraordinary.

In detailing the duties of the assistant, in his letter of May 6th, I have what may be the only time he ever did so by letter and in his own hand. Beatty described the position as his cageboy as quite a job.

> . . . Here's a few things he does, besides working around the arena doing the act. First thing in the morning, he sees that the ground and space where the arena will be located is completely level and no holes, and if grass is too high then it must be mowed. He keeps all props repaired and painted including Guns and whips, looks after my wardrobe and boots, drives my car and trailer and takes care of them, it seems like a lot of work, but after you get the hang of it and the routine it's not so much, the most diffcult job will be working around the arena during my act. This will take a little time, in learning my movements and knowing the animals. . . .

He was still trying to secure better quarters for me, but by now I answered that I would take a spot in

Mabel Stark. A characteristic shot of Mabel's daily dress, with her beloved lead cat, Goldie (nicknamed Lady Bug). —*Kathy Wheeler; Roger Smith Collection*

78 Wagon, the cat truck.

The fifteen dollars from the show netted me $13.10 a week. After two weeks, Beatty got me a raise to $20. Then, I took home $18.17. The extra money he mentions was never less than $15, and often was $25. It was most welcome and useful when I could slip off the lot for a needed extra meal. Cookhouse ran supper from 2:30 to 4:00 p.m., and by the time we tore down the chutes and loaded the props after the night show, I was ravenous. Our stops at the diners enroute at night were out when Jane and Clyde, Jr., joined the show. She cooked for him at nights then, and we only stopped for Clydie's ice cream desserts. Some of the boys told me Beatty often "forgot" to tip them. He may have, since most of them were 40-milers. But my tip was there every week, and I saw him regularly tip the water man, the electrician, and everyone else who did anything for him in the old circus tradition.

By the time I received his letter of May 17th, I was healed up and ready to join. Once this letter arrived I lost no time in getting to Philadelphia.

Dave Price helped me to pinpoint the exact date I was drawn to the profession by sending me the 1947 route. It brought back a flood of memories. There were some very personal reasons for Beatty to have such an impact on my imagination then, but I remember the night even though I was only four years old. It was Monday, August 25th, and I was that night introduced to my future.

On a separate page, I have written out my career by the years. This will best reflect the careers of many independent trainers who contract with many producers rather than become a fixture on any one title. Pat Anthony worked this way most of his career. In fact, most of us do. We'd all like to see something like twenty years on a show, but today there aren't the shows anymore. Above all, I want another place like Thousand Oaks, the old Jungleland.

Goebel's Lion Farm opened in the Oaks, in 1925. Later, it became World Jungle Compound, and in 1965, Jungleland. It survived eleven managements including intermittent ones by Goebel, who always took the place back when others failed or moved on. Among them were Jimmy Woods, probably the best businessman; the Ruhe brothers, Heinz and Lutz; and lastly, the ones who sent it into ruin, Thurston M. "Tex" Scarbrough, and Roy G. Kabat as manager.

For years, the place enjoyed little competition as chief supplier for movie animals, and the best trainer of such animals was my friend Mel Koontz, who was something of a legend in Hollywood circles. Mel was in demand by DeMille when wild animals were needed, and in DeMille's *Samson and Delilah* another young trainer was tapped: none other than Pat Anthony doubled for Victor Mature when Samson wrestled the lion. Almost everyone on the payroll eventually went to the studios for some picture or other.

The original Cheetah chimp came from the Compound and was trained by Henry Tyndall, who had trained chimps for Beatty at the Fort Lauderdale Zoo. Henry also trained the chimps for Ronald Reagan's albatross, *Bedtime for Bonzo.* Henry worked on many of the Weissmuller films, and later in the Lex Barker *Tarzan* series. To list the films made with our animals would be almost impossible, but it kept the place alive for forty-four years.

Many greats from the Corporation shows had worked in Thousand Oaks. Louis Roth trained there from 1933 to 1945. In 1933, Goebel hired a man who became the mainstay of the Compound until the finish. His name was Benny Bennett. Roth demanded Bennett's presence every time he broke new acts, and Benny became Mabel's No. 1 man for thirty-one years. All through the years, it was Benny, everyone's Uncle Ben, who taught us the ways of Roth, told us inside secrets to the work, taught us to cut meat and properly feed, and when we needed it he bailed us out of jackpots and kept us safe. It was Benny who finally got me on the good side of Mabel Stark. To show the value of Benny Bennett, no one less than Roth wanted only him when an order came in to break an act in 45 days. Roth said, "Give me Benny and I can do it." The act consisted of five lions and four tigers. The year was 1945.

John "Chubby" Guilfoyle broke Pat Anthony in there and proved a terrible but highly competent taskmaster. Frank Phillips, the "Mountain Lion King," trained there. Up until his near-fatal mauling in 1965, Chet Juszyk was the Compound's Head Trainer. Don Carr was a contemporary of mine. John Richards (Writtinghouse) was present for a time. Others included Lou Regan, Cheryl Shawver, and a man who became, with Bennett, my finest benefactor, Dick McGraw.

Dick, besides being my greatest pal, was the best

trainer on the place in many years. He was tutored by Phillips and Bennett (of course) and became my mentor on male lions. Beatty learned of Dick and watched him work. He tried for years to hire Dick, always at times when Dick had firmed up other commitments.

The last major film we had out there was *Dr. Dolittle*, 20th Century-Fox's biggest multi-million-dollar flop in years. But the trainers who worked on the film for over two years all made themselves windfall salaries, and the infighting for jobs on the picture was part of the great undoing of the Compound.

Rather than pay Goebel, Scarbrough and Kabat raked in the profits and refused payments. Goebel, after five years, filed suit. The original purchase price of Jungleland was $1,035,000, and the new owners never even touched the interest payments. They went into receivership under A.J. Bumb Company and lapsed into bankruptcy. There was a great gathering for the funeral, and we watched, during August 9th and 10th, 1969, the last moments of an institution.

For a time, there was some talk of Goebel coming in once again and bringing back the old place. But it was all over. Animals we had worked and known were trucked away, cages dismantled and loaded, and props and arenas taken by successful bidders. I was stunned and sickened at the spectacle. Most of us were thrown out of work. But the worst came when I visited the old site in 1972, while playing the Shrine Auditorium in Los Angeles with Castle. Bulldozers had razed the remaining structures, and the offices had been occupied by the Conejo Refuse Company.

· · ·

I felt that from the outset I understood Mabel Stark. Everyone knew I was coming; after all, everyone else who worked cats had been in there at one time or another. After the death of Beatty, I squeezed in another quick stretch at Texas Tech, got from it what I wanted, and finalized talks with Scarbrough to make the jump to the Coast. I was coming in as a new trainer. Mabel didn't like it very much.

By this time, Mabel Stark boasted 54 years with tigers. She was in her last years as even she often jokingly admitted. But any new trainer might just be the one the office could use in their long-running battle with the old star to put her out. She was keenly aware of their efforts. So for the first six months around there, I couldn't get "Good morning" out of the old lady.

When I arrived, there was a cage hand for each of the four strings, or cage lines. Then, one kid quit and I immediately volunteered to take over his work and maintain my own string. Everyone thought it would be too much, but it was easily done by coming in an hour earlier than the other guys. This put me there at 7:00 a.m., exactly the same time Mabel and Benny began work on her cages. Seeing me get done at nine, the same time as she, Mabel asked Benny, "What's that little bastard trying to do? Be a wise guy?" At least, I was noticed.

Next, one of the first things I did was make friends with Uncle Ben. I stayed with him in that slaughterhouse like glue. Very soon, he was letting me help him skin, cut the meat and, honor of honors, sharpen his own knives, an unheard of privilege. He kept Mabel up to date with my progress. She still wasn't convinced.

Mabel had broken in when no woman ever had the ambitions she professed to Al G. Barnes. She became supreme with tigers, and recognition came to her as a true pioneer. Her rise was unstoppable. But she had also seen many come and go who never had the determination she lived by. She had no reason to be impressed even when I took over still another string, the long string, and kept all three as spotless as hers.

When I began to work the McGraw lions, she was in evidence every time. After the first successful run-through, I became a fixture, and the next morning, at seven sharp, she called out a hearty greeting. After our cages were done, I was invited to sit at her special table in the snack bar, and my stock rose dramatically within the company.

But the best of my times with her were when she saw something in my work that needed guidance. She would take me on little walks, away from ears she considered undeserving, and teach me shortcuts on tricks and formations that became rare and great lessons to me. I knew that what I was hearing was privileged—deep secrets and insights born of this incomparable half-century of achievement. It was not lost on either of us that the scene looked like an E.F. Hutton television commercial, with many finding excuses to saunter along closely, trying to listen. When others came too close, Mabel would stop suddenly and turn to face them. She scattered them with an icy, "Yes? Do you want something?" Then she would take me by the arm and continue talking in conspiratorial tones about the lesson of the day.

Now this didn't help my personal popularity at work. For a time, I was badgered backstage and in the dressing room about what Mabel had to say. When it got back to Mabel that I had respected her confidence, we became close then as friends, and one day, to the utter amazement of every eye and ear, she even let me buy the two of us a beer.

Mabel's professionalism set examples that were impeccable. Her big maroon and white Buick rolled to a stop in her special parking place every morning at 6:20. She unlocked her dressing room, set down her gigantic leather purse, touched at her tight blonde curls and set to work at 6:30. By seven, when Benny or I invariably showed up on the dot, she had shifted one tiger into the arena in back and another, her head cat Goldie, into the exercise pen, thus giving us two empty cages to clean, and had placed all the cage tools in their exact position. In everything that Mabel did, there was an exact location and a precise time for everything. Should anything be moved or delayed, the violator caught living hell for it. Benny had warned me about this and I had made a half-dozen trips to her cages to reconnoiter the set-up. By 7:30, her ten animals were fed; they were boned out and bedded down by nine; and the cage work was finished for the morning. But to accomplish this, her day had started much earlier.

Mabel arose at 4:45 daily. She then bathed, dressed in her familiar garb of specially made trousers, a blouse with long, full sleeves, and her inevitable heavy brooch centered at the open neckline. Her breakfast was another ritual: one slice of corn meal mush, fried golden brown, two pieces of dry toast, two strips of bacon and two cups of strong black coffee, and Mabel Stark was ready for the world.

One of her great specialties, aside from training firsts, was the rearing of cubs. In my string, I had a highly reliable breeding pair, Hanzie and Emir. Mabel taught me how and when to let them breed, all the things to look for during gestation, security for mother and cubs, and the correct rearing of the little tigers themselves. Emir was an excellent mother. She nursed her own, and Mabel took me through her and Emir's care of them each step in time. When other tigers had cubs, we had to remove them and do it all ourselves—another story

entirely. Together, Mabel and I saw sixteen cubs to adulthood with a survival rate of one hundred percent. The woman was a masterful professional.

One afternoon, Mabel stayed later than usual. I was a little surprised by her still being there. It was a disruption to her routine. She was pensive and quiet for a long time. Finally, she began to speak reflectively, all the while gazing out at the arena, the cages and the animals quiet in the twilight.

"It couldn't have worked out with the others. Never did." She thought a while. "I don't know it all . . . you never will either, Roger. I've had you three years now. Taught you everything I know. Keep it going for us." And she rose and walked out through the door and turned and walked around the path to the main gate.

Ina Scarbrough and Roy Kabat at length succeeded in railroading Mabel out of Jungleland. Don Carr and I helped her move out of her dressing room and took her things home for her. On that day, she gave me the last buggy whip and hickory pole she used to work her tigers, among many other personal mementoes.

She lived six months longer. Mabel died sometime during the week of April 20th, 1968.

APPENDIX

The following two letters are reproduced in their entirety. They demonstrate the diversity of opinion still existing today concerning wild animal acts. The authors express such interesting views, allowing them to speak for themselves seemed the best choice.

Alice Herrington is the president of Friends of Animals. This organization was formed in 1957, and presently has a $2 million budget for various animal protection projects. The group's lobby in Washington is the Committee for Humane Legislation. Ms. Herrington was asked her opinion of wild animal acts.

Robert L. Parkinson is the chief librarian and historian of the Circus World Museum in Baraboo, Wisconsin. This museum, owned by the State Historical Society of Wisconsin, is the leading center of circus research in the United States. Mr. Parkinson was asked to expatiate on the position of the modern American circus toward wild animal acts and protective legislation.

friends of animals, inc. *11 West 60th Street, New York, N.Y. 10023* • *(212) 247-8120*

December 14, 1978

Ms. Joanne Joys
The University of Toledo
Publications Office
2801 West Bancroft Street
Toledo, Ohio 43606

Dear Ms. Joys:

Friends of Animals believes that the exploitation of wildlife in performing acts at circuses, carnivals and the like is a violation of animal rights. The training of wildlife to behave like humans, jump through flaming hoops, do balancing acts, etc. is generally accomplished through great cruelty and deprivation. Those who enjoy such spectacles are thoughtless people - throwbacks to Elizabethan times when mad humans were caged in the thoroughfares for the public to tease and taunt.

Sincerely yours,

Alice Herrington

President

AH:vl

CIRCUS WORLD MUSEUM

BARABOO, WISCONSIN
53913

608-356-8341

Robert L. Parkinson
Chief Librarian and Historian
January 31, 1979

Ms. Joanne Joys
The University of Toledo
2801 West Bancroft Street
Toledo, Ohio   43606

Dear Joanne:

A while back you asked for my views on the endangered species-performing animal
question and debate. This letter may be reaching you rather tardy, but here are my
views, in any event.

The primary cause of any species of animal becoming endangered, rests in the conditions prevailing in the natural habitat of the animal; namely, uncontrolled killing,
encroachment of civilization and the simple shrinkage of land areas of the natural
habitat.   Where those habitats are in foreign places such as Kenya, Bengal and
Burma, there is no way whatsoever that legislation by the United States Congress
(or the states,) can do anything to save the animals in their natural habitats.   That
must be done by the governments and people in those habitats or it will not be done
at all.   The truth is that the inevitable growth of the World's population has long
ago destined these natural habitats to surrender to the march of civilization. We
can no more expect the people of the Sudan to sacrifice their own human needs for the
sake of animals, than have we done in America and Western Europe.   A few thousand
acres of natural forrests or parks for animals? Yes.   But adequate mass lands for
the natural roamings and life conditions of elephants, lions etc? Never.

Experience has demonstrated that many of these animals, including the big cats,
reproduce and thrive in captivity; yet, the current course of legislation in the
U.S.A. has been to restrict the sale, transportation and use of animals within our
borders. This apparently is on the premis that if the demand for and use of these
endangered animals is reduced in the United States, that will lessen the demand
for their removal from their natural habitats, and contribute to their survival
on their home soil.   This premis overlooks two facts - the expansive natural
habitats are doomed to becoming civilized and that upon that taking place. the only

hope for the survival of these animals is that they may do so in captivity.

As the World shrinks and its population grows, that which survives will do so because it has a purpose to humans.   This thought may agonize the theorists of animal rights, but their pleadings will not change the facts.   Man will not accept starvation and unemployment while critters occupy millions of square miles of wild lands and deny natural resources.

It is one thing for idealists in the developed Western nations to preach about saving the lands for the elephant, lion and ape - - when those lands are someone else's. It is quite something else to expect the undeveloped countries where those habitats exist, to forego their own prosperity and development in order to reserve half their national lands for roaming animals.

Recent legislation has aimed to try to protect animals by making them unuseful and unavailable to men.   By this course, legislation has done nothing to save animals in their natural habitat, but has undertaken to destroy the one last hope of preserving expiring species.

What is needed is a realization that indeed, the very salvation of these endangered species remains only in civilization's ability to preserve them in captivity. If their natural habitats are destined to disappear, due to conditions the United States Congress cannot legislate; then the only recourse is to preerve them in captivity under conditions the U. S. Congress can legislate.   If it were not for preservation in captivity and domestication, the American bison and common horse may now have been gone, or certainly endangered.

Such a realization means that U.S. legislation should encourage possession, use, breeding, transport and sale of domestic bred cats in the U.S.A.   The realization should be broadcast that the present base of big cats in the United States today is domestic bred - - existing at no expense to the animal populations elsewhere in natural habitats.   They exist in domestic conditions because circuses, trainers and zoos have use of them, and the public finds their display and performing exhibition to be both entertaining and educational.

Indeed, remove wild animals from view and accessability to the American public, and in time, the public's concern and care for animals will also disappear.   The public responds today to the appeal of environmentalists because the public finds wild animals to be interesting, beautiful and exotic.   They are responsive to a fear that they may lose these creatures.   But, actually, "losing" the animals, really means losing them from public access and view.   In fact, environmentalists and legislators may take animals from public view long before the deterioration of their habitats does so.

If the public loses sight of, and care for, animals; and if the purposeful use and exhibition of animals is prohibited by law, all incentive for animal preservation will also disappear.   Again, it bears repeating, that if animals are to survive on this overcrowded earth, they must be useful to man.

The question of survival of animals is often confused with the issue of cruelty to animals or "animals rights."   These subjects are quite independent of each other, and quite interpretable. What you may call "cruel" and what I may call "cruel" can be quite different.   We can agree that it is wrong to be cruel to animals, but then fall apart on how that common feeling should be applied to actual legislation.   I, for instance, believe the greatest cruelty to animals would be to render them useless to man, therefore not worth caring about.   There are indeed, cruel ways to break and train animals, but the simple fact that they are broken and trained is not cruel. Exhibition and performing of animals is no more cruel than is the self-imposed routine of the exhibition and performing of people themselves.   Only in the degree of pain and abuse applied in a specific instance of training, should the element of cruelty become a factor, and therein you will find agreement and support from most circus people and animal trainers.

Circuses and trainers have been attentive to the love and care of animals over a hundred years before the phrase "endangered species" was created. Circuses and trainers will be the first to acknowledge that there are some amongst their midst who are rightfully subject to critisism in their manner of handling animals, and animals should be protected from them. As an industry or profession, however, circuses and trainers are truly the animals' best champions and should, for the best interests of the animals, should be encouraged and consulted in the quest for animal preservtaion.

The conservationists (on the one hand,) and circuses, trainers and zoos (on the other hand) should be made to look upon each other as allies in a common cause, not antagonists. Both have knowledge and lessons to learn from each other. As long as either seek the elimination of the other, they are in either instance undoing their own cause, by seeking to eliminate a true friend and champion of animals. The sooner they gain respect for each other, and learn to work together to create a domestic environment in which endangered animals can survive in captivity in an overcrowding world, the surer will be the preservation of the species.

Yours truly,

Robert L. Parkinson
Chief Librarian & Historian
Circus World Museum

Wild Animal Acts in America

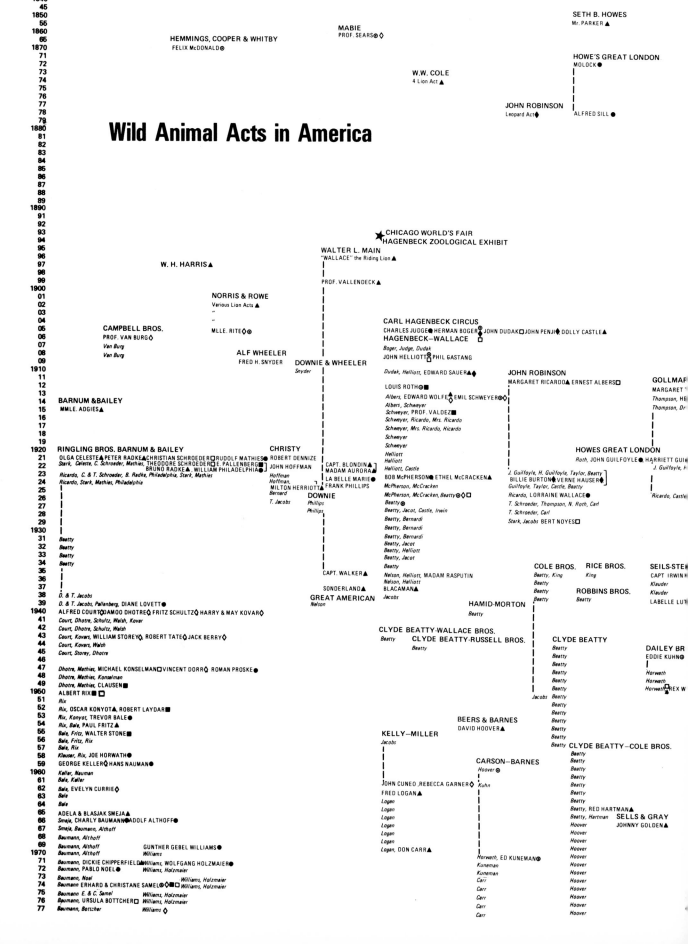

1830
35
1840
45
1850
55
1860
65
1870
71
72
73
74
75
76
77
78
79
1880
81
82
83
84
85
86
87
88
89
1890
91
92
93
94
95
96
97
98
99
1900
01
02
03
04
05
06
07
08
09
1910
11
12
13
14
15
16
17
18
19
1920
21
22
23
24
25
26
27
28
29
1930
31
32
33
34
35
36
37
38
39
1940
41
42
43
44
45
46
47
48
49
1950
51
52
53
54
55
56
57
58
59
1960
61
62
63
64
65
66
67
68
69
1970
71
72
73
74
75
76
77

TAMER ENTERED DEN OR CAGE

TRANSITION PERIOD

AMUSEMENT PARKS AND CARNIVALS PREDOMINANT
(ACTUAL PERFORMING ANIMALS)

ZOOLOGICAL INSTITUTE
★ ISAAC VAN AMBURGH▲
popularized caged man
an animal act in America

VAN AMBURGH & CO.
PROF. LANGWORTHY⊚

FRENCH GREAT ORIENTAL
GEORGE W. HALL▲
FRENCH
HERR PAUL SCHOFF▲

```
KEEPERS BEFORE VAN AMBURGH
1829 WILLIAM SHERMAN (Rufus Welch), 1834 (Purdy, Welch & Co.)
1829 CHARLES WRIGHT (New Caravan), 1830 (Carley, Purdy & Wright)
1831 SOLOMON BAILEY (Purdy, Carley & Bailey), 1834 (J.T. & J.P. Bailey)
1833 MR. ROBERTS (National Menagerie)
1833 JOHN SEARS (New England Caravan)
1833 MR. PUTNAM (Purdy, Welch, Macomber & Co.)
1833 MR. GRAY (Raymond & Ogden)
1833 MR. FLINT (Tufts, Waring & Co.), 1834 (same)
1834 AGRIPPA MARTIN (S. Butler & Co.)
1834 MR. WORD (Miller, Mead & Delavan)
1834 JOHN SCHAFFER (Purdy, Welch & Co.)
```

FOREPAUGH
★ Col. Edgar Daniel Boone &
★ Miss Carlotta — First steel arena▲
GEORGE ARSTINSTALL▲ ALBERT STADLER▲◆

★ CAPT. FRANK C. BOSTOCK

FOREPAUGH-SELLS
Various Polar Bear Acts until 1910 □

★ PAN AMERICAN EXHIBIT
JACK BONAVITA▲ MMLE LOUISE MORELLI◊ HERMAN WEEDON◊⊚
EDWARD DEYERLING▲ CHARLES DAY◊ RICHARD 'DUTCH' RICARDO (WARNER)▲

COL. FRANCIS FERARI

AL G. BARNES
Al G. BARNES⊚ ◊■

SELLS—FLOTO
Ricardo , MRS RICARDO
Mrs. Ricardo, LUCIA ZORA
Zora
Zora
Zora
|
|
STELLA ROWLAND◊
|
Jacot , MISS JACOT◊ ALLEN KING▲
AAGE CHRISTANSEN⊚
Christiansen, T.Schroeder,Helliott
Christiansen
T. Schroeder
Helliott, Taylor
Jacot, Stark, King

SPARKS
FRITZ BRUNNER▲
Brunner
Brunner
Brunner
Brunner

FRANZ WOSKA⊚ STEVE BATTY▲
Woska, Batty
Woska, Batty, MRS. BATTY◆
Woska, Batty, H. Guilfoyle
Hauser, Guilfoyle, Woska
Hauser, Guilfoyle, Woska, H. Guilfoyle
Hauser, H. Guilfoyle, JOHN RENICK□
Woska, Phillips
Hauser, Woska

Roth, MABLE STARK■ BOB THORNTON■
MARTHA FLORINE◆ FRED VALLIE■
Roth, Stark, Thornton, Florine, Vallie
Roth , Stark●
Stark
|
Ricardo, Stark, PEARL HAMILTON◆■
Ricardo, Stark, ROY STEVENS□ VERN VENABLE▲
|
Roth, NELLIE ROTH , MABLE GARDNER ,
AGNES LAUSTON , MARGARET GRAHAM ,
BESSIE DUFOR , JOHN BACKMAN◆ BERT NELSON□
Roth, Nelson, HERMAN ZIGLER⊚ ALMA TAYLOR◊
Roth, Taylor, Meyers , BETTY ROTH⊚ BOBBY TODD▲
Stark, Metcalf, Jacot
Stark, Meyers, Jacobs, MILDRED DOUGLAS●
Jacobs, Stark, Meyers
Jacobs, Stark, Meyers
Jacobs, Stark
Jacobs, Stark
Jacobs, Stark, Nelson
Nelson, Stark
Stark, Phillips, D. & T. Jacobs

JONES & WILSON
PETER TAYLOR▲ ZIRA◆
Taylor, Zira

YANKEE ROBINSON
JULES JACOT▲
Jacot
Jacot

GREAT PATTERSON
H Guilfoyle, JOHNNY MEYERS▲
GENTRY—
PATTERSON   HONEST BILL
Meyers   WILLIAM STOKES
Meyers

GOLDEN
Bernard, Jacot
TESSIE FLAKENDORF⊚
Bernard, Florine, IONE CARLA⊚◊
ADOLPH HILEBRUNER▲
ALETHA FLETCHER
LEE
King, T. Jacobs
King, T. Jacobs

RHODA ROYAL
HARRY HALL▲

WORLD
WILLIAM BERNARD
ROBBINS
LOUIS FURTELL
Furtell
Furtell
Furtell
Furtell
T. Jacobs

ILONIS
LTZ▲
TON▲

LEWIS BROS.
JEROME SMITH▲
Smith
Smith
Smith

WPA
ERNEST ENGERER▲

KAY BROS.
BOB MATTHEWS▲

GREAT DAN RICE
MANUAL KING▲
M. King

PATTERSON
MADAM BEZONIA▲

FAMOUS ROBBINS
SWEDE JOHNSON ▲
Johnson
Johnson WORLD BROS.
Johnson

BUD ANDERSON
CAPT. HART▲

GILBERT
T. Jacobs

AUSTIN
T. Jacobs

SPARKS
Dhotre

RUSSELL BROS.
Clemens

JAMES M. COLE
CAPT. CHRISTY▲

SELLO
RUTH ROY▲

ROGERS
Horwath, Kuhn

BRADLEY & BENSON
Engerer, GLADYS GILLEM

AYRES & DAVIES
Christy

DIANO
Singe

CAMPA
ARIUM SINGE▲

WALLACE BROS.
FRED DELMAR▲
Engerer

BAILEY BROS.
DICK CLEMENS▲
D. Jacobs
Engerer, Gillem
Gillem

BILLER BROS.
PRINCE EL-KI-GOR⊚
Prince El-Ki-Gor
El-Ki-Gor

ILLS BROS.
ARLES ZERBINI⊚
HN ZERBINI⊚
rbini

CRISTIANI
Kuhn
Kuhn

Note: Perhaps thirty or more
independent cage acts exist
today. These acts contract
with various Shrine circus
producers or amusement
parks.

```
LEGEND
▲ LIONS
● TIGERS
⊚ LIONS AND TIGERS
◆ LEOPARDS
◊ MIXED SMALL CATS
   (Leopards, Pumas, Black Panthers, etc.)
■ BEARS (Other than Polar)
□ POLAR BEARS
```

STEBBINGS
LILI KRISTENSEN◆

VARGAS
PAT ANTHONY⊚
Anthony

Information derived from:
Pfening, Jr., Fred D. "Masters of the Steel Arena." *Bandwagon* 16 (May-June 1972).
Thayer, Stuart. "The Keeper Will Enter the Cage, Early American Wild Animal Trainers."

ENDNOTES

Chapter I

THE WILD ANIMAL TRAINER IN AMERICA
THE EARLY YEARS

1. Mildred Sandison Fenner and Wolcott Fenner, eds., *The Circus—Lure and Legend* (Englewood Cliffs, N.J.: Prentice-Hall, Inc., 1970), p. 127.

2. Roman Proske, *Lions, Tigers and Me* (New York: Henry Holt & Co., 1956), p. 16.

3. Orrin E. Klapp, *Heroes, Villains, and Fools* (Englewood Cliffs, N.J.: Prentice-Hall, Inc., 1962), pp. 29–30.

4. *Ibid.*, p. 35.

5. *Ibid.*, pp. 70–71.

6. *Ibid.*, p. 55.

7. Marcello Truzzi, "The American Circus as a Source of Folklore: An Introduction," *Southern Folklore Quarterly*, 30 (December 1966), pp. 289–300.

8. E. S. Hallock, "The American Circus," *Century*, 70 (August 1905), p. 568.

9. R.W.G. Vail, *Random Notes of the History of the Early American Circus* (American Antiquarian Society, 1933), pp. 117–131.

10. John and Alice Durant, *Pictorial History of the American Circus* (New York: A. S. Barnes & Co., 1957), p. 26.

11. Chang Reynolds, *Pioneer Circuses of the West* (Los Angeles: Western Lore Press, 1966), pp. 128–129.

12. R.W.G. Vail, "This Way to the Big Top," *The New York Historical Society Quarterly Bulletin*, 29 (July 1945), pp. 146–147.

13. Stuart Thayer, *Annals of the American Circus: 1793–1829* (Manchester, Mich.: Rymark Printing, 1976), pp. 69–70.

14. Mel Miller, *Ringling Museum of the Circus* (Sarasota, Fla.: John and Mable Ringling Museum of Art, 1963), no page numbers.

15. Isaac F. Marcosson, "Sawdust and Goldust—The Earnings of Circus People," *Bookman*, 31 (June 1910), p. 403.

16. Earl Chapin May, *The Circus from Rome to Ringling* (New York: Dover Publications, Inc., 1932), pp. 24–30.

17. Vail, *Random Notes*, p. 45.

18. George L. Chindahl, *A History of the Circus in America* (Caldwell, Idaho: Caxton Printers, Ltd., 1959), pp. 30–32.

19. Stuart Thayer, "The Keeper Will Enter the Cage, Early American Wild Animal Trainers" (unpublished manuscript).

20. Vail, *Random Notes*, p. 148.

21. Durant, p. 32.

22. Thayer, "The Keeper."

23. Ephraim Watts, *The Life of Van Amburgh: The Brute Tamer* (London 1838), pp. 15, 18–27.

24. *Ibid.*, p. 36.

25. *Ibid.*, p. 14.

26. *Ibid.*, p. 39.

27. *Ibid.*, p. 42.

28. Thayer, "The Keeper."

29. Marian Murray, *Circus: From Rome to Ringling* (New York: Appleton-Century-Crofts, Inc., 1956), p. 139.

30. Durant, p. 33.

31. Elbert R. Bowen, "The Circus in Early Rural Missouri," *Bandwagon*, 9 (September-October, 1965), p. 13.

32. Durant, p. 33.

33. Vail, *Random Notes*, p. 151.

34. Marian Murray, *Circus! From Rome to Ringling* (New York: Appleton-Century-Crofts, Inc., 1956), p. 139.

35. Watts, p. 30.

36. R. Toole Stott, *Circus and Allied Arts* (Derby, England: Harpur & Sons, Ltd., 1957), p. 134.

37. *A Concise Account Interspersed with Anecdotes of Van Amburgh's Celebrated Collection of Trained Animals*, J. W. Peel, Printer (Lambeth, 1841).

38. Marcosson, p. 403.

39. Watts, p. 36.

40. Watts, p. 42.

41. Thomas Frost, *Circus Life and Circus Celebrities (1875)* (Detroit: Singing Tree Press, 1970), p. 89.

42. Marcosson, p. 403.

43. Frost, p. 90.

44. Dembeck, p. 307.

45. Robert Kitchen, "Grizzly Adams: Fearless Menagerie, Circus Star," *The White Tops*, 50 (March-April 1977), pp. 8–9.

46. Richard Dillon, *The Legend of Grizzly Adams* (New York: Berkley Publishing Co., 1966), p. 3.

47. Kitchen, p. 9.

48. Dillon, p. 3.

49. Kitchen, p. 9.

50. Dillon, pp. 176–177.

51. Kitchen, pp. 9–10.

52. Dillon, pp. 187–189.

53. Kitchen, p. 10.

54. Bowen, p. 14.

55. Dillon, p. 195.

56. Dillon, p. 195.

57. Kitchen, p. 10.

58. Thayer, "The Keeper."

59. Hallock, p. 572.

60. Thayer, "The Keeper," addenda.

61. Richard E. Conover, *Wisconsin's Unique Heritage* (Baraboo, Wis.: Circus World Museum, 1967), p. 38.

62. Frost, pp. 73–78.

63. Ex-Lion King, "Lions and Lion Taming," *Every Saturday*, 12 (February 17, 1872), p. 175.

64. Frost, pp. 128–130.

65. George Conklin, *The Ways of the Circus* (New York: Harper & Bros., 1921), p. 56.

66. Frost, pp. 131–134 and 264–270.

67. Ex-Lion King, pp. 173–176.

68. *New York Times*, 15 April 1878, p. 15.

69. W. J. Rouse, "The Adventures of a Lion Tamer," *Cosmopolitan*, 5 (September 1888), p. 380.

70. *Ibid.*

71. *Ibid.*

72. *Ibid.*

73. *Ibid.*, p. 384.

74. W. C. Coup, *Sawdust and Spangles* (Chicago: Herbert S. Stone & Co., 1901), p. 18.

75. *Ibid.*, p. 169.

76. *Ibid.*

77. *Ibid.*, pp. 169–170.

78. *Ibid.*, p. 173.

79. *Ibid.*, p. 181.

80. *Ibid.*, pp. 184–185.

81. Fenner, p. 47.

82. Conklin, p. 52.

83. *Ibid.*, pp. 37–39.

84. *Ibid.*, pp. 53–56.

85. Robert Edmund Sherwood, *Here We Are Again* (Indianapolis: Bobbs-Merrill Co., 1926), pp. 100–102.

86. Murray, p. 192.

87. Carl Hagenbeck, *Beasts and Men*, edited and abridged by Hugh S. R. Eliot and A. G. Thatcher (London: Longmans, Green & Co., 1909), pp. v–x.

88. Jack Rennert, *100 Years of Circus Posters* (New York: Darien House Books, 1974), p. 10.

89. *New York Times*, 12 December 1879, p. 3.

90. Hagenbeck, p. 30.

91. Hagenbeck, p. 118.

92. *Ibid.*, pp. 98–111.

93. *Ibid.*, pp. 118–121, 126, 134.

94. *Ibid.*, pp. 136, 143.

95. *Ibid.*, pp. 34–36.

96. Murray, pp. 192–193.

97. *New York Times*, 14 January 1894, p. 20.

98. *New York Times*, 3 July 1894, p. 5.

99. *New York Times*, 11 July 1894, p. 8.

100. *New York Times*, 15 July 1894, p. 16.

101. Harold J. Shepstone, "Trained Animals at the World's Fair," *Scientific American*, 91 (August 6, 1904), p. 97.

102. Harold J. Shepstone, "The Scientific Training of Wild Animals," *Scientific American*, 87 (October 18, 1902), pp. 260–261.

103. Hermann Boyer, "Training Wild Beasts," *The Independent*, 55 (October 29, 1903), p. 2556.

104. Joe McKennon, *A Pictorial History of the American Carnival* (Sarasota, Fla.: Carnival Publishers of Sarasota, 1972), p. 49.

105. *Ibid.*, pp. 48–57.

106. David Lano, *A Wandering Showman, I* (Lansing: Michigan State University Press, 1957), pp. 132–133.

107. McKennon, p. 118.

108. E. H. Bostock, *Menageries, Circuses and Theatres* (New York: Frederick A. Stones Co., 1928), p. 303.

109. Frank C. Bostock, "The Brute in Captivity," Frank Leshe's *Popular Monthly*, 53 (December 1901), p. 172.

110. Hjalmar Hjorth Boyesen, "Training Wild Animals," *Cosmopolitan*, 34 (December 1902), pp. 125–126.

111. Ellen Velvin, "Hairbreadth Escapes in a Wild Animal Show," *Ladies Home Journal*, 23 (February 1906), p. 15.

112. Ellen Velvin, *Behind the Scenes with Wild Animals* (New York: Moffat, Yard & Co., 1906), pp. 50–51.

113. *New York Times*, 15 May 1911, p. 7.

114. Frank C. Bostock, *The Training of Wild Animals*, ed. Ellen Velvin (New York: The Century Company, 1920).

115. Samuel Hopkins Adams, "The Training of Lions, Tigers, and Other Great Cats," *McClure's*, 15 (September 1900), pp. 386–398.

116. Bostock, pp. 185–220.

117. *Ibid.*, pp. 185–220.

118. Sherwood, p. 103.

119. Bostock, p. 189.

120. *Ibid.*

121. Velvin, *Behind the Scenes*, pp. 47–52.

122. Bostock, pp. 185–220.

123. Jack Bonavita, "How I Became a Wild Animal Trainer," *The Delineator*, 74 (September 1909), p. 254.

124. Edo McCullough, *Good Old Coney Island* (New York: Charles Scribner's Sons, 1957), pp. 192–194.

125. Velvin, *Behind the Scenes*, p. 68.

126. Oliver Pilat and Jo Ranson, *Sodom by the Sea* (Garden City, N.Y.: Doubleday, Doran & Co., 1941), pp. 164–167.

127. *New York Times*, 27 May 1911, p. 1.

128. *New York Times*, 28 May 1911, p. 1.

129. Bostock, pp. xiv–xvi.

130. F. G. Aflalo, "The Ethics of Performing Animals," *Fortnightly*, 73 (March 1900), pp. 382–391.

131. Harvey Sutherland, "Training of Wild Beasts," *Current Literature*, 32 (June 1902), p. 709.

132. The Hon. George W. Peck, *Peck's Bad Boy With the Circus* (Chicago: Thompson and Thomas, 1906), pp. 76–77.

133. Sutherland, p. 709.

134. Aflalo, pp. 382–391.

135. S. L. Bensuan, "The Torture of Trained Animals," *English Illustrated Magazine* (April 1846), p. 26.

136. *Ibid.*, p. 130.

137. Joseph and Barne Klaitts (editors), *Animals and Man in Historic Perspective* (New York: Harper and Row, 1974), p. 157.

138. James Turner, *Reckoning with the Beast* (Baltimore: The Johns Hopkins University Press, 1980), p. 77.

139. Sutherland, p. 709.

140. "The Complete Lion Tamer," *Harper's Weekly*, 55 (January 28, 1911), p. 33.

141. Edward Lyell Fox, "When the Jungle Goes to School," *Harper's Weekly*, 56 (November 30, 1912), p. 18.

142. Maurice Brown Kirby, "The Gentle Art of Training Wild Beasts," *Everybody's Magazine*, 19 (October 1908), pp. 435–445.

143. J. Edward Leithead, "The Anatomy of Dime Novels," *Dime Novel Round-Up*, 37 (September 15, 1968), pp. 92–102.

144. *Ibid.*, p. 100.

145. Henry Gallup Paine, "The Lion Tamer," *Harper's*, 94 (May 1897), p. 964.

146. Hal Standish, "Fred Fearnot and the Wild Beast Tamer," *Work and Win*, 364 (November 24, 1905), pp. 16–27.

147. Berton Bertren, "Barnum's Young Sandow," *Pluck and Luck*, 413 (May 2, 1906), pp. 6–16.

148. "Among the Nomads or Life in the Open," *Brave and Bold*, 340 (June 26, 1909), p. 2.

149. Andrew Sinclair, *Jack – A Biography of Jack London* (New York: Harper & Row, 1977), p. 123.

150. The author claims London fused his own suppressed nature with that of a beast in his animal books. *Ibid.*, pp. 91, 133.

151. Jack London, *Michael, Brother of Jerry* (New York: Grosset and Dunlap, 1917), pp. v–vii.

152. *Ibid.*, pp. 200–218.

153. *Ibid.*, p. 304.

154. Boyce Rensberger, *The Cult of the Wild* (Garden City, N.Y.: Anchor Press/Doubleday, 1978), pp. 46–47.

155. Joan London, *Jack London and His Times* (Seattle: University of Washington Press, 1939), pp. xiv–xviii.

156. Richard O'Connor, *Jack London, A Biography* (Boston: Little, Brown & Co., 1964), pp. 368–387.

157. Joan London, p. 363.

158. Jimmy Chipperfield, *My Wild Life* (New York: G. P. Putnam's Sons, 1976), p. 52.

159. "Cruelty Charged in Training Trick Animals for Stage and Movies," *The Literary Digest*, 66 (September 25, 1920), p. 112.

160. "Breaking of Performing Animals," *The Literary Digest*, 73 (May 6, 1922), pp. 80–82.

161. Ludwig Lewisohn, "The Circus," *The Nation*, 114 (April 12, 1922), pp. 446–447.

162. *New York Times*, 31 March 1925, p. 20.

163. *New York Times*, 31 March 1925, p. 20.

164. *New York Times*, 1 April 1925, p. 22.

165. Richard Thomas, *John Ringling* (New York: Pageant Press, Inc., 1960), p. 129.

166. John Ringling, "We Divided the Job – But Stuck Together," *American Magazine*, 88 (September 1919), pp. 56–58.

167. *New York Times*, 4 December 1926, p. 17.

168. Fred D. Pfening, Jr., "Masters of the Steel Arena," *Bandwagon*, 16 (May-June 1972), p. 11.

Chapter II

THE TRAINED WILD ANIMAL CIRCUS

1. George L. Chindahl, *A History of the Circus in America* (Caldwell, Idaho: Caxton Printers, Ltd., 1959), pp. 125–126.

2. Gordon Borders, "Al G. Barnes Winterquarters at Culver City, California," *Bandwagon*, 11 (July-August, 1967), pp. 10–12.

3. Essie Forrester O'Brien, *Circus: Cinders to Sawdust* (San Antonio, Tex.: The Naylor Co., 1959), p. 88.

4. Dave Robeson as told by Al G. Barnes, *Al G. Barnes, Master Showman* (Caldwell, Idaho: Caxton Printers, Ltd., 1935), pp. 7–9.

5. Dave Robeson, *Louis Roth—Forty Years with Jungle Killers* (Caldwell, Idaho: Caxton Printers, Ltd., 1945), p. 199.

6. John and Alice Durant, *Pictorial History of the American Circus* (New York: A. S. Barnes & Co., 1957), p. 73.

7. W. C. Thompson, *On the Road with a Circus* (n.p.: Goldmann, 1903), pp. 137–138.

8. Francis Metcalfe, "Side Show Studies," *Outing*, 45 (March 1905), pp. 715–716.

9. Claire Heliot, "Diary of a Lion-Tamer," *Cosmopolitan*, 41 (September 1906), p. 464.

10. *New York Times*, 29 October 1905, part 3, p. 1.

11. Courtney Ryley Cooper, "The Lady of the Steel Arena," *Ladies Home Journal*, 38 (July 1921), p. 94.

12. Courtney Ryley Cooper, *Under the Big Top* (Boston: Little, Brown & Co., 1923), pp. 163–164.

13. George Brinton Beal, *Through the Back Door of the Circus* (Springfield, Mass.: McLoughlin Bros. Inc., 1938), pp. 108–113.

14. Connie Clausen, *I Love You Honey, but the Season's Over* (New York: Holt, Rinehart & Winston, Inc., 1960), pp. 119–120.

15. Beal, p. 142.

16. D. R. McMullin, "Tiger Lady Mabel Stark," *WomenSports*, 3 (January 1976), pp. 19–22.

17. Mabel Stark as told to Gertrude Orr, *Hold That Tiger* (Caldwell, Idaho: Caxton Printers, Ltd., 1938), p. 13.

18. *Ibid.*, pp. 13–21.

19. Fred Bradna as told to Hartzell Spence, *The Big Top* (New York: Simon & Schuster, 1952), p. 147.

20. *New York Times*, 26 March 1922, p. 20.

21. *New York Times*, 2 April 1922, Section 2, p. 9.

22. Stark, pp. 177–180.

23. *New York Times*, 28 March 1925, p. 8.

24. *New York Times*, 31 March 1925, p. 20.

25. Bill Ballentine, *Wild Tigers and Tame Fleas* (New York: Rinehart & Co., Inc., 1958), p. 94.

26. Emmett Kelly with F. Beverly Kelley, *Clown* (New York: Prentice-Hall, Inc., 1954), p. 101.

27. Stark, p. 213.

28. *New York Times*, 23 November 1905, p. 5.

29. Robert H. Gollmar, *My Father Owned a Circus* (Caldwell, Idaho: Caxton Printers, Ltd., 1965), p. 76.

30. "Ben Wallace and the Early Circus in Peru, Indiana," *Seventeenth Annual Souvenir*

Program—Peru Circus City Festival, 1976, p. 50; *Peru* (Indiana) *Tribune—Circus City Souvenir Edition*, July 20, 1976, p. 3; Chalmer Condon, "B. E. Wallace," *Bandwagon*, 8 (July-August, 1964), pp. 3–6.

31. Fred D. Pfening, Jr., "How Wallace Bought Hagenbeck," *Bandwagon*, 8 (July-August, 1964), pp. 11–12.

32. Joe McKennon, *Horse Dung Trail* (Sarasota, Fla.: Carnival Publishers of Sarasota, 1975), p. 241.

33. John W. O'Malley, S. J., *The Story of the West Baden Springs Hotel* (Master's Thesis, Loyola University, 1957), pp. 74–85.

34. "Recreation of an Era," *Indiana History Bulletin*, 48 (September 1971), p. 131.

35. John W. O'Malley, S. J., "The Story of the West Baden Springs Hotel," *Orange County Heritage* (Paoli, Indiana), pp. 119, 126–127.

36. O'Malley, Thesis, p. 87.

37. O'Malley, *Orange County Heritage*, p. 128.

38. Joseph T. Bradbury, "The Circus Winterquarters in West Baden, Indiana," *Bandwagon*, 16 (September-October, 1972), pp. 7–8.

39. Frank Braden, "An Interesting Interview with Jerry Mugivan—1921," *Bandwagon*, 5 (March-April, 1961), pp. 15–18.

40. Charles Wirth, "The New Circus 'Home' at Peru," *Bandwagon*, 8 (July-August, 1964), pp. 13, 15.

41. Joseph T. Bradbury, "Howe's Great London Circus—Season of 1921," *Bandwagon*, 8 (September-October, 1964), pp. 4–13.

42. Julia Shawell, "Clyde Beatty Says Women Are Like Tigers," *Pictorial Review*, 35 (March 1934), p. 4.

43. Joseph T. Bradbury, "Gollmar Bros. Circus Season of 1922," *Bandwagon*, 9 (January-February, 1965), pp. 4–13.

44. Chang Reynolds, "Hagenbeck-Wallace Circus, 1922," *Bandwagon*, 9 (November-December, 1965), pp. 4–6.

45. McKennon, pp. 326–334.

46. Bradbury, "Gollmar," p. 13.

47. Chang Reynolds, "John Robinson's Circus 1824—For 100 Years has kept Faith with the Public—1923," *Bandwagon*, 6 (September-October, 1962), pp. 3–6.

48. Cleveland *Plain Dealer*, 6 May 1923, p. 3.

49. Arthur E. McFarlane, "Deceptive Showman," *Colliers*, 42 (January 9, 1909), p. 19.

50. Anthony Hippisley Coxe, *A Seat at the Circus* (London: Evans Bros. Ltd., 1951), pp. 129, 132–133.

51. Cooper, *Under the Big Top*, pp. 113–116, 123.

52. Courtney Ryley Cooper, *Lions 'N' Tigers 'N' Everything* (Boston: Little, Brown & Co., 1924), pp. 7–8, 17–20.

53. *Ibid.*, p. 153.

54. Courtney Ryley Cooper, *Circus Day* (New York: Farrar & Rinehart, Inc., 1925), pp. 48–52.

55. *Ibid.*, pp. 87, 89.

56. Peter Taylor, "Training Wild Animals for Circus and Stage Not Cruel," *Billboard*, 30 June 1925, p. 62.

57. John T. Benson, "How Wild Animals Are Picked and Trained for Circus Jobs," *American Magazine*, 99 (March 1925), pp. 48, 192.

58. Al Priddy, *The Way of the Circus* (Chicago: The Platform World, 1930), pp. 43–50.

59. Garner Wilson and Robert Hickey, "The Circus Program Metamorphosis," *Billboard*, 12 April 1924, no page numbers.

60. Ballentine, pp. 137–138.

61. Edward Hoagland, *The Courage of Turtles* (New York: Random House, 1968, 1969, 1970), p. 37.

62. Charles Phillip Fox and Tom Parkinson, *The Circus in America* (Waukesha, Wis.: Country Beautiful, 1969), p. 223.

63. Clyde Beatty with Edward Anthony, *Facing the Big Cats* (New York: Doubleday & Co., 1965), pp. 1–2.†

64. Dave Price, "The Building of a Legend . . . Clyde Beatty: Man or Myth," *White Tops*, 47 (July-August, 1974), p. 13.

65. Beal, p. 151.

66. Paul L. Reddin, *Wild West Shows: A Study in the Development of Western Romanticism* (Ph.D. Dissertation, University of Missouri, 1970), pp. 205–206, 215–221.

67. *New York Times*, 8 June 1934, p. 18.

68. Ballentine, p. 20.

69. Clyde Beatty with Edward Anthony, *The Big Cage* (New York: The Century Co., 1933), p. 169.

70. *Detroit News*, 14 February 1926, Metro section, p. 5.

71. *Ibid.*

72. Beatty, *Big Cage*, pp. 60–61.

73. *Ibid.*, pp. 59–71.

74. *New York Times*, 9 January 1931, p. 26.

75. *New York Times*, 4 September 1929.

76. Joseph T. Bradbury, "John Ringling's Circus Empire," *White Tops*, 46 (November-December, 1973), p. 7.

77. *Peru* (Indiana) *Daily Tribune*, 26 April 1930, p. 1.

78. "Personal Glimpses—How the Cat Man Fights Off Claws and Fangs," *The Literary Digest*, 108 (January 24, 1931), pp. 32–33.

79. McKennon, pp. 393, 395.

80. *Hagenbeck-Wallace Circus Program*, 1931, p. 14.

81. *New York Times*, 3 April 1931, no page number.

82. *New York Times*, 23 April 1931, p. 7.

83. *New York Times*, 25 April 1931, p. 6.

84. *Toledo Blade;* 25 February 1933.

85. Beatty, *Facing the Big Cats*, pp. 15–19.

86. Beatty, *Big Cage*, p. 268.

87. Clyde Beatty and Earl Wilson, *Jungle Performers* (New York: Robert M. McBride & Co., 1941), pp. 47–48.

88. Beatty, *Big Cage*, pp. 181–182.

89. *Ibid.*, p. 119.

90. Beatty, *Jungle Performers*, p. 92.

91. Helen Walsh Imer, "The Strange Germ that Lurked in the Lion's Bite," *Hagenbeck-Wallace Program—1932*, p. 16. (Reprint from *Everyweek Magazine*.)

92. *Peru* (Indiana) *Daily Tribune*, 30 January 1932, no page number.

93. "Clyde Beatty in Bad Shape," *Billboard* (February 1932), no page number.

94. Imer, p. 17.

95. *The Peru* (Indiana) *Republican*, 12 February 1932, p. 1.

96. *Peru* (Indiana) *Daily Tribune*, 25 January 1932, p. 1.

97. *The Peru* (Indiana) *Republican*, 29 January 1932, p. 1.

98. Edward Anthony, *This is Where I Came In* (New York: Doubleday & Co., 1960), pp. 257–276.

99. James R. Patterson, "Beatty and the Beasts," *Remember When*, 7 (August 1972), no page number.

100. Irvin S. Cobb, *Exit Laughing* (Indianapolis: Bobbs-Merrill Co., 1945), p. 341.

101. Beatty, *Jungle Performers*, pp. 33–34.

102. *Ibid.*, pp. 29, 83.

103. *Ibid.*, pp. 37–38.

104. Edwin T. Randall, "At Home with Clyde Beatty and His Lions and Tigers," *Cleveland Plain Dealer Magazine*, 17 February 1935, p. 5.

105. Beatty, *Facing the Big Cats*, p. 164.

106. Beatty, *Jungle Performers*, pp. 103–105.

107. "Clyde Beatty's Life is a Repetition of Thrills," *Cole Bros. Circus Program* (New York Hippodrome Edition), 1937, p. 2.

108. Joseph T. Bradbury, "A History of the Cole Bros. Circus 1935–1940," *Bandwagon*, 9 (May-June, 1965), pp. 4–6.

109. "3-Ring Investments," *Business Week*, 22 (April 27, 1935), pp. 22–23.

110. Henry Ringling North and Alden Hatch, *The Circus Kings* (New York: Doubleday & Co., 1960), p. 247.

111. Dexter W. Fellows, *This Way to the Big Show* (New York: Viking Press, 1936), p. 239.

112. Charly Baumann with Leonard A. Stevens, *Tiger, Tiger* (Chicago: Playboy Press, 1975), pp. 63–64.

113. Curry Kirkpatrick, "The Greatest Showman on Earth," *Sports Illustrated*, 47 (September 26, 1977), p. 89.

114. *New York Times*, 8 June 1935.

115. *New York Times*, 27 May 1936.

116. *New York Times*, 8 and 9 April 1937.

117. "Cat Man," *Time*, 29 (March 29, 1937), pp. 44–46.

118. Joseph T. Bradbury, "History of Cole Bros. Circus, 1935–1940, Pt. IX," *Bandwagon*, 10 (July-August, 1966), p. 16.

119. Joseph T. Bradbury, "History of Cole Bros. Circus, 1935–1940, Pt. VI," *Bandwagon*, 10 (March-April, 1966), pp. 20–21.

120. Bradbury, "Part IX," p. 18.

121. Joseph T. Bradbury, "History of Cole Bros. Circus, 1935–1940, Pt. XI," *Bandwagon*, 11 (March-April, 1967), pp. 14–24.

†*The Middletown* (Conn.) *Press* of July 3, 1925, told that Taylor (who works fourteen lions and three tigers) was hit in the head by the arena door as he entered the arena at the afternoon show on the second. He was taken to the local hospital and treated for a nerve strain in the neck but was aboard the train when it pulled out. The *Torrington* (Conn.) *Register* for the sixth reviewed the show and mentioned the Beatty act of mixed leopards, pumas, lions, hyenas, and black panther. It also said that the lion and tiger act did not appear since the trainer had been injured in Middletown.

There is also evidence that the arena shock story may be true. The Middletown write-up refers to an attack the previous winter and says that Taylor is fighting a bad case of nerves as well as the neck injury. This is confirmed by the January 17, 1925, *Billboard* report of Taylor's being confined for three weeks for a nervous breakdown.

Rumors abounded on the Hagenbeck-Wallace show that Taylor had left the show with someone's wife. He may have gone to Cuba, but he did return to have another act on Sells-Floto. Taylor supposedly settled down to run a riding school in Jacksonville, Florida, where he reportedly met his end when an irate husband shot and killed him.

Clyde Beatty did take over the Taylor act in 1925, but not as rapidly after Taylor's departure as legend would have it.

– Synopsis of information gathered by Dave Price.

Chapter III
THE RECENT YEARS

1. Bruce Bliven, Jr., "Long Live the Circus," *The New Republic*, 98 (April 26, 1939), p. 330.

2. "Circus Time," *Newsweek*, 15 (April 8, 1940), p. 18.

3. "Menagerie in Blue," *Time*, 37 (April 21, 1941), p. 61.

4. Henry Ringling North and Alden Hatch, *The Circus Kings* (New York: Doubleday & Co., 1960), p. 214.

5. "Ran Away from Stepmother at 12, Now He's a Lion Tamer," press release from Peru (Indiana) Public Library files.

6. *New York Times*, 31 March 1940, no page number.

7. Alfred Court, "Alfred Court in the U.S.A.," *White Tops*, 48 (March-April, 1975), p. 8.

8. "Greatest Show," *Time*, 35 (April 15, 1940), p. 75.

9. F. Beverly Kelley, "Here Kitty, Kitty," *Colliers*, 106 (July 20, 1940), pp. 23, 60.

10. Alfred Court, *My Life with the Big Cats* (New York: Simon & Schuster, 1955), p. 29.

11. *Ibid.*, pp. 32–33.

12. *Ibid.*, p. 39.

13. *Ibid.*, p. 37.

14. *Ibid.*, p. 45.

15. *Ibid.*, p. 130.

16. *Ibid.*, pp. 117–118.

17. Claire Fawcett, *We Fell in Love with the Circus* (n.p.: H. L. Lindquist Publications, 1949), p. 18.

18. Fred Bradna as told to Hartzell Spence, *The Big Top* (New York: Simon & Schuster, 1952), pp. 204–207.

19. John and Alice Durant, *Pictorial History of the American Circus* (New York: A. S. Barnes & Co., 1957), p. 227.

20. North, pp. 247–248.

21. Bill Ballentine, *Wild Tigers and Tame Fleas* (New York: Rinehart & Co., Inc., 1958), p. 77.

22. Alfred Court, "Noah's Ark: The Flight from War Torn Europe," *White Tops*, 49 (January-February, 1976), p. 16.

23. "Death Stops a Circus," *Newsweek*, 24 (July 17, 1944), pp. 31–32.

24. John Kobler, "Care to Train a Tiger?," *American Magazine*, 161 (June 1956), p. 24.

25. *New York Times*, 11 April 1959, p. 23.

26. *New York Times*, 14 April 1965, p. 36.

27. *Ringling Bros.–Barnum & Bailey Circus Magazine and Program*, 1977.

28. Edward Hoagland, *The Courage of Turtles* (New York: Random House, 1968), p. 70.

29. *New York Times*, 14 March 1976, Section 7, p. 26.

30. Charly Baumann with Leonard A. Stevens, *Tiger, Tiger* (Chicago: Playboy Press, 1975), p. 117.

31. *Ibid.*, p. 63.

32. *Ibid.*, p. 127.

33. Edward Hoagland, "The Soul of the Tiger," *Esquire*, 76 (July 1971), p. 130.

34. *New York Times*, 10 May 1971, p. 28.

35. "Big Cat with Big Cats," *Time*, 97 (May 24, 1971), p. 67.

36. *Ibid.*, jp. 67.

37. Hoagland, *Courage of Turtles*, pp. 64–65.

38. Phillips, p. 28.

39. *New York Times*, 13 May 1973, Section 6, p. 15.

40. Hoagland, "Soul of the Tiger," p. 130.

41. Phillips, p. 28.

42. Richard Schickel, "Gebel-Williams Burning Bright," *Harper's*, 243 (August 1971), p. 22.

43. Culhane, p. 17.

44. Curry Kirkpatrick, "The Greatest Showman on Earth," *Sports Illustrated*, 47 (September 26, 1977), p. 89.

45. *Ibid.*, p. 89.

46. *New York Times*, 3 June 1973, Section 6, p. 58.

47. Kirkpatrick, p. 89.

48. Culhane, p. 15.

49. Kirkpatrick, p. 90.

50. Hoagland, "Soul of the Tiger," p. 130.

51. Schickel, p. 23.

52. Schickel, p. 9.

53. Kirkpatrick, p. 90.

54. Jean Reed, "Circus Time is Here Again," *Siesta Key Pelican* (January 8, 1981), p. 38.

55. *Ibid.*

56. *The Peru* (Indiana) *Republican*, 12 February 1932, p. 2.

57. Leonard Traube, "Out in the Open," *Billboard* (February 1941), no page number.

58. Donald R. Carson, Walt Matthie, and Gordon Borders, "Clyde Beatty Circus—Season of 1946," *Bandwagon*, 14 (May-June, 1970), pp. 25–31.

59. Hazel L. Gable, "Clyde Beatty Wild Animal Circus—1945 Season," *White Tops*, 18 (March-April, 1945), p. 12.

60. Collie Small, "Lions 'N' Tigers 'N' Clyde Beatty," *Colliers*, 127 (April 7, 1951), pp. 60–61.

61. *Ibid.*, p. 60.

62. Mickey Spillane, "Sawdust in My Shoes," *Clyde Beatty Circus Program, 1957*, p. 18.

63. David O. Ives, "Entertainment Union Takes on the Big Top," *Wall Street Journal*, May 22, 1956, p. 1.

64. "Wintry Summer," *Wall Street Journal* (July 18, 1956), p. 10.

65. "End of the Trail," *Time*, 67 (May 28, 1956), p. 96.

66. Bruce R. Royal, epilogue by Roger Smith, *Speaking of Elephants* (n.p.: Texian Press, 1973), pp. 169–170.

67. *New York Times*, 9 November 1958, p. 73.

68. Frank Braden, "Move Over Pal," *Clyde Beatty–Cole Bros. Circus Program, 1960*, p. 1. (Quotes Robert Coleman, *New York Mirror*.)

69. Tom Parkinson, "Pros Operate All-Circus Beatty-Cole Aggregation," *Billboard*, 29 August 1960, p. 48.

70. *New York Times*, 24 November 1962, p. 17.

71. Irwin Kirby, "Beatty-Cole: It's Also the 'Big One'," *Amusement Business*, 26 April 1969, p. 20.

72. *Clyde Beatty–Cole Bros. Circus Program, 1960*.

73. Edward Anthony, "Clyde Beatty's Collaborator Closeup on Great Animal Trainer," *Variety*, 21 July 1965, pp. 34, 37.

74. Dale Carnegie, *Five Minute Biographies* (New York: Southern Publishers, Inc., 1937), p. 51.

75. Mark Hellinger, "That Fellow Beatty," *Sunday Mirror* (New York), 12 April 1936.

76. Drew Pearson and Robert S. Allen, "The Washington Merry-Go-Round," reprinted in 1937 *Cole Bros. Circus Program*.

77. G. Cornwell Spencer, "Clyde Beatty," *1938 Cole Bros. Circus Program*.

78. Ballentine, pp. 118–119.

79. Jane Beatty and Ann Pinchot, *Davey's Adventures with the Clyde Beatty Circus* (New York: Abelard-Schuman, 1965), p. 58.

80. *Ibid.*, p. 80.

81. *Ibid.*, p. 115.

82. *Ibid.*, p. 123.

83. Edwin T. Randall, "At Home with Clyde Beatty, His Lions and Tigers," *Cleveland Plain Dealer Magazine*, 17 February 1935, p. 5.

84. Clyde Beatty and Earl Wilson, *Jungle Performers* (New York: Robert M. McBride & Co., 1941), pp. 296–297.

85. Bernard Gavzer, "Raw Courage" (reprint of AP News feature), *Clyde Beatty–Cole Bros. Circus Program 1964*, p. 3.

86. Anthony, *Variety*, p. 57.

87. Beatty and Wilson, p. 18.

88. *Ibid.*, pp. 145–148.

89. *Detroit Free Press*, 18 March 1934, no page number.

90. Ballentine, p. 119.

91. Clyde Beatty with Edward Anthony, *Facing the Big Cats* (New York: Doubleday & Co., 1965), p. 17.

92. *Ibid.*, pp. 131–138.

93. *Ibid.*, p. 114.

94. Beatty, *Facing the Big Cats*, p. 152.

95. *Ibid.*

96. *Ibid.*, p. 211.

97. *Ibid.*, p. 211.

98. *Ibid.*, p. 233.

99. Anthony, *Variety*, p. 54.

100. Dave Price, "The Building of Legend . . . Clyde Beatty: Man or Myth," *White Tops*, 47 (July-August, 1974), pp. 13–14.

101. *Detroit News*, 14 February 1926, Metro section, p. 5.

102. *Kansas City Star*, 30 September 1928, Section c, p. 2.

103. *The Scioto Gazette* (Chillicothe, Ohio), 25 June 1929, no page number.

104. Toledo *Blade*, 27 January 1930, p. 1.

105. "How the Cat Man fights off Claws and Fangs," *The Literary Digest*, 108 (January 24, 1931), p. 31.

106. Paul Brown, "Beatty and the Beasts," *The American Magazine*, 114 (July 1932), p. 69.

107. Small, p. 60.

108. Randall, p. 1.

109. *Cole Bros.–Clyde Beatty Circus Magazine of 1935*.

110. *Detroit Free Press*, 20 July 1965, p. 1.

111. *Chillicothe* (Ohio) *Gazette*, 22 July 1966, p. 1.

112. Dave Price, "Harriett Beatty," *Bandwagon*, 18 (May-June, 1974), p. 15.

113. *Detroit News*, 14 February 1926, Metro section, p. 5.

114. "Working the Big Cats in the Kleig Lights," *The Literary Digest*, 115 (April 22, 1933), p. 26.

115. Clyde Beatty and Edward Anthony, "Bars and Stripes," *Colliers*, 102 (July 2, 1938), p. 14.

116. *Chillicothe* (Ohio) *Gazette*, 20 November 1941, no page number.

117. "Clyde Beatty's Playmates," *The Ohio Story* (radio script), May 31, 1955, no. 1266.

118. Ballantine, p. 137.

119. "The Cat Man," *Newsweek*, 61 (February 18, 1963), p. 92.

120. Clyde Beatty, "Don't Be Afraid to Live," *Detroit News Magazine*, 28 January 1962, p. 1.

121. Gavzer, pp. 3, 30.

122. *Detroit Free Press*, 20 July 1965, p. 1.

123. *New York Times*, 20 July 1965, no page number.

124. Leasure, p. 1.

125. An example of Beatty's name as a synonym for "wild animal trainer": "Each May it comes to life: a great rough beast, howling, snarling and belching. Each May it must be tamed, and it is in the style of that taming that the drama of the Indianapolis 500 takes shape. . . . Penske was in the best position of any car owner to play Clyde Beatty in this year's circus." Robert F. Jones, "Al Breaks 'Em in Right," *Sports Illustrated*, 48 (June 5, 1978), p. 22.

126. *Clyde Beatty-Cole Bros. Circus Program*, 1966.

127. Jerry Digney, "The Clyde Beatty Legend," *Clyde Beatty-Cole Bros. Circus Program*, 1977.

An interesting similarity exists between America's two most publicized wild animal trainers: Isaac Van Amburgh, the first really modern trainer and Clyde Beatty, who pioneered large mixed groups of lions and tigers of both sexes. They were born roughly a century apart, both in small towns—Van Amburgh in Fishkill, New York, Beatty in Bainbridge, Ohio. Both of their childhoods are relatively unknown and the subject of legend. Van Amburgh and Beatty began their circus careers as cageboys in large circus combines: The Flatfoot's Zoological Institute and the American Circus Corporation. They gained their chances at stardom when their English mentors (Roberts and Taylor) were injured and unable to perform. They burst upon the public scene in New York— Van Amburgh at the Richmond Hill Theatre in 1833, and Beatty in 1931 in Madison Square Garden. Their acts both stressed the killer nature of the big cats and man's dominance over them, especially through utilization of "sheer will" and the "hypnotic eye."

Following their big city debuts, they became involved in other ventures during the off-season. Van Amburgh gained parts in plays specially written for him and his animals and became the subject of a book and a song. Beatty was in motion pictures, wrote books, and later had a radio show. Early in his career, Van Amburgh's name was utilized as a circus title, although he did not own the show. This also occurred with Beatty and Cole Bros. in 1935. Van Amburgh proved an extremely shrewd businessman and was the first American circus performer to court personal publicity. Beatty, too, was extremely active in creating his own legendary status. Both later owned their own circuses. Van Amburgh, always an innovator, utilized showboats, parades, and introduced the American style tent show in Europe. Beatty was one of the final users of the street parade and had the last railroad tent show in America.

Little is recorded about either one's personal life. Late in their careers, they often were mistakenly reported killed by their cats. Both remained active until their deaths and neither died performing. Van Amburgh suffered a fatal heart attack in his hotel room in Philadelphia in 1865, Beatty died of cancer in a hospital in California in 1965. Both names were considered invaluable in circus titles. Van Amburgh's name remained active for ninety years, Beatty's has now been utilized for forty-eight years. Oddly enough, the full title of the show Beatty originally joined was Howe's Great London and Van Amburgh's Trained Wild Animal Circus—the last time this title was utilized. [Author's note.]

ENDNOTES

Chapter IV

THE WILD ANIMAL TRAINER IN AMERICA
HERO OR VILLAIN?

1. Eugene Wood, "Circus Day — A Reminiscence of 'Back Home,'" *McClure's*, 25 (September 1905), pp. 526, 531, 533.

2. *Ibid.*, p. 531.

3. *Ibid.*, p. 533.

4. Ellen Velvin, *Behind the Scenes with Wild Animals* (New York: Moffat, Yard & Co., 1906), p. 163.

5. Clyde Beatty and Edward Anthony, *Facing the Big Cats* (New York: Doubleday & Co., 1965), p. 219.

6. Clyde Beatty with Edward Anthony, *The Big Cage* (New York, The Century Co., 1933), p. 278.

7. Velvin, pp. 101–102.

8. Thomas W. Duncan, *Gus the Great* (Philadelphia: J. B. Lippincott Co., 1947), pp. 38–39.

9. *Ibid.*, p. 43.

10. *Ibid.*, p. 52.

11. *Ibid.*, p. 566.

12. *Ibid.*, p. 510.

13. *Ibid.*, p. 566.

14. Roman Proske, *Lion, Tigers and Me* (New York: Henry Holt & Co., 1956), p. 249.

15. Edward Hoagland, *Cat Man* (New York: Houghton-Mifflin Co., 1958), p. 99.

16. *Ibid.*, pp. 214–215.

17. *Ibid.*, p. 105.

18. *Ibid.*, p. 237.

19. *Ibid.*, p. 205.

20. Connie Clausen, *I Love You Honey, but the Season's Over* (New York: Holt, Rinehart & Winston, Inc., 1960), p. 144.

21. Clausen, pp. 147–148.

22. *Ibid.*, p. 148.

23. *Ibid.*, pp. 147–148.

24. Darryl Ponicsan, *The Ringmaster* (New York: Delacorte Press, 1978), p. 69.

25. J. Y. Henderson, D.V.M. and Richard Taplinger, *Circus Doctor* (Boston: Little, Brown & Co., 1951), p. 89.

26. Edward Hoagland, "The Soul of the Tiger," *Esquire*, 76 (July 1971), p. 130.

27. *Ibid.*

28. Lace Kendall, *Tigers, Trainers and Dancing Whales* (Philadelphia: MacRae Smith Co.), p. 74.

29. *Kansas City Star*, 30 September 1928, Section c, p. 1.

30. "The Super-Spectacular New 107th Edition of Ringling Bros. and Barnum & Bailey Circus is Coming with Superlatives Galore," *Marquee*, 1 (August 1978), p. 3.

31. Jim Tully, *Circus Parade* (New York: Literary Guild of America, 1927), pp. 8, 10, 17.

32. George Brinton Beal, *Through the Back Door of the Circus* (Springfield, Mass.: McLoughlin Bros. Inc., 1938), pp. 147–148.

33. Wesley L. Skillings, "Captain of the Big Cage," *Grit*, 25 (August 1974), pp. 18–19.

34. Marian Murray, *Circus: Rome to Ringling* (New York: Appleton-Century-Crofts, Inc., 1956), pp. 321–322.

35. Jimmy Chipperfield, *My Wild Life* (New York: G. P. Putnam's Sons, 1976), pp. 55–56.

36. *Ibid.*, p. 56.

37. Dr. H. Hediger, *Wild Animals in Captivity* (London: Butterworth's Scientific Publications, 1950), p. 23.

38. *Ibid.*, pp. 106–108.

39. *Ibid.*, pp. 166–167.

40. *Ibid.*, p. 46.

41. *Ibid.*, pp. 167–168.

42. *Ibid.*, p. 108.

43. *Ibid.*, p. 168.

44. *Ibid.*, p. 166.

45. *Ibid.*, p. 157. Hediger contends that since the great cats are occasional feeders, food stimuli play no real part in their training. *Ibid.*, p. 126.

46. Samuel Hopkins Adams, ed., "Notes from a Trainer's Book," *McClure's*, 24 (December 1904), p. 188.

47. *Ibid.*, p. 197.

48. *Ibid.*, p. 162.

49. Tully, p. 100.

50. Henderson, pp. 49–50.

51. Fred Powledge, *Mud Show: A Circus Season* (New York: Harcourt Brace Jovanovich, 1975), pp. 8, 77–78.

52. Frank Foster, *Pink Coat, Spangles and Sawdust* (London: Stanley Paul & Co. Ltd.), p. 125.

53. Velvin, pp. 108–110.

54. *Kansas City Star*, p. 3.

55. Philippe Diole, *The Errant Ark* (New York: G. P. Putnam's Sons, 1974), p. 64.

56. Juliet Bridgman, "The Headaches of a Circus Doctor," *Saturday Evening Post*, 222 (August 20, 1949), p. 99.

57. Henderson, pp. 49–50.

58. Skillings, p. 19.

59. Conversely, Gunther Gebel-Williams claims he has the ability to close a door mentally on the cats when he finishes his act and does not think about them again. Hoagland, "The Soul of the Tiger," p. 130.

60. Tully, p. 100.

61. Ernest Hemingway, *Death in the Afternoon* (New York: Charles Scribner's Sons, 1932), pp. 16, 21, 24, 58, 213, 222.

62. *Ibid.*, p. 58.

63. *Ibid.*, p. 84.

64. *Ibid.*, p. 213.

65. D. R. McMullin, "Tiger Lady Mabel Stark," *WomenSports*, 3 (January 1976), pp. 19–20.

66. Proske, p. 175.

67. *Ibid.*, p. 135.

68. *Ibid.*, pp. 18, 201.

69. Edward Hoagland, *The Courage of Turtles* (New York: Random House, 1968, 1969, 1970), p. 209.

70. Ponicsan, pp. 1–2.

71. *Ibid.*, pp. 1–6.

72. *Ibid.*, p. 67.

73. *Ibid.*, p. 283.

74. *Ibid.*, pp. 302–303.

75. Hemingway, p. 21.

76. Franz Schneider, "All the World's a Circus," *America*, 104 (December 24, 1960), p. 426.

77. Alfred Henry Bramilow, "The History of an 'African' Lion Tamer," *New Monthly Magazine*, 161 (1877), pp. 175–181.

78. *Ibid.*, p. 179.

79. *Ibid.*

80. *Ibid.*, p. 180.

81. *Ibid.*, jp. 181.

82. *Ibid.*, p. 176.

83. *Ibid.*, p. 181.

84. Schneider, p. 426.

85. Ruth Manning Sanders, *Luke's Circus* (Boston: Little, Brown & Co., 1940), pp. 21–22.

86. "Man-Killers and Man-Eaters," *Temple Bar*, 21 (1867), pp. 114–117.

87. "Three Months with a Lion King," *Gentleman's Magazine* (London, March 1873), p. 261.

88. E. S. Turner, *All Heaven in a Rage* (New York: St. Martin's Press, 1965), pp. 270–271.

89. Roland J. Gibbs, D.V.M., "Endangered Species Report—Legal Rights of Animals in America," *White Tops*, 52 (July-August, 1979), p. 34.

90. John G. Mitchell, "Bitter Harvest: Hunting in America—Book Two: In Another Country," *Audubon*, 81 (July 1979), pp. 70–73.

91. *New York Times*, 29 August 1950, p. 29.

92. Jeanne Roush, "Animals Under the Big Top," *The Humane Society of The United States News*, 26 (Spring 1981), p. 18.

93. *Ibid.*, p. 21.

94. Diole, p. 20.

95. *Ibid.*, p. 28.

96. *Ibid.*, p. 53.

97. *Ibid.*, pp. 51–54.

98. *Ibid.*, p. 146.

99. Boyce Rensberger, *The Cult of the Wild* (Garden City, N.Y.: Anchor Press/Doubleday, 1978), pp. 1–25.

100. *Ibid.*, p. 2.

101. *Ibid.*, pp. 201–216.

102. *Ibid.*, pp. 217–251.

103. Murray, p. 329.

104. Cleveland *Plain Dealer*, 26 January 1934, p. 17.

105. Chipperfield, p. 54.

106. *Ibid.*, p. 183.

107. Hermann Dembeck, *Animals and Men* (Garden City, N.Y.: Natural History Press, 1965), p. 318.

108. Velvin, pp. 84–85.

109. *Ibid.*, pp. 139–140.

110. Maitland Edey, *The Cats of Africa* (New York: Time-Life Books, 1968), pp. 35–36.

111. *Ibid.*, pp. 87–106.

112. Beatty, *The Big Cage*, p. 130.

113. Anthony Hippisley Coxe, *A Seat at the Circus* (London: Evans Bros. Ltd., 1951), p. 130.

114. *Ibid.*, pp. 72–73.

115. Hediger, pp. 4–12.

116. *Ibid.*, p. 44.

117. *Ibid.*, p. 53.

118. *Ibid.*, pp. 65–69.

119. *New York Times*, 26 February 1950, p. 1.

120. *New York Times*, 27 February 1950, p. 1.

121. Collie Small, "Lions 'N' Tigers 'N' Clyde Beatty," *Colliers*, 127 (April 7, 1951), p. 60.

122. Hediger, p. 155.

123. *Ibid.*, p. 156.

124. *Ibid.*, pp. 158–161.

125. Bertha Bennet Burleigh, *Circus* (New York: G. P. Putnam's Sons, 1938); Paul Eipper, "How Wild Animals Are Trained," *St. Nicholas*, 58 (October 1931), p. 840; Geraldine Kreml, *About the Circus*, Public Relations Department—Ringling Bros.-Barnum & Bailey Combined Shows, Inc., p. 5.

126. "Speeches of Felds—Father and Son—at Providence, R.I.," *White Tops*, 50 (January-February, 1977), pp. 39–40.

127. Kreml, pp. 3–5.

128. Hjalmar Hjorth Boyesen, "Training Wild Animals," *Cosmopolitan*, 34 (December 1902), p. 132.

BIBLIOGRAPHY

Articles

Adams, Samuel Hopkins. "The Training of Lions, Tigers and Other Great Cats." *McClure's* 15 (September 1900): 386–398.

Adams, Samuel Hopkins (editor). "Notes From a Trainer's Book." *McClure's* 24 (December 1904).

Aflalo, F. G. "The Ethics of Performing Animals." *Fortnightly* 73 (March 1900): 382–391.

"Among the Nomads or Life in the Open." *Brave and Bold* 340 (June 26, 1909): 1–31.

Beatty, Clyde and Anthony, Edward. "Bars and Stripes." *Colliers* 102 (July 2, 1938): 14.

———. "Don't be Afraid to Live." *Detroit News Magazine* (January 28, 1962): 1.

Benson, John T. "How Wild Animals Are Picked and Trained for Circus Jobs." *American Magazine* 99 (March 1925): 48, 192.

Bensuan, S. L. "The Torture of Trained Animals." *English Illustrated Magazine* (April 1896).

Bertren, Berton. "Barnum's Young Shadow." *Pluck and Luck* 413 (May 1906): 1–30.

"Big Cat with Big Cats." *Time* 97 (May 24, 1971): 67.

Bliven, Jr., Bruce. "Long Live the Circus." *The New Republic* 98 (April 26, 1939): 30.

Boger, Hermann. "Training Wild Beasts." *The Independent* 55 (October 29, 1902): 2551–2557.

Bonavita, Jack. "How I Became a Wild Animal Trainer." *The Delineator* 74 (September 1909): 254.

Borders, Gordon. "Al G. Barnes Winterquarters at Culver City, California." *Bandwagon* 11 (July-August, 1967): 10–12.

Bostock, Frank C. "The Brute in Captivity." *Frank Leslie's Popular Monthly* 53 (December 1901).

Bowen, Elbert R. "The Circus in Early Rural Missouri." *Bandwagon* 9 (September-October, 1965): 12–17.

Boyer, Hermann. "Training Wild Beasts." *The Independent* 55 (October 29, 1903): 2556.

Boyesen, Hjalmar Hjorth. "Training Wild Animals." *Cosmopolitan* 34 (December 1902): 132.

Bradbury, Joseph T. "The Circus Winterquarters in West Baden, Indiana." *Bandwagon* 16 (September-October, 1972): 7–8.

———. "Gollmar Bros. Circus, Season of 1922." *Bandwagon* 9 (January-February, 1965): 4–13.

———. "A History of the Cole Bros. Circus, 1935–1940." *Bandwagon* 9 (May-June, 1965): 4–6.

———. "History of Cole Bros. Circus, 1935–1940." Part VI. *Bandwagon* 10 (March-April, 1966): 20–21.

———. "History of Cole Bros. Circus, 1935–1940." Part IX. *Bandwagon* 10 (July-August, 1966): 16.

———. "History of Cole Bros. Circus, 1935–1940." Part XI. *Bandwagon* 11 (March-April, 1967): 14–24.

———. "Howe's Great London Circus—Season of 1921." *Bandwagon* 8 (September-October, 1964): 4–13.

———. "John Ringling's Circus Empire." *White Tops* 46 (November-December, 1973): 7.

Braden, Frank. "An Interesting Interview with Jerry Mugivan—1921." *Bandwagon* 5 (March-April, 1961): 15–18.

Bramilow, Alfred Henry (edited by). "The History of an 'African' Lion Tamer." *New Monthly Magazine* 161 (1877): 175–181.

"Breaking of Performing Animals." *The Literary Digest* 73 (May 6, 1922): 80–82.

Bridgman, Juliet. "The Headaches of a Circus Doctor." *Saturday Evening Post* 222 (August 20, 1949): 99.

Brown, Paul. "Beatty and the Beasts." *The American Magazine* 114 (July 1932): 69.

Browning, Henry. "The True History of A Great Pacificator." *New Monthly Magazine* (January 1839).

Carson, Donald R., Matthie, Walt, and Borders, Gordon. "Clyde Beatty Circus — Season of 1946." *Bandwagon* 14 (May-June, 1970): 25–31.

"Cat Man." *Time* 29 (March 29, 1937): 44–46.

"The Cat Man." *Newsweek* 61 (February 18, 1963): 92.

"Circus Time." *Newsweek* 15 (April 8, 1940): 18.

"The Complete Lion Tamer." *Harper's Weekly* 55 (January 28, 1911): 33.

Condon, Chalmer. "B. E. Wallace." *Bandwagon* 8 (July-August, 1964): 3–6.

Cooper, Courtney Ryley. "The Lady of the Steel Arena." *Ladies Home Journal* 38 (July 1921): 94.

Court, Alfred. "Alfred Court in the U.S.A." *White Tops* 48 (March-April, 1975): 8.

———. "Noah's Ark: The Flight from War Torn Europe." *White Tops* 49 (January-February, 1976): 16.

"Cruelty Charged in Training Trick Animals for Stage and Movies." *The Literary Digest* 66 (September 25, 1920): 102–110.

"Death Stops a Circus." *Newsweek* 24 (July 17, 1944): 31–32.

Eipper, Paul. "How Wild Animals Are Trained." *St. Nicholas* 58 (October 1931): 840.

"End of the Trail." *Time* 67 (May 28, 1956): 96.

Ex-Lion King. "Lions and Lion Taming." *Every Saturday* 12 (February 17, 1872): 172–176.

Fox, Edward Lyell. "When the Jungle Goes to School." *Harper's Weekly* 56 (November 30, 1912): 18.

Gable, Hazel L. "Clyde Beatty Wild Animal Circus — 1945 Season." *White Tops* 18 (March-April, 1945): 12.

Gibbs, Roland J., D.V.M. "Endangered Species Report — Legal Rights of Animals in America." *White Tops* 52 (July-August, 1979): 34.

"Greatest Show." *Time* 35 (April 15, 1940): 75.

Hallock, E. S. "The American Circus." *Century* 70 (August 1905): 568–585.

Heliot, Claire. "Diary of a Lion-Tamer." *Cosmopolitan* 41 (September 1906): 464.

Hoagland, Edward. "The Soul of the Tiger." *Esquire* 76 (July 1971): 130.

Kelley, F. Beverly. "Here Kitty, Kitty." *Colliers* 106 (July 20, 1940): 23, 60.

Kirby, Maurice Brown. "The Gentle Art of Training Wild Beasts." *Everybody's Magazine* 19 (October 1908): 435–445.

Kirkpatrick, Curry. "The Greatest Showman on Earth." *Sports Illustrated* 47 (September 26, 1977): 89.

Kitchen, Robert. "Grizzly Adams: Fearless Menagerie, Circus Star." *The White Tops* 50 (March-April, 1977): 8–9.

Kobler, John. "Care to Train a Tiger?" *American Magazine* 161 (June 1956): 24.

Leithead, J. Edward. "The Anatomy of Dime Novels." *Dime Novel Round-Up* 37 (September 15, 1968): 92–102.

Lewisohn, Ludwig. "The Circus." *The Nation* 114 (April 12, 1922): 446–447.

"Lions and Lion Tamers." *Bailey's Magazine* (September 1884).

"Lion Kings, Queens and Trainers." *Chambers Journal* (March 17, 1877).

McFarlane, Arthur E. "Deceptive Showmen." *Colliers* 42 (January 9, 1909): 19.

McMullin, D. R. "Tiger Lady Mabel Stark." *WomenSports* 3 (January 1976): 19–22.

"Man-Killers and Man-Eaters." *Temple Bar* 21 (1867): 114–117.

Marcosson, Isaac F. "Sawdust and Goldust — The Earnings of Circus People." *Bookman* 31 (June 1910): 402–410.

"Menagerie in Blue." *Time* 37 (April 21, 1941): 61.

Metcalfe, Francis. "Side Show Studies." *Outing* 45 (March 1905): 715–716.

Mitchell, John G. "Bitter Harvest: Hunting in America—Book Two: In Another Country." *Audubon* 81 (July 1979): 70–73.

Moffett, Cleveland. "Careers of Danger and Daring—The Wild Beast Trainer." *St. Nicholas* 28 (August 1901): 867–882.

Nelson, Bert. "Lion Taming's the Bunk." *Saturday Evening Post* (1935).

O'Malley, John W. "The Story of the West Baden Springs Hotel." *Orange County Heritage* (no date): 119–127.

Paine, Henry Gallup. "The Lion Tamer." *Harpers* 94 (May 1897): 962–968.

Patterson, James R. "Beatty and the Beasts." *Remember When* 7 (August 1972): no page numbers.

Peake, Elmore Elliott. "The Wrath of Afric." *Cosmopolitan* 34 (November 1920): 105–113.

"Personal Glimpses—How the Cat Man Fights Off Claws and Fangs." *The Literary Digest* 108 (January 24, 1931): 32–33.

Pfening, Jr., Fred D. "How Wallace Bought Hagenbeck." *Bandwagon* 8 (July-August, 1964): 11–12.

————. "Masters of the Steel Arena." *Bandwagon* 16 (May-June, 1972): 4–17.

Price, Dave. "The Building of a Legend . . . Clyde Beatty: Man or Myth." *White Tops* 47 (July-August, 1974): 13–14.

————. "Harriett Beatty." *Bandwagon* 18 (May-June, 1974): 15.

Randall, Edwin T. "At Home with Clyde Beatty and His Lions and Tigers." *Cleveland Plain Dealer Magazine* (February 17, 1935): 5.

"Recreation of an Era." *Indiana History Bulletin* 48 (September 1971): 131.

Reynolds, Chang. "Hagenbeck-Wallace Circus, 1922." *Bandwagon* 9 (November-December, 1965): 4–6.

————. "John Robinson's Circus 1824—For 100 Years has kept Faith with the Public—1923." *Bandwagon* 6 (September-October, 1962): 3–6.

Ringling, John. "We Divided the Job—But Stuck Together." *American Magazine* 88 (September 1919): 56–58.

Rouse, W. J. "The Adventures of a Lion Tamer." *Cosmopolitan* 5 (September 1888): 380–384.

Roush, Jeanne. "Animals Under the Big Top." *The Humane Society of The United States News* 26 (Spring 1981): 18–21.

Schickel, Richard. "Gebel-Williams Burning Bright." *Harpers* 243 (August 1971): 9.

Schneider, Franz. "All the World's a Circus." *America* 104 (December 24, 1960): 426.

Shawell, Julia. "Clyde Beatty Says Women Are Like Tigers." *Pictorial Review* 35 (March 1934): 4.

Shepstone, Harold J. "The Scientific Training of Wild Animals." *Scientific American* 87 (October 18, 1902): 260–261.

————. "Trained Animals at the World's Fair." *Scientific American* 91 (August 6, 1904): 97–98.

Skillings, Wesley L. "Captain of the Big Cage." *Grit* (August 25, 1974): 18–19.

Small, Collie. "Lions 'N' tigers 'N' Clyde Beatty." *Colliers* 127 (April 7, 1951): 60–61.

"Speeches of Felds—Father and Son—at Providence, R.I." *White Tops* 50 (January-February, 1977): 39–40.

Standish, Hal. "Fred Fearnot and the Wild Beast Tamer." *Work and Win* 364 (November 24, 1905): 16–27.

Sutherland, Harvey. "Training of Wild Beasts." *Current Literature* 32 (June 1902): 709.

"Three Months with a Lion King." *Gentleman's Magazine* (London), March 1873.

"Three-Ring Investments," *Business Week* 22 (April 27, 1935): 22–23.

Truzzi, Marcello. "The American Circus as a Source of Folklore: An Introduction." *Southern Folklore Quarterly* 30 (December 1966): 289–300.

————. "The Training of Lions, Tigers, and Other Great Cats." *McClure's* (1900).

Vail, R.W.G. "This Way to the Big Top." *The New York Historical Society Quarterly Bulletin* 29 (July 1945): 146–147.

Velvin, Ellen. "Hairbreadth Escapes in a Wild Animal Show." *Ladies Home Journal* 23 (February 1906): 15–16.

————. "Wild Beast Tamer." *St. Nicholas* (1901).

Wirth, Charles. "The New Circus 'Home' at Peru." *Bandwagon* 8 (July-August, 1964): 13–15.

Wood, Eugene. "Circus Day—A Reminiscence of 'Back Home.'" *McClure's* 25 (September 1905): 526–533.

"Working the Big Cats in the Kleig Lights." *The Literary Digest* 115 (April 22, 1933): 26.

Books

Anthony, Edward. *This is Where I Came In.* New York: Doubleday & Co., 1960.

Ballentine, Bill. *Wild Tigers and Tame Fleas.* New York: Rinehart & Co., Inc., 1958.

Baumann, Charly, and Stevens, Leonard A. *Tiger, Tiger.* Chicago: Playboy Press, 1975.

Beal, George Brinton. *Through the Back Door of the Circus.* Springfield, Mass.: McLoughlin Bros. Inc., 1938.

Beatty, Clyde, and Anthony, Edward. *The Big Cage.* New York: The Century Co., 1933.

————. *Facing the Big Cats.* New York: Doubleday & Co., 1965.

Beatty, Clyde, and Wilson, Earl. *Jungle Performers.* New York: Robert M. McBride & Co., 1941.

Beatty, Jane, and Pinchot, Ann. *Davey's Adventures with the Clyde Beatty Circus.* New York: Abelard-Schumann, 1965.

Bostock, E. H. *Menageries, Circuses and Theatres.* New York: Frederick A. Stones Co., 1928.

Bostock, Frank C. *The Training of Wild Animals.* New York: The Century Co., 1920.

Bradna, Fred, and Spence, Hartzell. *The Big Top.* New York: Simon & Schuster, 1952.

Burleigh, Bertha Bennet. *Circus.* New York: G. P. Putnam's Sons, 1938.

Chindahl, George L. *A History of the Circus in America.* Caldwell, Idaho: Caxton Printers, Ltd., 1959.

Chipperfield, Jimmy. *My Wild Life.* New York: G. P. Putnam's Sons, 1976.

Clausen, Connie. *I Love You Honey, but the Season's Over.* New York: Holt, Rinehart & Winston, Inc., 1960.

Cobb, Irvin S. *Exit Laughing.* Indianapolis: Bobbs-Merrill Co., 1945.

A Concise Account Interspersed with Anecdotes of Van Amburg's Celebrated Collection of Trained Animals. J. W. Peel, Printer. Lambeth, 1941.

Conklin, George. *The Ways of the Circus.* New York: Harper & Bros., 1921.

Cooper, Courtney Ryley. *Circus Day.* New York: Farrar & Rinehart, Inc., 1925.

————. *Lions 'N' Tigers 'N' Everything.* Boston: Little, Brown & Co., 1924.

————. *Under the Big Top.* Boston: Little, Brown & Co., 1923.

Coup, W. C. *Sawdust and Spangles.* Chicago: Herbert S. Stone & Co., 1901.

Court, Alfred. *My Life with the Big Cats.* New York: Simon & Schuster, 1955.

Coxe, Anthony Hippisley. *A Seat at the Circus.* London: Evans Bros., Ltd., 1951.

Dembeck, Hermann. *Animals and Men.* Garden City, N.Y.: Natural History Press, 1965.

Dillon, Richard. *The Legend of Grizzly Adams.* New York: Berkley Publishing Co., 1966.

Diole, Philippe. *The Errant Ark.* New York: G. P. Putnam's Sons, 1974.

Duncan, Thomas W. *Gus the Great.* Philadelphia: J. B. Lippincott Co., 1947.

Durant, John and Alice. *Pictorial History of the American Circus.* New York: A. S. Barnes & Co., 1957.

Edey, Maitland. *The Cats of Africa.* New York: Time-Life Books, 1968.

Fawcett, Claire. *We Fell in Love with the Circus.* H. L. Lindquist Publications, 1949.

Fellows, Dexter W. *This Way to the Big Show.* New York: Viking Press, 1936.

Fenner, Mildred Sandison and Wolcott. *The Circus—Lure and Legend.* Englewood Cliffs, N.J.: Prentice-Hall, Inc., 1970.

Foster, Frank. *Pink Coat, Spangles and Sawdust.* Stanley Paul & Co., Ltd.

Fox, Charles Phillip, and Parkinson, Tom. *The Circus in America.* Waukesha, Wis.: Country Beautiful, 1969.

Frost, Thomas. *Circus Life and Circus Celebrities (1875).* Detroit: Singing Tree Press, 1970.

Gollmar, Robert H. *My Father Owned A Circus*. Caldwell, Idaho: Caxton Printers, Ltd., 1965.

Hagenbeck, Carl. *Beasts and Men*. London: Longmans, Green & Co., 1909.

Hediger, Dr. H. *Wild Animals in Captivity*. London: Butterworth's Scientific Publications, 1950.

Hemingway, Ernest. *Death in the Afternoon*. New York: Charles Scribner's Sons, 1932.

Henderson, J. Y., and Taplinger, Richard. *Circus Doctor*. Boston: Little, Brown & Co., 1951.

Hoagland, Edward. *Cat Man*. New York: Houghton-Mifflin Co., 1958.

———. *The Courage of Turtles*. New York: Random House, 1968, 1969, 1970.

Hubbard, Freeman. *Great Days of the Circus*. New York: American Heritage Publishing Co., 1962.

Kelly, Emmett, and Kelley, F. Beverly. *Clown*. New York: Prentice-Hall, Inc., 1954.

Kendall, Lace. *Tigers, Trainers and Dancing Whales*. Philadelphia: MacRae Smith Co.

Klaitts, Joseph and Barne, ed. *Animals and Man in Historic Perspective*. Chicago: Harper and Row, 1974.

Klapp, Orrin E. *Heroes, Villains, and Fools*. Englewood Cliffs, N.J.: Prentice-Hall, Inc., 1962.

Lano, David. *A Wandering Showman, I*. Lansing: Michigan State University Press, 1957.

London, Jack. *Michael, Brother of Jerry*. New York: Grosset and Dunlap, 1917.

London, Joan. *Jack London and His Times*. Seattle: University of Washington Press, 1939.

McCullough, Edo. *Good Old Coney Island*. New York: Charles Scribner's Sons, 1957.

McKennon, Joe. *Horse Dung Trail*. Sarasota, Fla.: Carnival Publishers of Sarasota, 1975.

———. *A Pictorial History of the American Carnival*. Sarasota, Fla.: Carnival Publishers of Sarasota, 1972.

May, Earl Chapin. *The Circus From Rome to Ringling*. New York: Dover Publications, Inc., 1932.

Millette, Ernest Schlee, and Wyndham, Robert. *The Circus That Was*. Philadelphia: Dorrance & Co., 1971.

Murray, Marian. *Circus! From Rome to Ringling*. New York: Appleton-Century-Crofts, Inc., 1956.

North, Henry Ringling, and Hatch, Alden. *The Circus Kings*. New York: Doubleday & Co., 1960.

O'Brien, Essie Forrester. *Circus: Cinders to Sawdust*. San Antonio, Tex.: The Naylor Co., 1959.

O'Connor, Richard. *Jack London, A Biography*. Boston: Little, Brown & Co., 1964.

Peck, The Hon. George W. *Peck's Bad Boy With the Circus*. Chicago: Thompson and Thomas, 1906.

Pilat, Oliver, and Ranson, Jo. *Sodom by the Sea*. Garden City, N.Y.: Doubleday, Donan & Co., 1941.

Ponicsan, Darryl. *The Ringmaster*. New York: Delacorte Press, 1978.

Powledge, Fred. *Mud Show: A Circus Season*. New York: Harcourt Brace Jovanovich, 1975.

Priddy, Al. *The Way of the Circus*. Chicago: The Platform World, 1930.

Proske, Roman. *Lions, Tigers and Me*. New York: Henry Holt & Co., 1956.

Rennert, Jack. *100 Years of Circus Posters*. New York: Darien House Books, 1974.

Rensberger, Boyce. *The Cult of the Wild*. Garden City, N.Y.: Anchor Press/Doubleday, 1978.

Reynolds, Chang. *Pioneer Circuses of the West*. Los Angeles: Western Lore Press, 1966.

Robeson, Dave. *Louis Roth—Forty Years with Jungle Killers*. Caldwell, Idaho: Caxton Printers, Ltd., 1945.

Robeson, Dave, and Barnes, Al G. *Al G. Barnes, Master Showman*. Caldwell, Idaho: Caxton Printers, Ltd., 1935.

Royal, Bruce R. *Speaking of Elephants*. Texian Press, 1973.

Sanders, Ruth Manning. *Luke's Circus*. Boston: Little, Brown & Company, 1940.

Sherwood, Robert Edmund. *Here We Are Again*. Indianapolis: Bobbs-Merrill Co., 1926.

Sinclair, Andrew. *Jack—A Biography of Jack London*. New York: Harper & Row, 1977.

Stark, Mabel, and Orr, Gertrude. *Hold That Tiger*. Caldwell, Idaho: Caxton Printers, Ltd., 1938.

Stott, R. Toole. *Circus and Allied Arts*. Derby, England: Harpur & Sons, Ltd., 1957.

Thayer, Stuart. *Annals of the American Circus: 1793–1829*. Manchester, Mich.: Rymark Printing, 1976.

Thomas, Richard. *John Ringling*. New York: Pageant Press, Inc., 1960.

Thompson, W. C. *On the Road with a Circus*. Goldmann, 1903.

Tully, Jim. *Circus Parade*. New York: Literary Guild of America, 1927.

Turner, E. S. *All Heaven in a Rage*. New York: St. Martin's Press, 1965.

Turner, James. *Reckoning with the Beast*. Baltimore: The Johns Hopkins University Press, 1980.

Vail, R.W.G. *Random Notes of the History of the Early American Circus*. American Antiquarian Society, 1933.

Velvin, Ellen. *Behind the Scenes with Wild Animals*. New York: Moffat, Yard & Co., 1906.

Watts, Ephraim. *The Life of Van Amburgh: The Brute Tamer*. London, 1838.

Newspapers, Trade Papers, Programs, Guides

Amusement Business, 1969.

Billboard, 1909, 1924, 1925, 1932, 1960.

Chillicothe Gazette, 1941, 1966.

Cleveland *Plain Dealer*, 1923, 1934.

Clyde Beatty Circus Program, 1957.

Clyde Beatty–Cole Bros. Circus Program, 1960, 1964, 1966, 1977, 1978.

Cole Bros.–Clyde Beatty Circus Magazine for Seasons of 1935, 1937, 1938.

Columbus Dispatch, 1965.

Conover, Richard E. *Wisconsin's Unique Heritage*. Baraboo, Wis.: Circus World Museum, 1967.

Detroit Free Press, 1934, 1965.

Detroit News, 1926, 1960, 1962.

Hagenbeck-Wallace Circus Program, 1931, 1932.

Kansas City Star, 1928.

Kreml, Geraldine. *About the Circus*. Public Relations Department: Ringling Bros.– Barnum & Bailey Combined Shows, Inc.

Marquee, 1978.

Miller, Mel. *Ringling Museum of the Circus*. Sarasota, Fla.: John and Mabel Ringling Museum of Art, 1963.

New York Times, 1878, 1879, 1894, 1905, 1911, 1922, 1925, 1926, 1931, 1934, 1940, 1950, 1958, 1959, 1962, 1965, 1971, 1973, 1976.

Peru Circus City Festival Souvenir Program, 1976.

Peru Daily Tribune (Indiana), 1930, 1932, 1966.

Peru Republican, 1932.

Ringling Bros.–Barnum & Bailey Circus Magazine and Program, 1954, 1977.

Scioto Gazette (Chillicothe), 1929.

Siesta Key Pelican, January 8, 1981.

Toledo *Blade*, 1930, 1933.

Variety, 1965.

Wall Street Journal, 1956.

Unpublished Manuscripts

O'Malley, John W. *The Story of the West Baden Springs Hotel*. Master's Thesis: Loyola University (Chicago), 1957.

Polacsek, John F. *The Development of the Circus and Menagerie: 1825–1860*. Master's Thesis: Bowling Green State University, 1974.

Reddin, Paul L. *Wild West Shows: A Study in the Development of Western Romanticism.*
    Ph.D. Dissertation: University of Missouri, 1970.
Thayer, Stuart. "The Keeper Will Enter the Cage, Early American Wild Animal Trainers."

INDEX

RINGLING AND BARNUM BROS COMBINED SHOWS & BAILEY

TERRELL JACOBS

EARTH'S FOREMOST TRAINER of SAVAGE WILD BEASTS

PRESENTS ...

FURIOUSLY FEROCIOUS KILLERS of the JUNGLE HITHERTO UNTAMEABLE and UNCONQUERABLE

THE WORLD'S FIRST AND ONLY GROUP OF PERFORMING BLACK LEOPARDS

CAPTURED IN MALAYAN FASTNESSES BY *BRING 'EM BACK ALIVE* FRANK BUCK FOR THE GREATEST SHOW ON EARTH

RINGLING AND BARNUM BROS COMBINED SHOWS & BAILEY

FIRST TIME ON THIS CONTINENT - THE GREATEST WILD ANIMAL DISPLAY IN HISTORY

PRESENTED BY **ALFRED COURT** WORLD'S FOREMOST TRAINER

DIRECT FROM EUROPE ...

THREE OF THE MOST AMAZING MIXED GROUPS OF JUNGLE ENEMIES EVER ASSEMBLED!